REIKI AND THE POWER OF THE JOINT POINTS

UNLOCKING ENERGY PATHWAYS FOR HEALING

REIKI WISDOM SERIES
Beyond the Symbols — The Path to True Mastery

Sacred Symbol of Reiki Wisdom

The sacred combination of the **circle, triangle, intersecting lines**, and **pentagram** represents the harmonious flow of spiritual and physical energy.

- The **circle** symbolizes **wholeness** and **spiritual protection**, reflecting the infinite and interconnected nature of Reiki energy.
- The **triangle** embodies **creation** and **balance**, representing the three pillars of Reiki — **mind, body,** and **spirit** — working in harmony.
- The **three converging lines** reflect **unity** and **focused intent**, directing energy flow through the chakras and meridians.
- The **pentagram** signifies **mastery of the elements** (earth, fire, water, air, and spirit) and the awakening of spiritual wisdom.

This symbol represents the manifestation of divine energy into physical reality through balance, alignment, and focused intention. It reflects the path to enlightenment — where mind, body, and spirit align to unlock deep healing and spiritual mastery.

Grand Master, Constance Santego

REIKI AND THE POWER OF THE JOINT POINTS

VOL. I OF THE REIKI WISDOM SERIES

Beyond the Symbols — The Path to True Mastery

Dr. Constance Santego

Maximillian Enterprises
Kelowna, BC

REIKI AND THE POWER OF THE JOINT POINTS
Copyright ° 2025 by Dr. Constance Santego.

Copy Editor and Interior Design: Constance Santego
Book Layout: °2017 BookDesignTemplates.com
Cover Design: Jennifer Louie

Ordering Information:
Quantity sales. Special discounts are available on quantity purchases by corporations, associations, and others. For details, contact the address below.

Trade paperback ISBN: 978-1-990062-57-5
eBook ISBN 978-1-990062-58-2

Created and published In Canada. Printed and bound in the United States of America

First Edition
Published by Maximillian Enterprises

Kelowna, BC Canada
www.constancesantego.ca

Dedication

To all Reiki instructors, practitioners, and healers — from beginners to masters — who dedicate themselves to the art of healing through energy. May this work deepen your connection to the universal flow and empower you to unlock greater wisdom, balance, and healing.

"Through wisdom and intention, your hands become a channel for healing and transformation."
—Dr. Constance Santego

ALSO BY DR. CONSTANCE SANTEGO

NOVELS

Illegitimate Grace

Okanagan Trilogy:

Beneath the Vineyards
Under the Okanagan Sun
Guardian of the Lake

The Nine Spiritual Gifts Series:
Journey of a Soul – (Vol 1 Michael)
Language of a Soul – (Vol 2 Gabriel)
Prophecy of a Soul – (Vol 3 Bath Kol)
Healing of a Soul – (Vol 4 Raphael)
Miracles of a Soul – (Vol 5 Hamied)
Knowledge of a Soul – (Vol 6 Raziel)
Wisdom of a Soul – (Vol 7 Uriel)
Faith of a Soul – (Vol 8 Pistis Sophia)

NONFICTION
The Intuitive Life, The Gift Of Prophecy, Third Edition
Fairy Tales, Dreams And Reality... Where Are You On Your
Path? Second Edition
Your Persona... The Mask You Wear
Angelic Lifestyle, a Vibrant Lifestyle
Angelic Lifestyle 42-Day Energy Cleanse
Archangel Michael's Soul Retrieval Guide
Tesla And The Future Of Energy Medicine
Beyond Tesla: *Advancing The Science Of Energy Healing*
Tesla's Code: *Mastering Energy, Frequency, And Creative
Power*

Scaling Beyond 6 Figures: *Strategies for Health & Wellness Professionals*
Beyond the Mind: *Harnessing the Power of Astral Projection for Creative Awakening*
Bend, Don't Break: *Finding Your Way Back to Abundance*
Ring Therapy: *A Guide to Healing and Balance*
Ring Therapy Pocket Guide
Floraopathy™: *The Art and Science of Vibrational Healing with Essential Oils*

SECRETS OF A HEALER, SERIES:
Magic Of Aromatherapy (Vol I)
Magic Of Reflexology (Vol II)
Magic Of The Gifts (Vol III)
Magic Of Muscle Testing (Vol IV)
Magic Of Iridology (Vol V)
Magic Of Massage (Vol VI)
Magic Of Hypnotherapy (Vol VII)
Magic Of Reiki (Vol VIII)
Magic Of Advanced Aromatherapy (Vol IX)
Magic Of Esthetics (Vol X)
The Reiki Master's Manual (Vol XI)

ADULT COLORING JOURNALS

SERIES-ZEN COLORING:
Quantum Energy and Mindful Living Journal (Vol 1)
Reiki Energy Journal (Vol 2)
Nine Spiritual Gifts Journal (Vol 3)
I Forgive Journal (Vol 4)

FOR CHILDREN
I am Big Tonight. I Don't Need the Light

Contents

Preface

Reiki Wisdom:
Unlocking Energy Pathways for Healing

Reiki has been a profound part of my life since 1999, when it was one of the first modalities taught at my healing school. I had no idea what Reiki was until my Reiki Master, Nefertiti, introduced me to Level I and II during a transformative weekend course. That experience changed everything.

At the time, Reiki was often dismissed as "woo-woo" or pseudoscience — misunderstood and even feared by those who couldn't perceive its benefits. Many people, limited by what they could see or explain, labeled Reiki as suspicious or even dangerous. But over time, perspectives have shifted. Reiki is now recognized and respected for its ability to reduce stress, promote healing, and improve overall well-being. It's even being integrated into medical settings, including cancer clinics, as a valuable tool for pain relief and emotional support.

This book, *Reiki and the Power of the Joint Points*, is part of the *Reiki Wisdom* series and takes Reiki practice to a deeper level — focusing on the energetic significance of the joints in the body. While chakras and meridians are well-known focal points in Reiki, the joints serve as powerful energy gateways where blockages often form. By working with Reiki to release these blockages, you can restore balance, increase mobility, and support emotional and physical healing.

My hope is that this book will expand your understanding of Reiki and empower you to apply it in new and transformative ways. Whether you are a beginner or an experienced practitioner, may this work deepen your connection to the universal flow of energy and help you unlock greater healing potential — for yourself and those you serve.

With gratitude and light,
Dr. Constance Santego
Grand Reiki Master

Note to Reader

Reiki is not intended to replace traditional medical techniques. Persons with physical, mental, emotional, and spiritual problems should seek the service of a professional psychologist or Doctor.

Your Doctor still plays a vital role in your health care. For example, if you break my leg, You will need a Doctor, all the nurses, and staff in the Hospital.

Integrated Medicine focuses on "**our**" significant role in caring for our health. What we put into our bodies, how hard we work our bodies, the stress level we allow into our everyday lives, and the positive or negative energy we attract around us all play a role in our well-being.

Reiki is an excellent technique for relaxation, stress relief, clearing the mind, improving self-awareness, self-empowerment, and possibly a miracle. However, you are ALWAYS in control of your health, and Reiki cannot heal you alone. Only you can do that.

A legal *(Signed by your Reiki Master)* Reiki Level 2 certificate is required if you are to "charge $" to "treat" others, and a Reiki Level 3 certificate is required if you are to "charge $" and "teach" others!

Learning Outcome

Reiki and the Power of the Joint Points: Unlocking Energy Pathways for Healing

This book is a specialized guide that explores the often-overlooked role of joints in Reiki healing. It provides a comprehensive understanding of how joints act as energetic crossroads where emotional, physical, and spiritual energy converge. By focusing on the flow of energy through the joints, this book teaches advanced techniques for identifying and releasing blockages, restoring balance, and enhancing overall well-being. Whether you are a beginner or an experienced Reiki practitioner, this book will expand your knowledge and empower you to integrate joint healing into your Reiki practice.

By the end of this book, you will have a thorough understanding of the following:

Part 1: Understanding the Energy of Joints

- The role of joints as energetic "crossroads" within the body's chakra and meridian systems.
- How energy flow through the joints influences emotional and physical health.
- The metaphysical meaning of specific joints and how they reflect life patterns and emotional states.

- The presence of secondary chakras in the joints and their connection to overall energy balance.

Part 2: Reiki Techniques for Joint Healing

- How to set intentions and identify energy blockages in joints before a session.
- Best hand positions and techniques for healing joint-related issues like inflammation, tension, and emotional imprints.
- How to combine Reiki with breathwork, visualization, and affirmations to enhance joint healing.
- Specialized techniques for working with specific joints, including the shoulders, elbows, wrists, hips, knees, ankles, fingers, and toes.

Part 3: Advanced Joint Healing with Reiki

- How to integrate Reiki with other modalities, such as reflexology, acupressure, and massage.
- Using sound healing, tuning forks, crystals, and essential oils to support joint release and healing.
- Techniques for addressing chronic joint issues like arthritis and inflammation from an energetic perspective.
- Methods for long-term energy balancing to maintain joint health and prevent future imbalances.

Part 4: Spiritual and Emotional Growth Through Joint Healing

- How joint issues reflect emotional and spiritual blocks.

- Techniques to release emotional trauma stored in the joints.
- Journaling exercises and guided meditations for emotional healing and spiritual growth.
- How to integrate joint healing into professional Reiki sessions and educate clients on the emotional and spiritual aspects of joint health.

This book will serve as a practical and spiritual guide for working with the body's structural and energetic systems through Reiki. It will empower you to deepen your practice, enhance your ability to release energy blockages, and align mind, body, and spirit through the powerful energy pathways of the joints. Whether you are just beginning your Reiki journey or are a seasoned practitioner, this book will elevate your understanding and ability to heal.

Introduction – The Hidden Power of Joints in Reiki

Reiki practitioners are often taught to focus on the chakras and meridians when working with energy. While these are essential components of the body's energetic system, joints are frequently overlooked — yet they hold immense potential for healing and balance. Understanding the energetic significance of joints and how Reiki can restore their flow is a powerful expansion of your Reiki practice.

Joints are more than just physical connectors; they act as energetic gateways where emotional, spiritual, and physical energy converge. The body has over 360 joints, including the knees, hips, shoulders, elbows, wrists, and ankles — all of which serve as key points where energy flow can either be supported or restricted. When energy becomes stagnant or blocked in these areas, it can manifest as physical pain, stiffness, inflammation, and emotional imbalance.

In Reiki practice, the goal is to create harmony and restore the free flow of energy throughout the body. When a joint is blocked energetically, it creates a disruption in this flow, similar to a kink in a hose that restricts the movement of water. This blocked energy can lead to emotional and physical discomfort, fatigue, and a sense of being stuck or limited.

The energetic significance of joints goes beyond their physical function. Each joint is linked to specific emotional and spiritual themes. For example, the hips are associated with emotional movement and creativity, while the knees reflect humility and trust in life's path. Stiffness or pain in these areas can often be traced back to emotional resistance or unresolved trauma. By directing Reiki energy into the joints, you can release these stored patterns, restore flexibility, and improve both physical and emotional well-being.

This book explores how to work with the energy of joints using Reiki, including techniques for identifying and releasing energetic blockages, balancing emotional energy, and improving physical mobility. You will learn how to apply Reiki to specific joints, understand the metaphysical meaning behind joint-related issues, and use advanced methods to enhance the body's natural healing process.

Whether you are a new practitioner or an experienced Reiki Master, this book will expand your understanding of Reiki and empower you to integrate joint healing into your practice. Working with joints allows Reiki energy to flow more freely through the body, creating a state of alignment where healing occurs naturally. Understanding the power of joints in Reiki practice will deepen your connection to the body's energetic system and open new pathways for healing and balance.

PART 1:
UNDERSTANDING THE
ENERGY OF JOINTS

Chapter 1: The Body as an Energy System

The body is more than just a physical structure; it is an intricate and dynamic energy system composed of chakras, meridians, and energy fields that work together to maintain balance and health. Reiki practitioners understand that physical and emotional well-being are rooted in the smooth and balanced flow of energy through this system. When energy is flowing freely, the body functions harmoniously, and emotional stability and mental clarity naturally follow. ***However, when energy becomes blocked or stagnant, it creates imbalances that can manifest as physical discomfort, emotional distress, and reduced vitality.***

Understanding Energy Pathways

Energy in the body flows through interconnected pathways that influence both physical and emotional health. There are three primary components of the body's energy system:

1. Chakras – These are the body's main energy centers. They act as both receivers and transmitters of energy, regulating emotional and physical health.
2. Meridians – These are the channels through which life force energy (ki) flows, connecting the organs and energetic structures of the body.
3. Joints – While often overlooked, joints act as *energetic intersections* where multiple meridians and energy pathways meet.

Joints serve a dual function in the body — they provide physical mobility and also regulate the flow of energy through the body's energetic network. When joints are blocked or out of alignment, they can disrupt the flow of energy through the meridians and chakras, leading to stiffness, pain, emotional instability, and even chronic health issues.

Blocked joints create an energetic **"traffic jam,"** where the natural movement of chi/ki (life force) is restricted. This not only causes physical discomfort but also affects emotional and mental clarity.

I trust the wisdom of my body. Energy flows freely through me, restoring balance and strength

For example, tightness in the hips may not just reflect muscular tension — *it could indicate a blockage in the Sacral Chakra or Liver Meridian*, signaling emotional holding or creative suppression.

By working with joints through Reiki, you can restore balance at a deeper level — not only relieving physical discomfort but also addressing the emotional and energetic imbalances that contribute to that discomfort.

The Chakra System

The chakra system is one of the foundational components of Reiki practice. Chakras are spinning wheels of energy located along the body's central axis, from the base of the spine to the crown of the head. Each chakra governs specific physical, emotional, and spiritual functions. When the chakras are open and balanced, energy flows smoothly through the body. When a chakra is blocked, it can cause physical tension, emotional instability, and spiritual disconnect.

The Seven Primary Chakras:

1. Root Chakra (Muladhara) – Located at the base of the spine. Governs security, survival, and grounding. When balanced, you feel secure and stable; when blocked, you may feel anxious, fearful, or unstable.

I trust the wisdom of my body. Energy flows freely through me, restoring balance and strength

2. Sacral Chakra (Swadhisthana) – Located just below the navel. Governs creativity, sexuality, and emotional flow. When balanced, you feel creative and emotionally open; when blocked, you may experience emotional numbness or creative blocks.

3.   – Located at the upper abdomen. Governs confidence, personal power, and digestion. When balanced, you feel empowered and confident; when blocked, you may experience self-doubt, insecurity, or digestive issues.

4. Heart Chakra (Anahata) – Located at the center of the chest. Governs love, compassion, and emotional balance. When balanced, you feel connected and open to love; when blocked, you may feel isolated or emotionally closed off.

5. Throat Chakra (Vishuddha) – Located at the throat. Governs communication, truth, and self-expression. When balanced, you can express yourself authentically; when blocked, you may struggle with communication or feel unheard.

6. Third Eye Chakra (Ajna) – Located between the eyebrows. Governs intuition, perception, and insight. When balanced, you trust your intuition; when blocked, you may feel mentally foggy or disconnected from your inner wisdom.

7. Crown Chakra (Sahasrara) – Located at the top of the head. Governs spiritual connection and enlightenment. When balanced, you feel aligned with your higher self; when blocked, you may feel spiritually disconnected or directionless.

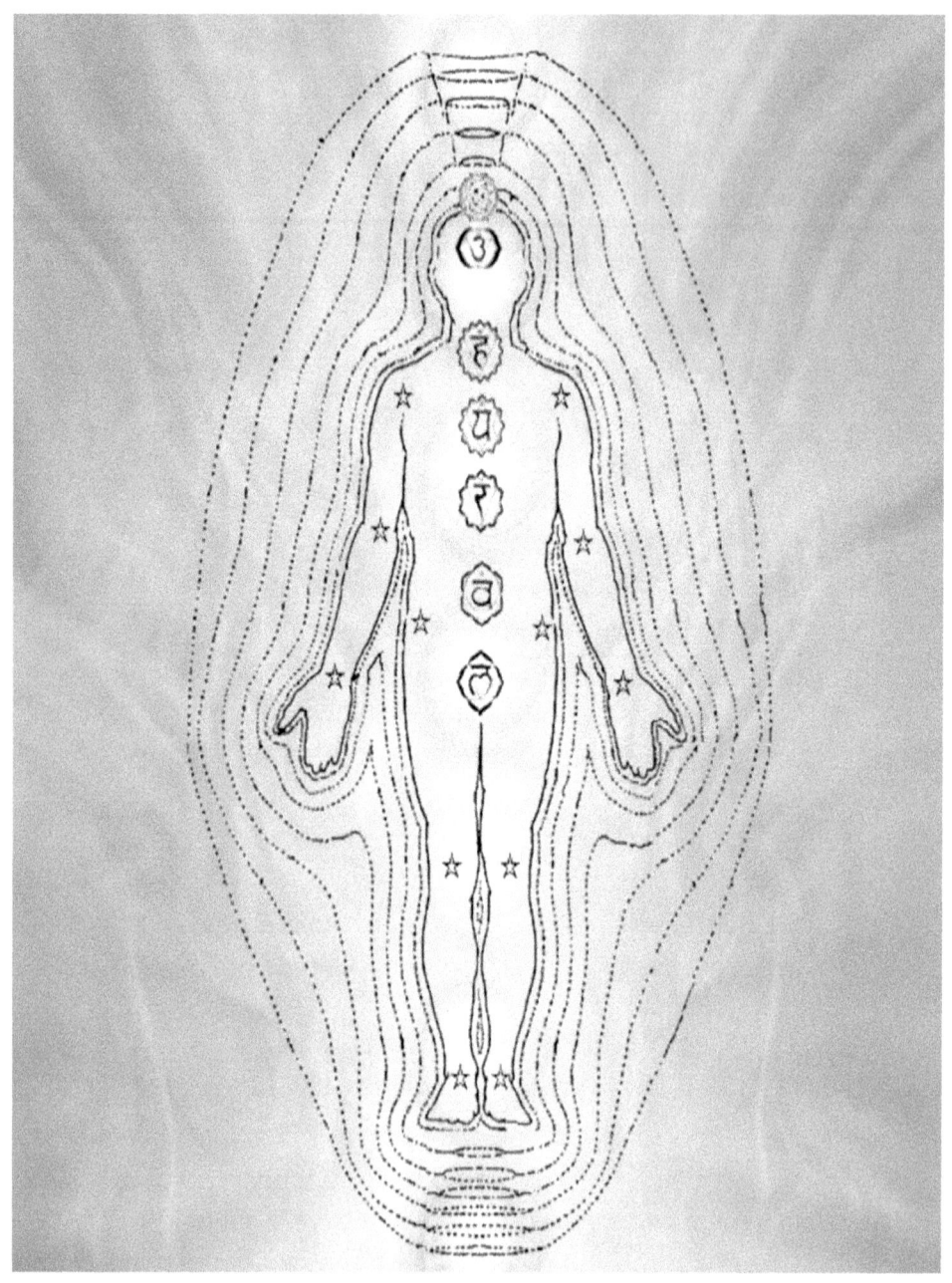

I trust the wisdom of my body. Energy flows freely through me, restoring balance and strength.

The Role of Chakras in Joint Health

Each joint is linked to one or more chakras, meaning that joint stiffness or pain can often be traced back to a chakra imbalance. Understanding these connections allows Reiki practitioners to address not only the physical discomfort but also the underlying energetic cause.

Joint	Chakra Connection	Emotional Theme
Shoulders	Heart Chakra	Carrying emotional burdens, self-expression
Elbows	Heart and Solar Plexus Chakra	Flexibility in relationships and self-worth
Wrists	Throat Chakra	Trust and communication
Hips	Sacral Chakra	Emotional movement and creative energy
Knees	Root and Solar Plexus Chakra	Fear of moving forward, humility, adaptability
Ankles	Root and Sacral Chakra	Grounding, balance, and stability
Fingers and Toes	Crown and Throat Chakra	Precision, control, and action

Blocked energy in a joint can indicate an imbalance in the related chakra. For example:

- Pain in the knees may reflect a blockage in the Root Chakra, signaling fear of moving forward or lack of trust in life.
- Stiffness in the hips may indicate an imbalance in the Sacral Chakra, representing creative or emotional suppression.
- Shoulder tension may reflect emotional heaviness or resistance to vulnerability, linked to the Heart Chakra.

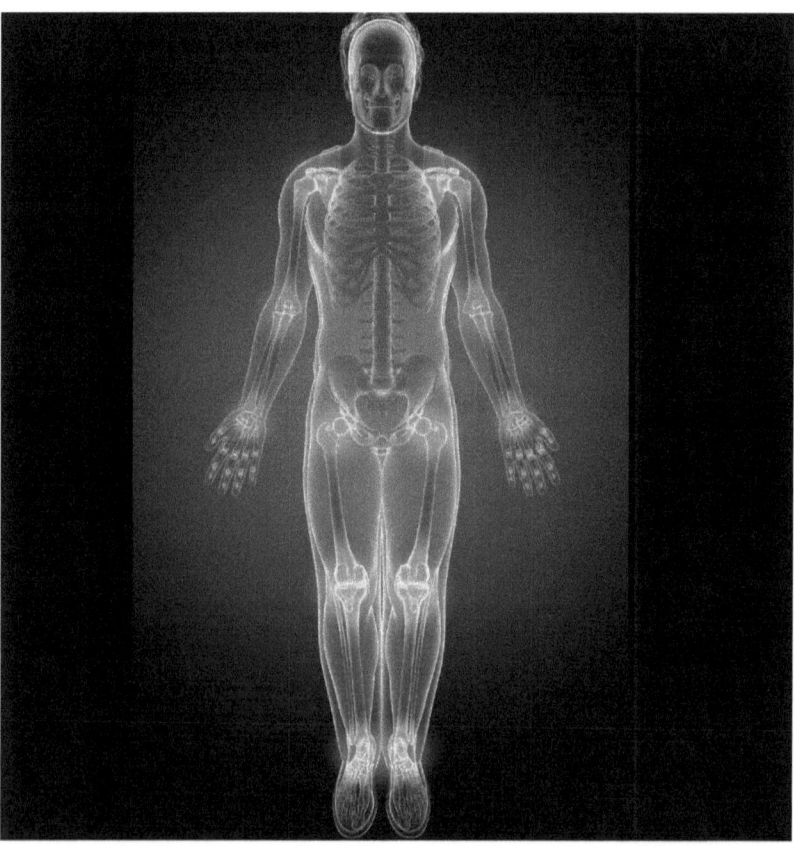

I trust the wisdom of my body. Energy flows freely through me, restoring balance and strength

Nadis

The Nadis are an essential part of the body's energetic anatomy, particularly in the context of Reiki, yoga, and Ayurveda. They are considered energy channels through which prana (life force energy) flows. Understanding the nadis helps to deepen the practice of Reiki, as working with them allows for more precise energy flow and greater balance within the body's subtle system.

What Are Nadis?

The word "nadi" comes from the Sanskrit root *nad*, which means "flow" or "channel." In the same way that blood vessels carry blood through the body, nadis are said to carry prana (life force energy) through the energetic body.

- Nadis are not physical structures — they are part of the subtle body (energy body).
- The human body is said to have between 72,000 to 350,000 nadis — depending on the spiritual tradition — but most teachings focus on the three primary nadis and 14 secondary nadis.
- Nadis intersect at points called chakras, which act as energy hubs where the energy flow is concentrated and distributed.
- When nadis are open and energy flows freely, the body and mind experience balance, health, and emotional stability. When nadis are blocked, it can lead to physical pain, emotional distress, and spiritual disconnection.

Three Primary Nadis

Although there are thousands of nadis in the body, three primary nadis are considered the most important in energetic healing and spiritual development:

1. Ida Nadi – The Lunar Channel (Left Side)

- Ida represents the feminine, cooling, and calming energy.
- It begins at the base of the spine (root chakra) and spirals upward along the left side of the spine, ending at the left nostril.
- Ida is connected to:
    - The moon (cooling and reflective energy)
    - Emotional and mental activity
    - Intuition and creativity
    - The parasympathetic nervous system (rest and relaxation)
- When Ida is overactive, it can cause emotional instability and mental fog.

2. Pingala Nadi – The Solar Channel (Right Side)

- Pingala represents the masculine, heating, and activating energy.
- It begins at the base of the spine and spirals upward along the right side of the spine, ending at the right nostril.
- Pingala is connected to:
    - The sun (warm and active energy)
    - Physical activity
    - Logical thinking

I trust the wisdom of my body. Energy flows freely through me, restoring balance and strength

○ The sympathetic nervous system (fight or flight)
- When Pingala is overactive, it can cause physical tension, restlessness, and anxiety.

3. Sushumna Nadi – The Central Channel (Spiritual Awakening)

- Sushumna is the most important nadi — it represents the path of spiritual awakening and higher consciousness.
- It runs straight up the center of the spine, from the base of the spine (root chakra) to the crown of the head.
- Sushumna remains dormant until Ida and Pingala are balanced.
- When prana begins to flow freely through Sushumna, it activates kundalini energy — the spiritual energy coiled at the base of the spine — leading to:
  - Higher consciousness
  - Deep meditation
  - Spiritual awakening
  - Emotional and physical balance
- Reiki energy often works through Sushumna, encouraging balance between Ida and Pingala and opening the pathway for spiritual growth.

How Reiki Affects the Nadis

Reiki works by channeling prana (life force energy) through the hands and into the body's energy system. When working with the nadis, Reiki can:

Clear Blockages – If a nadi is blocked, Reiki dissolves energetic knots and restores flow.
Balance Ida and Pingala – Reiki helps balance the feminine and masculine energies, encouraging alignment and stability.
Activate Sushumna – Reiki increases the flow of prana through Sushumna, encouraging spiritual growth.
Enhance Chakra Function – Since the nadis intersect at the chakras, clearing and balancing the nadis improves chakra function and overall energy flow.

14 Major Nadis (Secondary Nadis)

Beyond the three primary nadis, there are 14 major nadis that are considered important for physical and emotional balance. These nadis branch off from Sushumna and distribute prana to different parts of the body.

Nadi	Description	Function
Gandhari	Left eye	Controls vision and emotional perception.
Hasti-jihva	Right eye	Balances sight and mental clarity.

I trust the wisdom of my body. Energy flows freely through me, restoring balance and strength

Nadi	Description	Function
Yashasvini	Right ear	Enhances listening and communication.
Pusha	Left ear	Regulates inner guidance and emotional sensitivity.
Alambusha	Mouth	Governs speech and communication.
Kuhu	Reproductive organs	Manages creative and sexual energy.
Shankhini	Throat	Influences self-expression and truth.
Varuni	Large intestine	Affects digestion and emotional release.
Payasvini	Lips	Governs nourishment and emotional intake.
Vishvodhara	Skin	Governs touch and sensitivity.
Sarasvati	Tongue	Influences taste, nourishment, and speech.
Pingala	Right side of the body	Solar and masculine energy.

Nadi	Description	Function
Ida	Left side of the body	Lunar and feminine energy.
Sushumna	Central axis	Spiritual and energetic alignment.

How Blockages in the Nadis Affect Health

When nadis become blocked, the flow of prana is restricted, which can lead to:

- Emotional imbalance – Anxiety, depression, or emotional instability.
- Physical pain – Stiffness, joint pain, inflammation, or chronic illness.
- Mental confusion – Lack of focus, mental fog, and indecision.
- Spiritual disconnection – Feeling stuck, uninspired, or spiritually lost.

Example:

- If *Ida* is blocked — You may feel emotionally overwhelmed and mentally foggy.
- If *Pingala* is blocked — You may feel physically sluggish and lack motivation.
- If *Sushumna* is blocked — Spiritual growth and deeper awareness may feel inaccessible.

I trust the wisdom of my body. Energy flows freely through me, restoring balance and strength

How to Open and Balance the Nadis with Reiki

1. Reiki Hand Placement on the Spine

- Place one hand at the base of the spine (root chakra) and one at the crown.
- Visualize white light flowing through the spine, balancing Ida and Pingala.

2. Alternate Nostril Breathing (Nadi Shodhana)

- Close the right nostril and inhale through the left.
- Close the left nostril and exhale through the right.
- Repeat, alternating sides.
- This helps balance Ida and Pingala and opens Sushumna.

3. Third Eye Activation

- Place hands over the third eye (Ajna chakra).
- Visualize prana flowing through Ida and Pingala into the center of the forehead.
- This encourages energy to merge in Sushumna.

4. Using Reiki Symbols

- Cho Ku Rei – Clears blockages and increases energy flow.
- Sei He Ki – Balances emotional patterns held in the nadis.
- Dai Ko Myo – Opens Sushumna and promotes spiritual growth.

Why Nadis Matter in Reiki and Joint Healing

- Joints are energetic intersections where multiple nadis meet.
- When energy stagnates at a joint, it creates physical pain and emotional tension.
- Reiki restores the flow of prana through the nadis, clearing these intersections and restoring balance.
- Balancing the nadis enhances not only physical healing but also emotional and spiritual growth.

Key Takeaways

- Nadis are energy channels that transport prana through the body.
- Ida and Pingala balance feminine and masculine energy.
- Sushumna governs spiritual growth and higher consciousness.
- Reiki restores flow through the nadis, clears blockages, and promotes balance.
- Joint-focused Reiki works directly with the nadis to release stored energy and tension.

Understanding the nadis allows you to work more effectively with Reiki, improving both physical and emotional healing at the deepest level.

I trust the wisdom of my body. Energy flows freely through me, restoring balance and strength

The Meridian System and Energy Points

In Traditional Chinese Medicine (TCM), the body is viewed as an intricate network of energy pathways called meridians. These meridians form a complex map of the body through which **chi/**qi (life force energy) flows, supporting physical, emotional, and spiritual health. The meridian system is fundamental to acupuncture, acupressure, and many Eastern healing practices, and it aligns closely with the energetic principles of Reiki.

Understanding the meridian system enhances Reiki practice by providing insight into how energy travels through the body and where blockages might form. While chakras are seen as large energy centers along the body's central axis, the meridians serve as the channels that distribute this energy to every organ, joint, and tissue. Each point along a meridian is an access point to the body's energy system — much like a smaller chakra or energy node — making the meridian system a powerful tool for both physical and energetic healing.

The Twelve Primary Meridians

There are 12 primary meridians in the body, each linked to an internal organ and governed by specific physical and emotional functions. These meridians are organized into six pairs, with each pair consisting of a yin and a yang meridian. The yin meridians run along the front or inner side of the body, while the yang meridians run along the back or outer side of the body.

Meridian	Element	Function	Yin/Yang
Lung	Metal	Breath, grief, emotional release	Yin
Large Intestine	Metal	Letting go, digestion, absorption	Yang
Stomach	Earth	Nourishment, grounding, stability	Yang
Spleen	Earth	Transformation of food and energy	Yin
Heart	Fire	Love, emotional connection, circulation	Yin
Small Intestine	Fire	Sorting emotions and nutrients	Yang
Bladder	Water	Storage, fear, elimination	Yang
Kidney	Water	Willpower, security, reproduction	Yin
Pericardium	Fire	Emotional protection, circulation	Yin
Triple Warmer	Fire	Regulation of body temperature and stress	Yang
Gallbladder	Wood	Decision-making, courage	Yang

I trust the wisdom of my body. Energy flows freely through me, restoring balance and strength.

Meridian	Element	Function	Yin/Yang
Liver	Wood	Flexibility, emotional balance	Yin

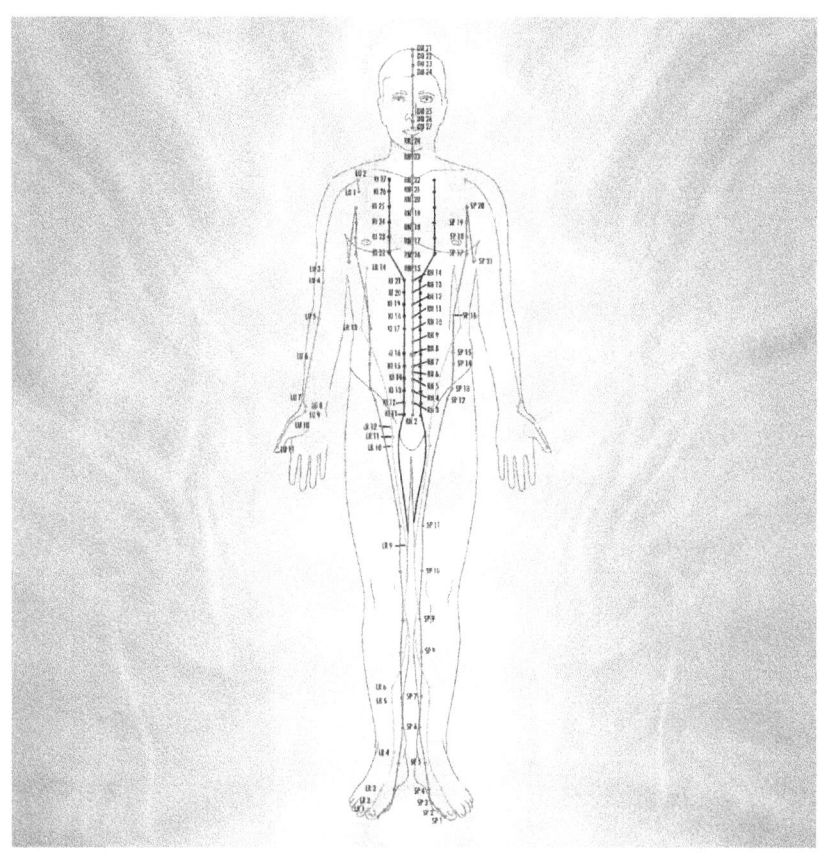

Flow of Energy Through the Meridians

Each meridian is part of a continuous cycle of energy flow, known as the Chinese Body Clock or Meridian Clock. Qi flows through each meridian during a two-hour period in a 24-hour cycle, meaning that each organ and meridian is most energized and receptive to healing during its corresponding time of day.

For example:

- The Liver Meridian is most active between 1:00 a.m. and 3:00 a.m.
- The Heart Meridian is most active between 11:00 a.m. and 1:00 p.m.

This cyclical flow of energy influences not only physical function but also emotional and mental states. Practicing Reiki or other energy work during the time when a meridian is most active can enhance the effectiveness of the treatment.

Tsubo Points – The Acupuncture/Acupressure Points

Along each meridian are tsubo points — specific points where energy can be accessed and influenced. These are the same points targeted in acupuncture and acupressure. Tsubo points are essentially smaller energy centers or secondary chakras where energy tends to pool, making them particularly sensitive to both touch and energy work.

I trust the wisdom of my body. Energy flows freely through me, restoring balance and strength

There are 361 classical tsubo points mapped across the 12 primary meridians and two additional channels known as the Ren Mai (Conception Vessel) and Du Mai (Governing Vessel):

- 12 Primary Meridians – 309 points
- Ren Mai (Conception Vessel) – 24 points
- Du Mai (Governing Vessel) – 28 points

Tsubo points are considered powerful access points for influencing the flow of qi through the meridians. Each point corresponds to a specific physical function, emotional state, and energetic quality. In the context of Reiki, these points serve as minor chakras — energetic "hubs" where focused energy work can bring profound healing effects.

How Tsubo Points Function Like Chakras

In Reiki, the chakras are viewed as the body's main energy centers. Similarly, tsubo points function as smaller energy receptors or secondary chakras within the meridian system. While the seven primary chakras govern broad energetic themes and emotional states, tsubo points allow for more targeted access to the body's energy system.

Key Similarities Between Chakras and Tsubo Points:

1. Energy Exchange: Both chakras and tsubo points act as receivers and transmitters of energy.
2. Emotional Storage: Just as emotions can be stored in the chakras, unresolved emotional patterns can accumulate at specific tsubo points.

3. Balance and Flow: When a chakra or tsubo point is blocked, it disrupts the flow of energy through the system, leading to physical or emotional symptoms.
4. Reiki Activation: Applying Reiki to a chakra or a tsubo point stimulates the flow of ki, helping to dissolve energetic blockages and restore harmony.

Example of Chakra and Tsubo Connection:

- The Heart Chakra governs emotional connection, love, and compassion.
- The Shen Men point in the ear (associated with the Heart Meridian) is used in acupuncture and auricular therapy to relieve stress, balance emotions, and promote relaxation.
- Applying Reiki to the Heart Chakra while also working with tsubo points along the Heart Meridian (such as Shen Men) can amplify emotional healing and release.

Tsubo Points and Joint Health

Many of the most powerful tsubo points are located near or on the joints, reinforcing the connection between joint health and overall energy flow.

Examples of Tsubo Points on or Near Joints:

- Knees:
    - SP-9 (Yin Ling Quan) – Located on the inner knee; associated with water retention and emotional release.

I trust the wisdom of my body. Energy flows freely through me, restoring balance and strength

- o ST-36 (Zusanli) – Located below the knee; associated with grounding and strengthening energy.
- Shoulders:
  - o LI-15 (Jian Yu) – Located on the shoulder; associated with releasing stored emotional burdens.
  - o SI-9 (Jianzhen) – Located at the back of the shoulder; connected to emotional flow and connection.
- Hips:
  - o GB-30 (Huantiao) – Located on the outer hip; associated with movement and emotional release.
- Elbows:
  - o LI-11 (Quchi) – Located on the outer elbow; used for releasing heat and tension.
- Wrists:
  - o PC-7 (Daling) – Located on the wrist; associated with emotional calming and balance.

In Reiki practice, focusing energy on these tsubo points can help to:

- Improve joint flexibility and mobility.
- Dissolve emotional patterns stored in the joints.
- Restore the natural flow of energy through the corresponding meridian.

The Integration of Meridians, Nadis, Tsubo Points, and Chakras in Reiki

Reiki practitioners often focus on the chakras as the primary energy centers in the body. However, incorporating the meridian system, nadis, and tsubo points into your Reiki practice allows for more precise and comprehensive energy work, enhancing the overall flow of energy and deepening the healing process.

How It Works:

- When you sense a blockage in a joint, you can direct Reiki not only to the joint itself but also to the related meridian, the intersecting nadi, and the corresponding tsubo points (pressure points).
- Meridians act as the primary energy highways that distribute qi (life force) throughout the body, while nadis form a more subtle energetic grid that governs the flow of prana (life energy).
- Tsubo points are key access points along the meridians — similar to secondary chakras — where energy can be stimulated and released.
- By aligning and balancing the flow of energy through the chakras, meridians, and nadis simultaneously, you create a deeper level of energetic harmony and physical balance.

Why Joints Are Key:

Joints serve as powerful intersections where multiple meridians and nadis converge. When a joint becomes stiff or painful, it often reflects blocked energy at the crossroads of these systems.

- Working on the joints through Reiki clears these "kinks" in the energy system, ensuring that qi and prana flow smoothly through both the physical and energetic body.
- When Reiki energy is directed through the joint, it not only restores physical movement but also releases emotional and spiritual blockages held within the intersecting energy channels.

Key Takeaways:

Meridians act as the primary channels that distribute qi (life force energy) throughout the body.
Nadis form the subtle energy pathways that regulate prana (life energy) and spiritual flow.
Tsubo points act as access points along the meridians — similar to secondary chakras — that can be used to release tension and restore flow. Joints serve as energetic crossroads where meridians and nadis intersect — clearing them restores both physical and emotional balance.

Combining chakra healing with meridian and nadi-focused Reiki enhances the depth and effectiveness of the healing process. By understanding and working with all three systems — meridians, nadis, and chakras — Reiki practitioners can refine their techniques and bring the body into a deeper state of alignment and balance.

Why Joints Are Important in Reiki

Joints are more than just physical connectors — they serve as vital regulators of energy flow between the body's chakras, meridians, and nadis. Each joint functions as an energetic crossroads where multiple pathways intersect, making them key points for maintaining balance and harmony within the body's energy system.

When a joint becomes blocked or stagnant, it creates a ripple effect that disrupts the flow of energy through the entire system. The stagnation or imbalance at the joint level can lead to physical discomfort, emotional instability, and spiritual disconnection.

How Blocked Joints Affect the Whole System:

- Mobility: Physical stiffness, reduced range of motion, and joint pain reflect stagnant energy.
- Emotional Balance: Emotional patterns, unresolved trauma, and stress often settle in the joints, leading to difficulty processing emotions.
- Mental Clarity: Blocked energy can manifest as mental fog, lack of focus, and indecision.
- Spiritual Connection: When energy flow through the nadis and meridians is restricted, it weakens the connection to higher consciousness and intuition.

I trust the wisdom of my body. Energy flows freely through me, restoring balance and strength

How Reiki Restores Joint Balance:

Reiki works by dissolving these energetic blockages and restoring the free flow of ki (life force energy) through the joints, meridians, and chakras.

- By directing Reiki to specific joints, you allow stagnant energy to release and flow more freely.
- As the energy begins to move through the body's pathways, physical flexibility improves, emotional tension lifts, and mental clarity sharpens.
- Balancing the energy flow at the joint level creates a harmonizing effect on the entire energy system — promoting healing at the physical, emotional, and spiritual levels.

Why Joints Matter in Reiki:

- Joints act as the meeting points for meridians and nadis — working on them affects the entire energy network.
- Clearing blockages in the joints allows the energy to flow more freely.
- Balanced joints reflect greater emotional adaptability, spiritual strength, and physical mobility.

By focusing on joint health in Reiki practice, you are not only enhancing physical movement — you are unlocking deeper layers of emotional and spiritual healing.

How Joints Act as Energetic Crossroads

Joints are more than physical connectors that allow for movement and flexibility — they serve as critical energetic gateways where multiple meridians and chakras intersect. From an energetic perspective, joints regulate the flow of energy through the body's meridians and play a significant role in storing and processing emotional experiences.

In Reiki practice, we often focus on the chakras and meridians independently, but the joints are where these two systems meet and influence each other. When energy becomes blocked or stagnant in a joint, it creates a ripple effect that disrupts the overall balance of the body's energetic field. Blocked joints not only restrict physical mobility but also create emotional and spiritual limitations, reducing your ability to process life's experiences with ease and flow.

By understanding the energetic role of joints and how to apply Reiki to them, you can unlock deeper levels of healing — both physical and emotional — and restore the smooth, harmonious flow of energy through the entire body.

I trust the wisdom of my body. Energy flows freely through me, restoring balance and strength

Three Key Roles of Joints in Energy Flow

1. Energy Convergence – Where the Chakras and Meridians Meet

Joints serve as energy convergence points where multiple meridians and energy pathways intersect. Think of them as traffic hubs or energy exchange stations. Just as major highways intersect at key junctions, meridians cross and exchange energy at the joints, making them powerful regulators of overall energy flow.

Each joint acts as a "switching station" where energy from different sources (chakras, meridians, emotional patterns) comes together and is redistributed throughout the body. If the energy at a joint is flowing freely, the body experiences balance, ease of movement, and emotional stability. However, when a joint is blocked — whether due to physical tension, emotional trauma, or energetic misalignment — the flow of energy is interrupted, causing downstream effects in both the physical and emotional body.

Examples of Energy Convergence at Joints:

- The shoulders are connected to the Lung Meridian, Heart Meridian, and Large Intestine Meridian. Tension or misalignment in the shoulders can disrupt the flow of energy to the heart and lungs, affecting emotional balance, breath, and circulation.
- The hips are connected to the Liver Meridian and Gallbladder Meridian, which govern emotional

release and decision-making. Tightness in the hips can lead to emotional stagnation and difficulty processing life changes.

- The knees are linked to the Kidney Meridian and Stomach Meridian, which influence grounding, stability, and emotional security. Knee pain or stiffness can reflect fear or insecurity about moving forward in life.

Because joints are intersections of multiple meridians, any blockage or tension in a joint creates a ripple effect, influencing the health and balance of the entire energetic system. A blocked shoulder may not only cause physical discomfort — it may also weaken the heart's energetic ability to give and receive love.

2. Emotional Storage – Joints as Energy Containers

Joints are not only points of energy exchange — they are also storage sites for emotional energy. Just as muscles store tension, joints hold onto unresolved emotions, trauma, and stress. When emotional experiences are not fully processed or released, they can become energetically "trapped" in the joints, creating physical stiffness and limiting the joint's range of motion.

In Traditional Chinese Medicine, it is understood that emotions are directly tied to the health of specific organs and meridians — and because these meridians intersect at the joints, emotions are often held in the joints as well.

I trust the wisdom of my body. Energy flows freely through me, restoring balance and strength

Examples of Emotional Storage in Joints:

- Shoulders – Carrying emotional burdens, responsibility, or unexpressed grief.
- Hips – Storing fear of change, creative blockages, and sexual suppression.
- Knees – Holding fear of moving forward or lack of trust in life's path.
- Elbows – Reflecting issues with giving and receiving support.
- Wrists – Storing fear of trusting others or expressing oneself.
- Ankles – Holding fear of losing balance or direction in life.

When emotional energy is held in a joint, it creates a physical and energetic "knot" that restricts both movement and emotional flow. For example, a person who has trouble expressing vulnerability may experience chronic tension or discomfort in the shoulders. Over time, this emotional pattern reinforces itself, creating both physical discomfort and emotional resistance.

Reiki works by sending healing energy directly into these energetic knots, helping to release stored emotional patterns and restore the natural flow of ki through the joint. When the emotional energy is released, the joint becomes more mobile, and the corresponding emotional state becomes more balanced.

How Emotional Storage Manifests in Physical Symptoms:

- A person who feels emotionally "weighed down" may experience tension or pain in the shoulders.
- Someone who resists emotional movement or creative expression may develop stiffness or tightness in the hips.
- A person who fears instability or lacks trust may experience weakness or pain in the knees or ankles.

Blocked emotional energy in the joints creates a feedback loop between the mind and body:

1. Emotional resistance → Physical stiffness or pain.
2. Physical discomfort → Emotional suppression.
3. Energetic block → Reduced flow of energy.

Reiki helps to break this cycle by addressing the emotional and energetic root of joint-related discomfort.

3. Physical and Emotional Flexibility – Movement as a Reflection of Inner Flow

Joints symbolize the ability to move through life with ease. Just as physical flexibility allows the body to adapt to different movements and postures, emotional and spiritual flexibility allows you to adapt to life's changes and challenges.

When joints are stiff, painful, or restricted, they often reflect emotional or spiritual rigidity. Difficulty in physical movement can correspond to emotional resistance — the inability to let go, accept change, or trust the flow of life.

I trust the wisdom of my body. Energy flows freely through me, restoring balance and strength

Examples of Physical and Emotional Rigidity:

- Stiff hips – Fear of change or resistance to emotional expression.
- Tight knees – Lack of confidence or trust in your life path.
- Frozen shoulders – Feeling emotionally burdened or restricted.
- Locked elbows – Resistance to giving or receiving help.

When joints are fluid and flexible, it reflects a balanced emotional state — the ability to embrace life's changes without fear or resistance.

Reiki helps restore both physical and emotional flexibility by:

- Releasing energetic blockages in the joints.
- Restoring flow through the meridians and chakras.
- Balancing the body's emotional energy, creating a greater sense of ease and adaptability.

Flexibility in the joints reflects emotional flow and spiritual openness. When the body can move freely, the mind and spirit can also adapt and flow more easily through life's challenges.

Blocked Energy in Joints Creates a Ripple Effect

Because joints are energetic crosspoints, blockages in the joints disrupt the flow of energy through the entire body.

Examples of How Joint Blockages Affect the System:

- If the hips are tight and restricted, energy flow to the Sacral Chakra may be weakened, leading to reduced creativity and emotional expression.
- If the shoulders are tense, the Heart Chakra's ability to give and receive love may be diminished, leading to emotional withdrawal.
- If the knees are stiff, the Root Chakra's grounding energy may be restricted, leading to feelings of insecurity and instability.

A blockage in a single joint can create a ripple effect throughout the entire energetic system. This is why joint-focused Reiki is so powerful — by releasing blockages at these key energetic crossroads, you restore the entire body's energetic flow.

Why Reiki for Joint Healing Works

- Reiki dissolves energetic knots stored in the joints.
- Restores the natural flow of energy through the meridians and chakras.
- Releases emotional patterns stored in the body.
- Improves physical mobility and emotional balance.
- Encourages greater emotional and spiritual flexibility.

Key Takeaways:

- Joints act as energetic crossroads where meridians and chakras intersect.
- Emotional trauma and unresolved conflict often settle in the joints.
- Blocked energy in the joints creates a ripple effect through the body's energetic system.
- Reiki clears joint blockages, restoring both physical and emotional balance.

Why Joint Health Reflects Emotional Well-Being

Joints are more than physical connectors that allow for movement — they are energetic and emotional mirrors, reflecting how we process and respond to life's challenges. The state of your joints — whether they are flexible, stiff, or unstable — provides deep insight into your emotional and spiritual health. When you experience pain, stiffness, or weakness in your joints, it is often a signal that there is an underlying emotional or energetic imbalance that needs to be addressed.

The body and mind are not separate; they are deeply interconnected through the flow of energy. Just as physical flexibility allows you to move through life with ease, emotional flexibility allows you to process and adapt to change. Likewise, physical stiffness reflects emotional rigidity, and instability in the joints reflects insecurity or lack of emotional grounding.

Reiki provides a powerful tool for working with these emotional and energetic patterns stored in the joints. By directing energy into specific joints, you can release emotional resistance, restore balance to the energetic system, and improve both physical and emotional well-being.

I trust the wisdom of my body. Energy flows freely through me, restoring balance and strength

The Emotional Language of Joint Health

Joints are key sites where the body stores emotional experiences and energetic patterns. Every movement you make requires cooperation from the joints, making them a physical reflection of how easily you move through life. When joints are flexible and pain-free, it indicates that you are emotionally adaptable and open to new experiences. Conversely, when joints become stiff, painful, or unstable, it often reflects emotional patterns of resistance, fear, or insecurity.

1. Fluidity in Movement = Flexibility in Life

When joints are flexible and balanced, it reflects emotional and spiritual openness.

- Flexibility in the body indicates that you are emotionally adaptable and able to flow with life's changes.
- Healthy, pain-free joints reflect an ability to let go, trust the process of life, and respond to challenges with ease.
- Flexibility in the joints reflects emotional resilience — the ability to process emotions, release attachments, and remain open to new possibilities.

Emotional Patterns Associated with Flexible Joints:

- Open hips reflect emotional freedom and creative expression.
- Free movement in the shoulders reflects the ability to give and receive love without fear or restriction.

- Flexible knees reflect trust in life's path and confidence in moving forward.

For example:

- A dancer or yoga practitioner who has fluid and balanced movement in their joints often exhibits emotional adaptability and creative flow.
- A person who easily adapts to change and is emotionally grounded will likely have strong but flexible joints, indicating a healthy energetic system.

2. Stiffness = Emotional Resistance

When joints become stiff or inflamed, it often reflects emotional rigidity and an inability to adapt to life's challenges. Stiff joints are a physical manifestation of emotional resistance — the body's way of signaling that you are holding on to old patterns, fear, or unresolved conflict.

- Stiffness in the hips reflects an unwillingness to emotionally or creatively open up.
- Tight shoulders reflect feeling emotionally burdened or unable to express vulnerability.
- Locked knees reflect fear of moving forward or distrust in life's unfolding path.

Emotional Patterns Associated with Stiff Joints:

- Fear of change or transition often manifests as tight hips or lower back stiffness.

I trust the wisdom of my body. Energy flows freely through me, restoring balance and strength.

- Emotional protection and fear of vulnerability often show up as shoulder tension.
- Emotional control and resistance to release often appear as tight wrists or locked elbows.

Stiffness is often tied to deeply ingrained emotional patterns:

- A person who has difficulty forgiving may experience tight shoulders and neck tension.
- Someone who feels creatively blocked or emotionally suppressed may experience tightness or discomfort in the hips.
- Fear of moving forward in life or making big decisions may appear as stiffness or instability in the knees or ankles.

Reiki can dissolve these energetic patterns by working with the emotional root cause behind the stiffness. When the emotional block is released, the joint often regains flexibility, and emotional balance is restored.

3. Instability in Joints = Lack of Grounding

When joints feel weak or unstable, it often reflects emotional insecurity or a lack of trust in life's direction. Instability in the joints reflects an underlying energetic weakness — the inability to feel emotionally or spiritually anchored.

- Unstable knees reflect uncertainty about life's path and a lack of confidence in one's decisions.

- Weak or unstable ankles reflect a fear of losing balance or direction.
- Loose or hypermobile joints reflect emotional instability or a lack of boundaries.

Emotional Patterns Associated with Unstable Joints:

- A person who struggles with insecurity or self-doubt may experience weak or unstable knees.
- A person who has difficulty finding emotional balance may experience instability in the hips or ankles.
- A person who lacks emotional boundaries or struggles with trusting others may experience loose or unstable shoulder or wrist joints.

Instability often reflects energetic misalignment at the level of the root chakra or solar plexus chakra — the energy centers associated with grounding, confidence, and personal power.

For example:

- A person who fears instability in their career or relationships may experience recurring knee or ankle issues.
- Someone who struggles with emotional boundaries or emotional safety may experience shoulder or hip instability.
- A person who lacks confidence or personal power may experience weakness in the core, hips, or lower back.

I trust the wisdom of my body. Energy flows freely through me, restoring balance and strength

Reiki works by restoring energetic alignment at the level of the chakras and meridians, helping the body regain stability and strength. When the energetic foundation is balanced, the joints naturally become more stable and aligned.

Emotional Patterns Reflected in Specific Joints

Each joint reflects a unique emotional or spiritual theme. When you experience discomfort or restriction in a specific joint, it often reflects an imbalance in the corresponding emotional or energetic pattern.

Joint	Emotional and Spiritual Theme
Shoulders	Carrying emotional burdens, responsibility, and vulnerability.
Hips	Emotional movement, creative flow, and fear of change.
Knees	Trust in life's path, humility, and fear of moving forward.
Ankles	Balance, stability, and trust in life's unfolding.
Elbows	Flexibility in relationships and giving/receiving support.
Wrists	Trust, communication, and creative expression.

When a joint becomes painful or restricted, it signals that there is an emotional pattern or unresolved issue stored at that energetic point.

For example:

- A person who feels emotionally overburdened may experience tension in the shoulders.
- Someone who is resisting creative or emotional movement may develop hip stiffness.
- A person who is uncertain about their life path may experience knee instability or pain.

How Reiki Restores Emotional and Physical Balance

Reiki works by addressing the energetic root cause of joint-related issues. Unlike conventional approaches to joint health that focus solely on the physical structure, Reiki works at the energetic and emotional level, releasing stored trauma and restoring the flow of energy through the joints.

How Reiki Helps:

- Dissolves energetic blockages stored in the joints.
- Balances the corresponding chakra or meridian connected to the joint.
- Releases emotional patterns tied to joint stiffness or instability.
- Restores flow and mobility in the joint by improving energetic alignment.
- Strengthens the body's energetic foundation, improving overall stability and flexibility.

I trust the wisdom of my body. Energy flows freely through me, restoring balance and strength

For example:

- Reiki applied to the hips can release creative blocks and improve emotional flow.
- Reiki focused on the shoulders can release emotional burdens and improve vulnerability.
- Reiki directed to the knees can strengthen emotional trust and confidence in life's path.

Key Takeaways:

- Joints are energetic mirrors of emotional and spiritual patterns.
- Stiffness reflects emotional resistance; instability reflects insecurity and lack of grounding.
- Reiki restores balance by dissolving energetic blockages and aligning the emotional body.
- Flexible, pain-free joints reflect emotional openness and spiritual flow.

The Reiki Approach to Joint Healing

Reiki is a powerful healing modality that works by restoring the natural flow of ki (life force energy) through the body's energetic system. While most conventional approaches to joint health focus on the physical structure — such as improving muscle strength, correcting alignment, or reducing inflammation — Reiki takes a holistic approach by addressing the energetic root cause of joint issues.

Joints serve as energetic gateways where multiple meridians and chakras intersect. Because joints are directly linked to the body's energetic flow, blockages in the joints disrupt the flow of energy through the meridians and chakras, creating both physical discomfort and emotional imbalance. Reiki works by dissolving these energetic blockages, releasing stored emotional tension, and restoring harmony to the body's energetic system.

When energy flows freely through the joints, the body becomes more physically flexible, emotional patterns are more easily processed, and spiritual alignment is restored. By working on the joints through Reiki, you are not only relieving physical discomfort but also addressing the emotional and spiritual patterns that contribute to that discomfort.

I trust the wisdom of my body. Energy flows freely through me, restoring balance and strength.

How Reiki Works on Joints

Reiki is based on the principle that the body's natural state is one of balance and harmony. When energy becomes blocked or stagnant — whether due to physical injury, emotional trauma, or stress — it creates an energetic imbalance that disrupts both physical and emotional health.

Reiki works by channeling universal life force energy into the body, dissolving these blockages and encouraging the body to restore its natural state of balance. When applied to joints, Reiki helps to:

1. Dissolve Energetic Blockages in the Joint

Joints act as energy convergence points where multiple meridians intersect. When a joint is tight or restricted, it often reflects a blockage in the energetic flow at that intersection.

- Reiki works by directing energy into the joint, breaking up stagnant energy patterns.
- The practitioner channels Reiki energy into the joint, which acts like a gentle but powerful "flow of light" that penetrates the energetic blockage and clears it out.
- As the energy blockage dissolves, the joint becomes more relaxed, tension is released, and mobility improves.

Blocked joints often store emotional patterns — such as fear, resistance, or grief — alongside physical tension.

Reiki clears both the physical and emotional components of the blockage, creating a sense of release and ease in the joint.

Example:

- A person with tight hips due to fear of emotional vulnerability may experience both emotional release and improved hip flexibility after a Reiki session focused on the Sacral Chakra and hip joint.
- A person with stiff shoulders due to carrying emotional burdens may feel both physical relief and emotional lightness after Reiki dissolves the blockage.

2. Restore the Natural Flow of Energy Through the Meridians

When a joint is blocked, the flow of energy through the meridians is disrupted. This creates an imbalance not only in the joint itself but also in the surrounding muscles, tissues, and organs.

Reiki works by restoring the natural flow of ki through the meridians by:

- Opening the energetic pathways at the joint.
- Removing resistance or stagnation in the energy flow.
- Allowing energy to circulate freely through the body's entire meridian system.

I trust the wisdom of my body. Energy flows freely through me, restoring balance and strength.

When the energy flow through the meridians is restored, the body's natural healing mechanisms are activated. This supports improved circulation, reduced inflammation, and enhanced muscle and joint function.

Example:

- Tightness in the knee may reflect a blockage in the Kidney or Stomach Meridian.
- When Reiki dissolves this blockage, the flow of energy through the knee improves, leading to reduced pain and greater mobility.
- As energy flow through the meridians improves, related physical and emotional issues — such as fear or digestive problems — may also resolve.

3. Release Stored Emotional Tension

Joints are emotional "storage containers" where unresolved emotional experiences and trauma are held. When an emotional experience is not fully processed, it can become lodged in the body's energetic field — often settling in the joints.

Reiki works to release emotional tension by:

- Sending healing energy directly into the joint.
- Dissolving the energetic imprint of past emotional experiences.
- Helping the body integrate and release emotional patterns that are no longer serving the individual.

Emotional patterns stored in the joints are often linked to specific energetic themes:

- Shoulders – Carrying emotional burdens or feeling responsible for others.
- Hips – Fear of emotional movement or creative expression.
- Knees – Fear of moving forward in life or lack of confidence.
- Ankles – Feeling ungrounded or uncertain about life's direction.

When Reiki releases the stored emotional energy, the joint often becomes more mobile and pain-free. The emotional release creates a profound sense of lightness and emotional clarity.

Example:

- A person with tight hips may release stored grief or creative blocks after a focused Reiki session.
- Someone with knee pain related to fear of change may feel both emotional relief and physical strength after the energetic blockage is dissolved.

4. Improve Joint Mobility and Reduce Inflammation

Inflammation in the joints is often linked to both physical and energetic stagnation. When energy cannot circulate freely through the joint, it creates heat and pressure, leading to inflammation and pain.

I trust the wisdom of my body. Energy flows freely through me, restoring balance and strength

Reiki improves joint health by:

- Reducing heat and inflammation through the flow of cooling energy.
- Releasing pressure caused by blocked energy.
- Enhancing the flow of blood and synovial fluid to the joint.
- Improving muscle relaxation and alignment around the joint.

The physical release created by Reiki improves range of motion, reduces swelling, and allows the joint to function more smoothly.

Example:

- A person with arthritis in the knees may experience reduced inflammation and improved flexibility after consistent Reiki sessions targeting the knee joint and Kidney Meridian.
- Someone with shoulder stiffness may experience improved range of motion and reduced tension after Reiki clears the energetic blockage.

5. Enhance Overall Emotional Balance and Resilience

Because joints are linked to both physical and emotional health, balancing the energy in the joints creates a sense of emotional resilience and stability. When the joints are free of tension and energy is flowing smoothly, you feel more emotionally balanced and grounded.

Reiki enhances emotional well-being by:

- Restoring the natural flow of emotional energy.
- Strengthening the emotional body's ability to process and release difficult emotions.
- Creating a sense of emotional lightness and clarity.
- Enhancing the ability to adapt to life's challenges with confidence and ease.

Example:

- A person with chronic hip pain related to emotional holding patterns may experience increased emotional openness and creative flow after Reiki clears the blockage.
- Someone with tight shoulders due to stress and emotional burden may experience both physical relief and emotional lightness after a Reiki session focused on the Heart and Lung Meridians.

Why Reiki Is Effective

Most conventional approaches to joint health — such as physical therapy, chiropractic care, and medication — focus on the physical structure of the joint. While these methods can improve physical function, they often fail to address the **energetic and emotional root causes** of joint pain and stiffness.

I trust the wisdom of my body. Energy flows freely through me, restoring balance and strength

Reiki differs because it:

- Works at the level of the energetic field to release emotional and spiritual patterns.
- Balances the body's energy flow through the meridians and chakras.
- Addresses both the physical and emotional aspects of joint health.
- Creates lasting improvements in both physical mobility and emotional resilience.

Conventional Approach:

- Focus on muscles, ligaments, and bones.
- Relieves pain through medication, rest, or physical therapy.
- May temporarily improve mobility but often does not address emotional causes.

Reiki Approach:

- Focus on energetic flow and emotional patterns.
- Restores natural energy balance through the joints.
- Creates emotional release and improved physical function simultaneously.

Key Takeaways:

- Reiki works by dissolving energetic blockages stored in the joints.
- Restores the natural flow of energy through the meridians and chakras.
- Releases emotional tension and stored trauma from the joints.
- Improves physical mobility, reduces inflammation, and enhances emotional balance.
- Balances the emotional and spiritual patterns that underlie joint health issues.

I trust the wisdom of my body. Energy flows freely through me, restoring balance and strength

Chapter 2: The Metaphysical Meaning of Joints

How Joints Represent Flexibility and Adaptability

Joints are not only essential for physical movement and support — they also serve as energetic symbols of flexibility and adaptability in life. The state of your joints reflects your ability to navigate change, adjust to challenges, and remain open to new experiences.

Just as physical flexibility allows the body to bend, rotate, and extend without strain, emotional and spiritual flexibility allows you to adapt to life's inevitable ups and downs with ease. When your joints are healthy and mobile, energy flows freely through the body's energetic system, supporting emotional resilience and mental clarity. On the other hand, stiffness, tension, or instability in the joints can signal emotional resistance, fear of change, or an inability to adjust to new circumstances.

Understanding the connection between joint health and emotional adaptability allows you to use Reiki not only to improve physical mobility but also to enhance emotional openness and spiritual flow. By restoring balance and energy flow to the joints, you create greater ease and adaptability in both the physical body and the emotional self.

The Symbolism of Joints as Points of Flexibility

Joints represent the body's ability to move and adapt. Every time you bend your knee, rotate your shoulder, or twist your wrist, you are physically demonstrating flexibility and openness to movement.

From an energetic perspective, joints symbolize the body's ability to adjust and flow with the changing currents of life. When joints are healthy and fluid, they reflect an open and balanced energetic state — a willingness to release the past, embrace change, and remain grounded while moving forward.

However, when joints become stiff or painful, it reflects resistance — both physically and emotionally:

- Fear of change.
- Attachment to the past.
- Inability to let go of old patterns.
- Emotional rigidity or defensiveness.

Reiki works to restore physical and emotional flexibility by dissolving the energetic patterns that create joint stiffness or misalignment.

I trust the wisdom of my body. Energy flows freely through me, restoring balance and strength

Physical Flexibility = Emotional Adaptability

Physical flexibility — the ability of the joints and muscles to move freely without restriction — mirrors emotional flexibility and adaptability. When joints are open and mobile, energy flows freely through the body, supporting emotional resilience and a sense of ease.

What Physical Flexibility Reflects Energetically:

- Fluidity – An open flow of emotional and spiritual energy.
- Adaptability – A willingness to embrace change and adjust to new situations.
- Balance – Emotional and physical alignment, with the ability to respond rather than react.
- Strength – A sense of inner security that allows you to face challenges without resistance.

When your body can bend and stretch without pain or tension, it reflects emotional openness and spiritual flow. A person who is physically flexible is often emotionally adaptable — able to process life's challenges without holding onto resistance or fear.

For example:

- A yoga practitioner who can flow effortlessly through poses is often someone who is emotionally fluid and open to life's changes.
- A person who maintains flexible joints through mindful movement and energy work is more likely

to remain emotionally balanced during times of stress or uncertainty.

Joint Flexibility as a Reflection of Emotional Flexibility

When joints are flexible, they reflect an emotional state of:

- Openness — Willingness to embrace new experiences and perspectives.
- Adaptability — Ability to adjust to changing circumstances without stress.
- Emotional Resilience — The capacity to remain grounded even when life's circumstances shift.
- Creative Flow — The ability to express yourself emotionally and creatively without fear.

When you can physically move your body with ease, you are more likely to experience emotional ease and adaptability in life. Flexible joints reflect an internal state of openness, trust, and creative flow.

Stiffness = Emotional Rigidity and Resistance

Just as physical flexibility reflects emotional adaptability, joint stiffness reflects emotional resistance. When a joint becomes stiff, inflamed, or limited in movement, it often signals that there is a corresponding emotional blockage or resistance to change.

What Physical Stiffness Reflects Energetically:

- Fear of Change – Resistance to letting go or stepping into the unknown.

I trust the wisdom of my body. Energy flows freely through me, restoring balance and strength

- Emotional Rigidity – Difficulty processing or accepting new emotional experiences.
- Attachment to the Past – Holding onto old patterns or beliefs that no longer serve you.
- Control Issues – A tendency to micromanage life rather than trust the natural flow.

Stiffness in the joints creates a feedback loop between the body and the mind:

1. Emotional resistance creates energetic blockages in the joints.
2. Blocked energy in the joints leads to physical stiffness and discomfort.
3. Physical discomfort reinforces emotional patterns of control, fear, or rigidity.

Examples of Emotional Rigidity Manifesting as Joint Stiffness:

- Tight shoulders reflect the emotional burden of responsibility and an unwillingness to ask for help.
- Stiff hips reflect a fear of vulnerability or emotional expression.
- Locked knees reflect an unwillingness to move forward or embrace life's unfolding path.
- Limited wrist mobility reflects creative blocks or fear of expressing one's true self.

Reiki works to dissolve these patterns by targeting both the physical and emotional root causes of joint stiffness.

For example:

- A person who struggles with creative expression may experience tightness in the hips and wrists. Reiki applied to the Sacral Chakra and related meridians can help release these emotional blocks, improving both mobility and creative flow.
- A person who resists emotional vulnerability may experience shoulder stiffness. Reiki applied to the Heart Chakra and shoulder joints can help release emotional tension and improve flexibility.

Instability in Joints = Lack of Emotional Grounding

While stiffness reflects emotional rigidity, joint instability reflects emotional insecurity and a lack of grounding. When a joint feels weak or unstable, it often reflects an underlying sense of fear, lack of confidence, or emotional imbalance.

What Joint Instability Reflects Energetically:

- Lack of Trust – Difficulty trusting the flow of life or feeling emotionally secure.
- Emotional Instability – Difficulty maintaining emotional balance during times of stress.
- Insecurity – Feeling unsupported or uncertain about life's direction.
- Lack of Grounding – Feeling disconnected from one's physical body or spiritual path.

I trust the wisdom of my body. Energy flows freely through me, restoring balance and strength

Examples of Emotional Instability Manifesting as Joint Weakness:

- Weak knees reflect fear of stepping forward or making life decisions.
- Unstable ankles reflect difficulty maintaining emotional or spiritual balance.
- Loose shoulders reflect emotional vulnerability and lack of self-protection.

Reiki helps restore emotional balance and security by:

- Strengthening the energetic flow through the joints.
- Restoring balance to the related chakras and meridians.
- Creating a sense of inner security and emotional strength.

Reiki and the Restoration of Flexibility

Reiki is uniquely suited to improve flexibility and adaptability because it works at the energetic level — where emotional patterns and physical alignment intersect.

Reiki helps to:

- Dissolve energetic blockages causing stiffness.
- Release stored emotional patterns that create resistance.
- Strengthen the flow of ki through the meridians, supporting natural mobility.

- Align the emotional body with the physical body, improving resilience and adaptability.

Reiki Techniques for Flexibility:

1. Apply Reiki to the Chakras – Work on the Root Chakra for grounding and the Sacral Chakra for creative flow.
2. Use Reiki Symbols – Use Cho Ku Rei for power and Sei He Ki for emotional release.
3. Direct Reiki to the Joints – Place hands directly on or near the joint, visualizing energy flowing through the joint and dissolving stiffness.
4. Combine Reiki with Breathwork – Encourage deep, rhythmic breathing to enhance energy flow and emotional release.
5. Set the Intention for Openness and Flexibility – Use affirmations and visualization to reinforce emotional flexibility.

I trust the wisdom of my body. Energy flows freely through me, restoring balance and strength

Emotional Storage in Joints and How This Affects Healing

Joints are not just physical connectors that enable movement — they are also emotional storage sites where unresolved emotions, stress, and trauma are held in the body. The body and mind are deeply interconnected, and emotional experiences that are not fully processed often become embedded in the physical body, particularly in the joints.

In Reiki and other forms of energy healing, it is understood that emotional energy moves through the body along the meridians and is processed through the chakras. When an emotion is not fully expressed or released, the energy of that emotion becomes "trapped" in the body, often settling in the joints where multiple energy pathways intersect.

This stored emotional energy creates blockages in the flow of ki (life force energy), leading to stiffness, inflammation, and pain in the joints. It also reinforces emotional patterns, such as fear, resentment, or grief, which can limit emotional growth and flexibility. Healing joint-related issues through Reiki requires not only addressing the physical discomfort but also releasing the underlying emotional energy that is stored in the joint.

When Reiki is applied to joints, it works to dissolve these stored emotional patterns, restoring the free flow of energy through the meridians and chakras and encouraging emotional release and healing.

How Emotional Energy Becomes Stored in Joints

Every emotional experience carries an energetic charge. When you experience an emotion — such as fear, sadness, anger, or joy — that emotional energy moves through the body's energetic system, influencing the flow of ki.

When emotional energy is processed in a healthy way, it moves through the system, is integrated, and then released. However, when emotional energy is not fully processed — due to trauma, stress, or emotional resistance — it becomes trapped in the body's energetic field.

Three Primary Ways Emotional Energy Becomes Stored in Joints:

1. Unprocessed Emotional Experiences
     o When a traumatic or emotionally intense experience occurs, the body's nervous system and energetic system respond by contracting or "freezing."
     o If the emotional charge from the experience is not processed or expressed, the energy becomes stuck in the body, often settling in the joints.
     o This stored emotional energy creates muscle tension, joint stiffness, and restricted range of motion.
2. Emotional Defense Mechanisms

I trust the wisdom of my body. Energy flows freely through me, restoring balance and strength.

- o The body develops physical patterns to protect itself from emotional pain.
- o If you experience repeated emotional hurt — such as rejection or betrayal — the body may create a protective holding pattern in the joints.
- o This pattern creates physical stiffness or misalignment, reinforcing the emotional defense.
- o For example, someone who has experienced emotional rejection may tighten their shoulders as a form of emotional self-protection, leading to chronic tension or limited range of motion.

3. Energetic Imprints from Childhood or Past Lives
    - o Emotional patterns are often imprinted early in life or even carried from past life experiences.
    - o If emotional lessons are not fully processed or healed, the energetic imprint can remain in the body's energy field — especially in the joints — creating emotional and physical limitations.
    - o For example, someone who was taught to fear emotional vulnerability may carry that fear in the form of tight, restricted shoulders.

Why Joints Are Vulnerable to Emotional Storage

Joints are particularly prone to emotional storage because they serve as energy intersections where multiple meridians and energy pathways meet. This makes them energetically "sensitive" to the flow of emotional energy through the body.

When an emotional pattern creates tension or restriction in the body's energy system, the blockage often "settles" at the joints, where energy flow is naturally slower due to the complex intersection of pathways.

Reasons Joints Store Emotional Energy:

- Intersection of Meridians – Multiple meridians meet at the joints, making them natural storage points for energy.
- Slower Energy Flow – Joints have slower energetic circulation due to their structural function, making them more likely to retain stagnant energy.
- Protection Mechanism – The body "locks down" joints in response to emotional pain or trauma as a way of protecting itself.
- Emotional Patterns Reinforce Structural Patterns – Emotional holding patterns create muscle tension, which reinforces joint misalignment and stiffness.

For example:

- Emotional patterns related to security and stability often store themselves in the knees and hips because these joints are linked to the Root Chakra.
- Emotional patterns related to communication and trust often store themselves in the wrists and elbows because these joints are connected to the Throat Chakra and Heart Chakra.

I trust the wisdom of my body. Energy flows freely through me, restoring balance and strength

- Emotional patterns related to emotional burdens often store themselves in the shoulders because this joint is connected to the Heart and Lung Meridians.

Emotions Commonly Stored in Specific Joints

Each joint in the body is connected to a particular energetic and emotional theme. The type of emotion stored in a joint often reflects the joint's metaphysical function and its connection to specific chakras and meridians.

Joint	Chakra Connection	Emotional Theme
Shoulders	Heart Chakra	Carrying emotional burdens, resistance to vulnerability.
Elbows	Heart and Solar Plexus Chakra	Flexibility in relationships, giving and receiving support.
Wrists	Throat Chakra	Trust, communication, creative flow.
Hips	Sacral Chakra	Emotional movement, creativity, and sexual expression.

Joint	Chakra Connection	Emotional Theme
Knees	Root and Solar Plexus Chakra	Fear of moving forward, trust in life's path.
Ankles	Root and Sacral Chakra	Balance, direction, and stability.
Fingers and Toes	Crown and Throat Chakra	Precision, action, and control.

Examples of Emotional Storage in Joints:

1. Shoulders – A person who feels emotionally burdened or responsible for others may develop chronic shoulder tension.
2. Hips – A person who fears emotional vulnerability or creative expression may experience tightness or pain in the hips.
3. Knees – A person who feels insecure about their future or fearful about life's path may develop weakness or instability in the knees.
4. Ankles – A person who feels off balance or uncertain about their life's direction may experience repeated ankle sprains or instability.
5. Wrists – A person who fears expressing themselves creatively or verbally may develop stiffness or pain in the wrists.

I trust the wisdom of my body. Energy flows freely through me, restoring balance and strength.

How Stored Emotional Energy Affects Healing

Emotional energy stored in the joints creates an energetic blockage that disrupts the flow of ki through the body's meridians and chakras. This affects both the body's physical structure and emotional balance.

Impact of Stored Emotional Energy on Healing:

- Physical Resistance – Stiff joints and limited range of motion.
- Energetic Resistance – Reduced flow of energy through the meridians and chakras.
- Emotional Holding Patterns – Fear, grief, or anger may become habitual emotional responses.
- Delayed Recovery – The body's ability to heal itself is reduced when energy flow is restricted.

How Reiki Releases Stored Emotional Energy in Joints

Reiki is uniquely suited to work with emotional storage in the joints because it addresses the issue at the energetic level. Reiki works by:

- Directing ki (life force energy) into the joint.
- Dissolving the energetic block and emotional imprint stored in the joint.
- Restoring the natural flow of energy through the joint.
- Releasing the emotional pattern connected to the joint.
- Improving physical mobility and emotional resilience.

Reiki Techniques for Releasing Emotional Storage:

1. Use Reiki symbols – Sei He Ki (emotional healing) and Cho Ku Rei (power) can dissolve emotional patterns stored in the joints.
2. Place hands directly on the joint – Channel energy into the joint to release emotional knots.
3. Use breathwork and intention – Direct the client to breathe deeply to facilitate the release of emotional energy.
4. Visualize emotional release – Imagine the emotional energy dissolving and flowing out of the joint.

Key Takeaways:

- Emotional energy often becomes trapped in the joints.
- Reiki releases stored emotional energy and restores balance.
- Dissolving emotional blocks improves both physical and emotional health.
- Flexible joints reflect emotional flow and adaptability.

I trust the wisdom of my body. Energy flows freely through me, restoring balance and strength.

Connection Between Joints and Life Patterns

Joints are not only physical connectors — they serve as mirrors of life's emotional and spiritual patterns. Every joint in the body corresponds to a specific emotional or spiritual theme, which reflects how you process life experiences, navigate challenges, and embody emotional resilience. When a joint becomes stiff, weak, or painful, it often signals a disruption in the underlying life pattern connected to that joint.

From a metaphysical perspective, the joints function as gateways where the body stores emotional experiences and life lessons. These life patterns are connected to the body's energy system through the chakras and meridians. When energy is blocked or misaligned in a joint, it reflects an unresolved emotional issue or resistance to a life lesson.

Reiki addresses this connection by working at the energetic level — helping to dissolve the emotional patterns stored in the joint and restore the natural flow of energy. When you heal a joint through Reiki, you are not only improving physical mobility but also helping the individual integrate and resolve the life patterns tied to that joint.

The Body as a Reflection of Life's Journey

Your body is a physical manifestation of your emotional and spiritual state. Just as your physical posture reflects your emotional state (e.g., slouching when feeling defeated or standing tall when feeling confident), the condition of your joints reflects how you engage with life's challenges and transitions.

Joints are located at the places where the body bends and adapts — symbolizing the ability to adjust to life's changes and challenges. When a joint becomes blocked or restricted, it reflects emotional or spiritual resistance to that aspect of life.

For example:

- If your knees are stiff and painful, you may be struggling with humility or resisting change.
- If your hips are tight or misaligned, you may be holding onto fear of emotional vulnerability or creative expression.
- If your shoulders feel tense and heavy, you may be carrying emotional burdens or feeling overwhelmed by responsibility.

Understanding the emotional and spiritual symbolism behind each joint allows you to approach joint healing with greater depth and insight. Reiki works to dissolve these patterns and restore both emotional and physical flexibility.

I trust the wisdom of my body. Energy flows freely through me, restoring balance and strength

Joints as Gateways to Emotional and Spiritual Lessons

Each joint holds a specific life theme tied to the body's energetic and emotional system. These themes reflect both personal and collective life lessons. When a joint becomes blocked, it signals that there is an emotional or spiritual lesson that has not yet been integrated or resolved.

Healing the joint through Reiki helps the individual process and release these life lessons, creating greater emotional and spiritual freedom.

Connection Between Specific Joints and Life Patterns

1. Knees – Humility, Trust, and Moving Forward

The knees are connected to the Root Chakra and Solar Plexus Chakra, which govern security, confidence, and trust in life's unfolding path.

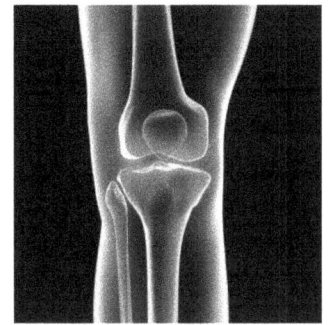

Emotional and Spiritual Themes:

- Trust in life's path.
- Confidence in decision-making.
- Humility and surrender to life's flow.
- Fear of vulnerability and instability.

Blocked Knee Energy Reflects:

- Fear of moving forward in life.

- Lack of confidence in your decisions.
- Stubbornness or resistance to change.
- Emotional rigidity or unwillingness to let go of control.

Example:

- A person who experiences recurring knee pain may feel stuck in life, fearful of stepping into new territory or uncertain about life's direction.
- Reiki applied to the knees helps dissolve fear and restore confidence, allowing the person to feel more secure and emotionally grounded.

2. Hips – Emotional Movement, Creativity, and Sexual Expression

The hips are connected to the Sacral Chakra, which governs emotional flow, creativity, and relationships.

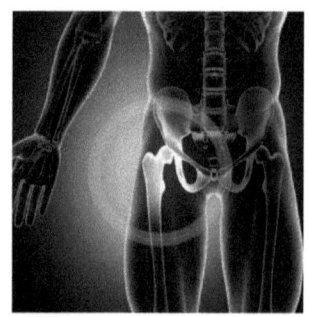

Emotional and Spiritual Themes:

- Emotional movement and expression.
- Creative flow and sexual energy.
- Openness to change and life's transitions.
- Fear of emotional vulnerability or intimacy.

Blocked Hip Energy Reflects:

- Creative blocks or difficulty expressing emotions.
- Fear of emotional vulnerability.

I trust the wisdom of my body. Energy flows freely through me, restoring balance and strength

- Resistance to new experiences or changes in relationships.
- Holding onto past trauma or emotional pain.

Example:

- A person with tight or painful hips may struggle with emotional intimacy or creative expression.
- Reiki focused on the hips and Sacral Chakra helps release emotional blockages and restore creative and emotional flow.

3. Shoulders – Emotional Burdens and Self-Expression

The shoulders are connected to the Heart Chakra and Throat Chakra, which govern emotional connection, love, and communication.

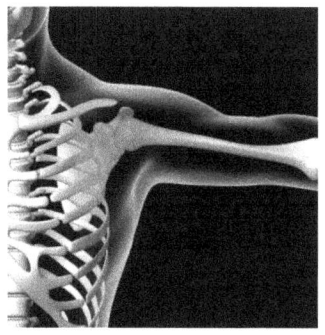

Emotional and Spiritual Themes:

- Carrying emotional burdens or responsibilities.
- Resistance to vulnerability and emotional openness.
- Difficulty expressing feelings or asking for help.
- Fear of rejection or emotional exposure.

Blocked Shoulder Energy Reflects:

- Feeling overburdened or responsible for others' emotional well-being.

- Emotional withdrawal or suppression.
- Difficulty asking for support or setting emotional boundaries.
- Fear of opening the heart or expressing vulnerability.

Example:

- A person with chronic shoulder tension may be carrying the emotional burden of family or relationship issues.
- Reiki applied to the shoulders and Heart Chakra helps release emotional heaviness and restore emotional openness.

4. Elbows – Flexibility in Relationships and Life's Direction

The elbows are connected to the Heart Chakra and Solar Plexus Chakra, which govern emotional strength and adaptability.

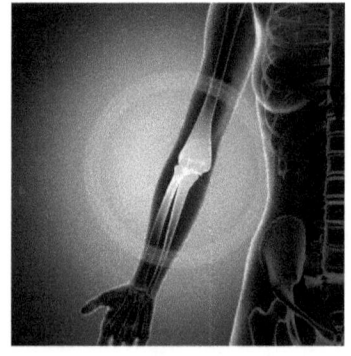

Emotional and Spiritual Themes:

- Flexibility in relationships and personal identity.
- Ability to give and receive emotional support.
- Trust in life's unfolding path.
- Willingness to adjust to new circumstances.

Blocked Elbow Energy Reflects:

- Resistance to giving or receiving emotional support.
- Difficulty adapting to changing circumstances.
- Emotional control issues.
- Inability to trust others or life's flow.

Example:

- A person with stiff elbows may struggle with trusting others or accepting help.
- Reiki focused on the elbows helps dissolve emotional resistance and restores emotional flow.

5. Wrists – Trust and Creative Flow

The wrists are connected to the Throat Chakra and Sacral Chakra, which govern communication and creative expression.

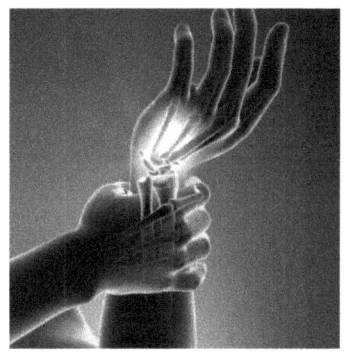

Emotional and Spiritual Themes:

- Trust in personal expression.
- Creative freedom and emotional openness.
- Ability to adapt to life's flow.
- Fear of exposure or creative vulnerability.

Blocked Wrist Energy Reflects:

- Fear of expressing creativity or personal truth.
- Feeling emotionally or creatively restricted.

- Resistance to change in personal identity.

Example:

- A person with weak or painful wrists may feel creatively blocked or fearful of speaking their truth.
- Reiki applied to the wrists helps restore creative and emotional flow.

6. Ankles – Balance, Grounding, and Trust in Life

The ankles are connected to the Root Chakra and Sacral Chakra, which govern grounding, balance, and stability.

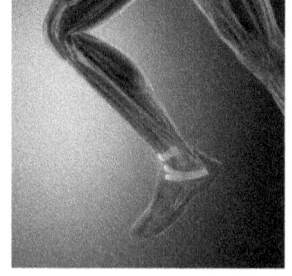

Emotional and Spiritual Themes:

- Stability and security.
- Trust in life's unfolding process.
- Emotional and physical balance.
- Ability to adjust to life's direction.

Blocked Ankle Energy Reflects:

- Fear of losing balance or security.
- Resistance to change or transition.
- Emotional instability.

Example:

I trust the wisdom of my body. Energy flows freely through me, restoring balance and strengt

- A person with weak or unstable ankles may feel emotionally ungrounded or uncertain about life's direction.
- Reiki focused on the ankles and Root Chakra helps restore emotional balance and grounding.

7. Fingers and Toes – Precision and Action

The fingers and toes are connected to the Crown Chakra and Throat Chakra, which govern personal expression and higher consciousness.

Emotional and Spiritual Themes:

- Precision and confidence in action.
- Trust in personal expression and decision-making.
- Spiritual alignment and trust in intuition.

Blocked Finger or Toe Energy Reflects:

- Lack of confidence in personal decisions.
- Feeling disconnected from intuition.
- Fear of expressing oneself or taking action.

Example:

- A person with weak or stiff fingers may struggle with expressing creativity or making decisions.

- Reiki focused on the fingers and Crown Chakra helps restore confidence and trust in personal expression.

How Reiki Restores Life Patterns Through Joint Healing

- Reiki clears emotional patterns stored in the joints.
- Reiki restores energetic flow through the chakras and meridians.
- Reiki helps integrate life lessons connected to joint health.
- Reiki restores emotional and spiritual balance.

Key Takeaways:

- Joints reflect emotional and spiritual life patterns.
- Stiffness and weakness reflect emotional and energetic resistance.
- Reiki restores flow, flexibility, and alignment.
- Healing joints helps integrate emotional and spiritual lessons.

I trust the wisdom of my body. Energy flows freely through me, restoring balance and strength

Chapter 3: Secondary Chakras/Energy Points in Joints

While the seven primary chakras are widely known and understood in Reiki practice, the body also contains a network of secondary chakras and energy points that are equally significant for maintaining balance and health. These secondary energy centers are often located at the joints — the elbows, knees, shoulders, wrists, ankles, and hips — where multiple energy channels (meridians) intersect.

Joints serve as energetic crosspoints where the body's energy flow is regulated and redirected. The secondary chakras located in these joints act as smaller energy hubs that influence physical mobility, emotional flow, and spiritual alignment. When the energy in a joint becomes blocked, it creates both physical stiffness and emotional or energetic resistance.

Understanding the role of secondary chakras in joint health allows Reiki practitioners to work more effectively with the body's subtle energy system, helping to dissolve blockages and restore balance at a deeper level.

The Role of Secondary Chakras in Energy Flow

The body's energy system is made up of two primary components:

1. Chakras – Large, spinning wheels of energy that govern physical, emotional, and spiritual health.
2. Meridians – Pathways that distribute energy throughout the body and connect the chakras to the muscles, tissues, and organs.

The seven primary chakras form the body's central energy column, but the flow of energy throughout the rest of the body depends on the smaller secondary chakras and energy points located at the joints. These secondary chakras act like "satellite stations" that regulate the flow of ki through the body's meridian network.

When a secondary chakra at a joint is open and balanced, energy flows freely, supporting physical mobility and emotional ease. However, when a secondary chakra becomes blocked or misaligned, it disrupts the flow of energy through the related meridians and the primary chakra system — leading to physical stiffness, emotional imbalance, and reduced spiritual connection.

Why Joints Hold Secondary Chakras

Joints are ideal locations for secondary chakras because they function as connection points where different energy channels and physical structures meet.

I trust the wisdom of my body. Energy flows freely through me, restoring balance and strength.

- Meridians intersect at the joints, making them high-traffic areas for energetic flow.
- Emotional energy and stress often collect at the joints due to the slower circulation of energy at these points.
- Joints act as energetic "hinges" — allowing for both physical and emotional movement and adjustment.
- When emotional patterns become stuck, they often settle in the joints, creating physical tension and energetic blockages.

For example:

- A blocked secondary chakra at the knee may restrict the flow of energy through the Root Chakra, creating a feeling of instability or insecurity.
- A blocked secondary chakra at the shoulder may reduce the flow of energy through the Heart Chakra, limiting emotional openness and vulnerability.
- Tightness in the hip joint may reflect a blockage in the Sacral Chakra, reducing creative flow and emotional expression.

Reiki works by dissolving these energetic knots, restoring the flow of energy through both the secondary chakras and the primary energy system.

The Lesser-Known Energy Centers at the Joints

The secondary chakras located at the joints are just as important to energetic health as the primary chakras. Each joint represents a specific emotional and energetic theme, tied to both physical and emotional flexibility.

1. Elbow Chakra – Flexibility in Giving and Receiving

The elbows are connected to the Heart Chakra and the Solar Plexus Chakra.

Emotional and Spiritual Themes:

- Ability to give and receive emotional support.
- Flexibility in relationships and personal boundaries.
- Willingness to adjust to changing emotional circumstances.

Blocked Elbow Chakra Reflects:

- Difficulty trusting others.
- Emotional defensiveness.
- Resistance to asking for or receiving help.
- Feeling "closed off" or emotionally guarded.

Example:

- A person with stiff or painful elbows may feel emotionally inflexible and unwilling to receive support from others.

I trust the wisdom of my body. Energy flows freely through me, restoring balance and strength

- Reiki directed to the elbows and Heart Chakra can restore emotional balance and improve trust and connection in relationships.

2. Shoulder Chakra – Carrying Emotional Burdens

The shoulders are connected to the Heart Chakra and the Throat Chakra.

Emotional and Spiritual Themes:

- Responsibility and emotional burdens.
- Self-expression and vulnerability.
- Emotional protection and openness.

Blocked Shoulder Chakra Reflects:

- Feeling emotionally overburdened or responsible for others.
- Difficulty expressing vulnerability.
- Emotional heaviness or tension.
- Fear of emotional rejection or exposure.

Example:

- A person with tense shoulders may be "carrying the weight of the world" emotionally.
- Reiki directed to the shoulders and Heart Chakra can release emotional burdens and restore emotional ease.

3. Knee Chakra – Humility and Trust in Life's Path

The knees are connected to the Root Chakra and the Solar Plexus Chakra.

Emotional and Spiritual Themes:

- Trust in life's unfolding path.
- Confidence in personal decisions.
- Humility and emotional surrender.

Blocked Knee Chakra Reflects:

- Fear of moving forward.
- Resistance to change.
- Lack of emotional confidence or trust in life's direction.

Example:

- A person with chronic knee issues may feel emotionally insecure or resistant to life changes.
- Reiki directed to the knees and Root Chakra helps restore confidence and emotional trust.

4. Hip Chakra – Emotional Movement and Creative Flow

The hips are connected to the Sacral Chakra and the Root Chakra.

Emotional and Spiritual Themes:

- Emotional flow and adaptability.

I trust the wisdom of my body. Energy flows freely through me, restoring balance and strength

- Creativity and personal expression.
- Sexual and emotional vulnerability.

Blocked Hip Chakra Reflects:

- Fear of emotional or creative expression.
- Emotional holding patterns related to past trauma.
- Resistance to change or personal growth.

Example:

- A person with tight or painful hips may feel emotionally guarded or creatively blocked.
- Reiki focused on the hips and Sacral Chakra can dissolve emotional resistance and restore creative flow.

5. Wrist Chakra – Trust and Communication

The wrists are connected to the Throat Chakra and the Sacral Chakra.

Emotional and Spiritual Themes:

- Trust in emotional and creative expression.
- Ability to communicate openly and honestly.
- Flexibility in relationships and creative flow.

Blocked Wrist Chakra Reflects:

- Fear of expressing oneself.
- Feeling creatively blocked or restricted.
- Emotional resistance to communication.

Example:

- A person with weak or painful wrists may struggle with expressing their true thoughts or emotions.
- Reiki focused on the wrists and Throat Chakra helps restore creative and emotional balance.

6. Ankle Chakra – Balance and Direction

The ankles are connected to the Root Chakra and the Sacral Chakra.

Emotional and Spiritual Themes:

- Stability and balance.
- Emotional grounding and security.
- Trust in life's path and unfolding process.

Blocked Ankle Chakra Reflects:

- Fear of losing balance or control.
- Emotional instability.
- Resistance to personal or professional change.

Example:

- A person with weak or unstable ankles may feel emotionally or spiritually ungrounded.
- Reiki focused on the ankles and Root Chakra helps restore stability and emotional strength.

I trust the wisdom of my body. Energy flows freely through me, restoring balance and strength.

How Reiki Works with Secondary Chakras

Reiki helps restore balance to the secondary chakras by:

- Dissolving energetic blockages in the joint.
- Restoring the flow of ki through the meridians and chakras.
- Releasing stored emotional patterns.
- Strengthening the joint's physical and energetic alignment.

Reiki Techniques for Secondary Chakras:

1. Hand Placement on Joints – Place hands directly on the joint to channel Reiki.
2. Sei He Ki Symbol – Use the emotional healing symbol to dissolve emotional resistance.
3. Cho Ku Rei Symbol – Use the power symbol to strengthen the joint's energetic flow.
4. Visualization – Imagine the joint filling with light and energy, clearing all blockages.

Key Takeaways:

- Secondary chakras are located at the joints.
- Blocked secondary chakras reflect emotional patterns and resistance.
- Reiki restores balance by dissolving energetic blockages and restoring flow.
- Healing secondary chakras creates physical, emotional, and spiritual harmony.

The Flow of Energy Through Joints and Its Connection to Chakras

The body's energy system operates through a network of chakras and meridians that distribute life force energy (ki) throughout the body. While the primary chakras act as the body's main energy centers, the meridians function as channels that carry this energy to every muscle, organ, and tissue.

Joints serve as crossroads where multiple energy pathways intersect. This makes them essential for regulating and distributing energy throughout the body. The flow of energy through the joints directly affects not only physical mobility but also emotional balance and spiritual alignment.

When energy flows smoothly through the joints, the body experiences flexibility, strength, and emotional ease. However, when energy becomes blocked or stagnant in a joint, it creates physical discomfort, emotional resistance, and energetic misalignment. Understanding the flow of energy through the joints — and its connection to the chakras — allows Reiki practitioners to work more effectively to restore balance and flow at the deepest level.

I trust the wisdom of my body. Energy flows freely through me, restoring balance and strength

The Role of Joints in Energy Flow

In the body's energy system, chakras and meridians work together to create a dynamic and balanced flow of energy.

- The primary chakras regulate the major aspects of physical, emotional, and spiritual health.
- The meridians carry energy from the chakras to specific areas of the body, including the muscles, tissues, and joints.
- The secondary chakras located at the joints act as key distribution points, regulating how energy circulates through the body.

Joints serve as high-traffic areas for energy flow because they are where multiple meridians and energy channels meet. This makes joints highly sensitive to both physical and emotional imbalances.

How Energy Flows Through the Joints:

1. Energy originates in the chakras.
2. The chakras send energy into the meridians.
3. The meridians direct energy through the joints and distribute it to the muscles, tissues, and organs.
4. When energy is flowing freely, the joints remain flexible, strong, and pain-free.
5. When energy becomes blocked at a joint, it creates physical stiffness and emotional resistance.

Example of Energy Flow in Action:

- When energy flows freely from the Root Chakra into the legs and knees, it creates a sense of stability and grounding.
- If energy becomes blocked in the knee joint, it can cause physical stiffness and emotional insecurity (reflecting a disruption in Root Chakra energy).
- Reiki helps restore balance by dissolving the blockage at the knee joint and encouraging energy to flow smoothly from the Root Chakra through the meridians to the legs.

Chakra Connection to Joint Health

Each joint is energetically linked to a specific chakra (or combination of chakras). The health and flexibility of the joint reflect the balance or imbalance of the related chakra.

When a chakra is open and balanced, energy flows smoothly through the corresponding joint, supporting physical mobility and emotional well-being. When a chakra becomes blocked or misaligned, energy flow through the joint becomes restricted, leading to stiffness, pain, or instability.

I trust the wisdom of my body. Energy flows freely through me, restoring balance and strength

Primary Chakra-Joint Connections

Joint	Primary Chakra Connection	Energetic Function
Shoulders	Heart Chakra, Throat Chakra	Emotional openness, giving and receiving love, self-expression
Elbows	Heart Chakra, Solar Plexus Chakra	Flexibility in relationships, personal boundaries
Wrists	Throat Chakra, Sacral Chakra	Trust, communication, creative expression
Hips	Sacral Chakra, Root Chakra	Emotional movement, creativity, grounding
Knees	Root Chakra, Solar Plexus Chakra	Stability, confidence, trust in life's path
Ankles	Root Chakra, Sacral Chakra	Balance, emotional security, direction in life
Fingers and Toes	Crown Chakra, Throat Chakra	Precision, decision-making, action

How Chakra Imbalances Affect Joint Health:

When a chakra becomes blocked, the energy flow to the related joint is weakened or distorted, creating both physical and emotional symptoms:

- Overactive Chakra: Too much energy directed toward the joint creates inflammation, tension, and overuse injuries.
- Underactive Chakra: Weak or limited energy flow leads to joint instability, weakness, and poor range of motion.
- Blocked Chakra: Completely stagnant energy flow creates stiffness, pain, and restricted movement.

Example:

- If the Root Chakra is blocked, the energy flow through the knees and ankles will be restricted, creating instability and feelings of insecurity.
- If the Heart Chakra is overactive, the shoulders may hold excessive tension, leading to tightness or limited range of motion.
- If the Throat Chakra is weak, the wrists and elbows may feel unstable or weak, reflecting difficulty in communication and creative expression.

I trust the wisdom of my body. Energy flows freely through me, restoring balance and strength

Energy Flow Through Specific Joints and Chakras

1. Shoulders – Heart and Throat Chakra Connection

- The shoulders reflect the flow of energy from the Heart Chakra and Throat Chakra.
- Blockages in the shoulders reflect difficulty giving and receiving love, emotional heaviness, and fear of vulnerability.
- An open Heart Chakra allows for emotional openness, while an open Throat Chakra supports authentic communication.

Example:

- A person with shoulder tightness may feel emotionally burdened and hesitant to express their feelings.
- Reiki applied to the shoulders and Heart Chakra dissolves tension and restores emotional flow.

2. Elbows – Heart and Solar Plexus Chakra Connection

- The elbows reflect emotional and relational flexibility.
- A blocked Heart Chakra or Solar Plexus Chakra can lead to stiffness in the elbows, reflecting difficulty adapting to change or accepting emotional support.

Example:

- A person with tight elbows may resist receiving help from others.
- Reiki focused on the elbows and Solar Plexus Chakra encourages emotional balance and trust.

3. Wrists – Throat and Sacral Chakra Connection

- The wrists reflect creative and emotional flow.
- A blocked Throat Chakra or Sacral Chakra can create stiffness or weakness in the wrists, reflecting creative suppression or fear of speaking one's truth.

Example:

- A person with wrist pain may feel creatively blocked or hesitant to express their ideas.
- Reiki directed to the wrists and Throat Chakra restores creative flow and confidence.

4. Hips – Sacral and Root Chakra Connection

- The hips reflect emotional movement and creative energy.
- A blocked Sacral Chakra or Root Chakra can cause tight hips, reflecting fear of emotional vulnerability or resistance to change.

Example:

- A person with tight hips may have unresolved emotional trauma or creative blocks.

I trust the wisdom of my body. Energy flows freely through me, restoring balance and strength

- Reiki applied to the hips and Sacral Chakra releases stored emotion and restores flow.

5. Knees – Root and Solar Plexus Chakra Connection

- The knees reflect emotional and physical stability.
- A blocked Root Chakra or Solar Plexus Chakra can create knee stiffness or weakness, reflecting fear of moving forward or insecurity.

Example:

- A person with knee pain may feel stuck or insecure about their life path.
- Reiki focused on the knees and Root Chakra restores stability and trust.

6. Ankles – Root and Sacral Chakra Connection

- The ankles reflect emotional and spiritual balance.
- A blocked Root Chakra or Sacral Chakra can create ankle weakness or instability, reflecting fear of losing control or feeling ungrounded.

Example:

- A person with ankle instability may feel emotionally unstable or directionless.
- Reiki applied to the ankles and Root Chakra restores emotional balance and confidence.

How Reiki Restores Energy Flow Through Joints and Chakras

Reiki restores the natural flow of energy through the joints by:

- Dissolving blockages at the joint and related chakra.
- Restoring the balance between overactive and underactive chakras.
- Realigning the flow of energy through the meridians and chakras.
- Strengthening the connection between the primary and secondary chakras.
- Enhancing emotional and physical flexibility.

Reiki Techniques to Restore Energy Flow:

- Direct Reiki to the Joint – Place hands directly on the joint to dissolve blockages.
- Use Reiki Symbols – Use Cho Ku Rei for power and Sei He Ki for emotional release.
- Work on the Related Chakra – Balance the primary chakra linked to the joint.
- Intention and Visualization – Imagine energy flowing smoothly through the joint and chakra.

I trust the wisdom of my body. Energy flows freely through me, restoring balance and strength

Key Takeaways:

- Joints reflect the flow of energy from the chakras through the meridians.
- Blocked joints reflect blocked chakra energy.
- Reiki restores balance by opening the joints and related chakras.
- Balanced joints create emotional, physical, and spiritual harmony.

How Working on Joints Influences the Whole-Body Energy Field

The body's energy field is an interconnected system where every part influences the whole. The chakras, meridians, and joints are not isolated — they function as part of a unified energy network. When you work on the joints through Reiki, you are not only addressing physical mobility and joint health, but also influencing the flow of energy throughout the entire energetic system.

Joints act as energetic gateways where multiple energy pathways intersect. Because they regulate the flow of energy through the meridians and into the muscles, tissues, and organs, any blockage or imbalance in a joint creates a ripple effect through the entire body. By restoring balance and alignment at the joints, you improve the overall flow of energy, promoting better emotional balance, physical strength, and spiritual alignment.

Reiki works by dissolving energetic blockages at the joints, improving the flow of ki (life force energy) through the meridians and chakras. This not only improves joint health and flexibility but also supports the healing of emotional patterns, energetic misalignments, and systemic health issues.

I trust the wisdom of my body. Energy flows freely through me, restoring balance and strength

The Whole-Body Impact of Joint Health

Joints serve as energetic "crossroads" where the body's energy channels (meridians) intersect and direct energy toward muscles, tissues, and organs. When energy flows freely through the joints, the body remains in a state of balance and harmony. When a joint becomes blocked or restricted, the disruption creates tension and misalignment that affects the entire body's energy system.

Three Primary Ways Joints Influence Whole-Body Energy:

1. Distribution of Energy Through the Meridians
   o Joints regulate the flow of energy from the chakras through the meridians.
   o When a joint is open and balanced, energy flows smoothly throughout the body, supporting health and vitality.
   o When a joint is blocked, energy becomes stagnant, creating physical and emotional symptoms.
2. Energetic Feedback Loop Between Joints and Chakras
   o Joints are connected to specific chakras through the meridians.
   o If energy is blocked at a joint, the corresponding chakra becomes misaligned or weakened.
   o For example, a blockage in the hips (connected to the Sacral Chakra) can restrict creative energy and emotional flow throughout the entire energy system.

3. Influence on Muscle Tone, Circulation, and Nerve Function
   - When energy is blocked at a joint, the muscles, tissues, and nerves surrounding that joint receive insufficient energy and circulation.
   - This creates muscle tightness, poor nerve function, and decreased flexibility, reinforcing the energetic blockage.
   - Restoring flow at the joint improves muscle tone, nerve response, and overall body alignment.

Example of Whole-Body Influence:

- If the hips are tight and blocked, it restricts the flow of energy from the Sacral Chakra through the Liver and Gallbladder Meridians.
- This disruption may lead to digestive issues, creative blocks, emotional stagnation, and muscle tension in the lower back and legs.
- Working on the hips through Reiki releases the blockage, restores the flow of energy, and improves not only hip mobility but also emotional expression and digestive health.

Joints as Structural and Energetic Anchors

Joints serve as both structural and energetic anchors for the body. They stabilize the skeletal system while also directing the flow of energy through the meridians.

I trust the wisdom of my body. Energy flows freely through me, restoring balance and strength

When a Joint Is Balanced:

- Energy flows freely through the meridians and muscles.
- Muscles remain relaxed, strong, and responsive.
- The body feels aligned and balanced.
- Emotional flow remains open and adaptable.

When a Joint Is Blocked:

- Energy becomes stagnant, creating muscle tension and misalignment.
- The surrounding muscles compensate, creating uneven posture and discomfort.
- Emotional energy becomes restricted, leading to stress and emotional stagnation.
- The body's energy field weakens, reducing vitality and immune function.

For example:

- A blocked knee joint causes the muscles in the upper leg and lower back to overcompensate, creating misalignment and poor circulation.
- The blocked energy creates emotional instability, feelings of insecurity, and difficulty trusting life's unfolding path (Root Chakra imbalance).
- Working on the knee with Reiki improves alignment and restores trust, emotional balance, and physical strength.

Meridian and Chakra Interaction Through Joints

Joints serve as energetic hubs where meridians and chakras intersect. When energy flows freely through the joints, it strengthens the entire energetic system by supporting the flow of energy through the related meridians and chakras.

1. The Hips and Sacral Chakra Connection

- The hips are linked to the Sacral Chakra and the Liver Meridian (connected to emotional flow).
- When the hips are tight or misaligned, the flow of creative and emotional energy becomes restricted.
- Reiki focused on the hips and Sacral Chakra restores emotional balance and creative expression.

2. The Shoulders and Heart Chakra Connection

- The shoulders are linked to the Heart Chakra and the Lung Meridian (connected to emotional openness and vulnerability).
- Shoulder tension reflects emotional protection or fear of vulnerability.
- Reiki directed to the shoulders and Heart Chakra dissolves emotional armor, allowing greater connection and emotional ease.

3. The Knees and Root Chakra Connection

- The knees are linked to the Root Chakra and the Kidney Meridian (connected to fear and survival).

I trust the wisdom of my body. Energy flows freely through me, restoring balance and strength

- Stiffness or weakness in the knees reflects insecurity and fear of moving forward.
- Reiki applied to the knees and Root Chakra restores confidence and emotional stability.

4. The Wrists and Throat Chakra Connection

- The wrists are linked to the Throat Chakra and the Pericardium Meridian (connected to communication and creative flow).
- Stiff or weak wrists reflect difficulty expressing personal truth or creative ideas.
- Reiki applied to the wrists and Throat Chakra restores creative flow and confidence in communication.

The Ripple Effect of Joint Healing

When Reiki dissolves a blockage in a joint, the release creates a ripple effect that impacts the entire body's energy system.

How a Single Joint Healing Influences the Whole Body:

1. Restores Energy Flow Through the Meridians – When a joint becomes unblocked, energy circulates more freely throughout the body's entire meridian network.
2. Balances the Chakras – Healing the energy flow at the joint restores balance to the related primary chakras.

3. Releases Emotional and Physical Tension – Muscle tension and emotional patterns stored at the joint are released.
4. Improves Physical Alignment and Posture – Restored joint mobility creates better structural alignment, improving overall body mechanics.
5. Enhances Emotional Balance and Mental Clarity – Restoring energy flow at the joint improves emotional resilience and cognitive focus.

Example of Ripple Effect:

- A person with shoulder stiffness (linked to the Heart Chakra) receives Reiki directed to the shoulders.
- The energy blockage in the shoulders dissolves, allowing greater emotional openness and reduced muscle tension.
- This improved energy flow through the Heart Chakra enhances the person's ability to give and receive love, feel more emotionally balanced, and breathe more deeply.
- Improved posture and alignment reduce discomfort in the upper back, improving overall body movement and balance.

I trust the wisdom of my body. Energy flows freely through me, restoring balance and strength

Reiki Techniques for Whole-Body Influence Through Joint Healing

- Direct Reiki to the Joint – Place hands directly on the joint to dissolve energy blockages.
- Use Reiki Symbols – Use Cho Ku Rei for power and Sei He Ki for emotional release.
- Balance the Related Chakra – Work on the related chakra to strengthen energy flow.
- Grounding and Centering – Direct energy from the Root Chakra through the legs and feet to restore whole-body alignment.
- Visualize the Entire Body's Energy Flowing Freely – Imagine the ripple effect of energy moving through the meridians and joints.

Key Takeaways:

- Joints regulate the flow of energy through the body's meridian system.
- Blocked joints create energetic stagnation and emotional imbalance.
- Reiki clears blockages, restoring energy flow and strengthening the whole body.
- Healing one joint creates a ripple effect that improves emotional, physical, and spiritual health.
- Balanced joints promote overall alignment, mobility, and emotional well-being.

By working with joints through Reiki, you are not only improving physical mobility but also creating harmony and balance within the entire body's energy field.

PART 2:
REIKI TECHNIQUES
FOR JOINT HEALING

Chapter 4: Preparing for a Joint-Focused Reiki Session

Working with joints in Reiki requires a specific approach because joints serve as energetic intersections where multiple energy pathways meet. Healing the joints through Reiki involves not only physical touch and energy work but also emotional and spiritual alignment. The process begins with setting a clear intention and creating a supportive environment that allows both the practitioner and the client to align energetically and mentally with the healing process.

When preparing for a joint-focused Reiki session, the goal is to:

- Establish a healing intention focused on the specific joint(s) being treated.
- Create a calm and balanced environment.
- Ground and center both the practitioner and the client.
- Clarify the emotional and energetic patterns associated with the joint.

- Direct energy to dissolve blockages, improve mobility, and restore emotional and physical balance.

A successful joint-focused Reiki session begins long before the hands-on work starts. The preparation phase ensures that the session is aligned with the client's highest good and that the practitioner is energetically grounded and focused.

Why Intention Matters in Reiki Healing

Intention is the foundation of Reiki practice. Reiki energy is guided by consciousness, and setting a focused intention creates a pathway for energy to flow with precision and purpose. When working with joints, the practitioner's intention focuses on:

- Directing Reiki energy into the specific joint.
- Clearing energetic blockages at the joint.
- Balancing the chakra connected to the joint.
- Releasing emotional patterns held within the joint.
- Restoring mobility and ease of movement.

In Reiki, intention acts like a compass — it directs the flow of energy and shapes the outcome of the session. Without clear intention, the energy may dissipate or flow in an unfocused way, reducing the effectiveness of the session.

Conscious breathwork and focused mantras help direct and amplify the flow of energy, promote balance and emotional release.

The Power of Focused Intention

Focused intention strengthens the practitioner's ability to direct energy where it's needed most. Intention also helps the client align mentally and emotionally with the healing process, creating a deeper sense of relaxation and receptivity.

Example:

- If a client is experiencing pain in the knees due to emotional resistance to moving forward, the intention might be:
  "My intention is to release the emotional fear and restore confidence and ease of movement through the knees."
- If a client is struggling with creative blocks linked to tight hips, the intention might be:
  "My intention is to release emotional resistance in the hips and restore creative flow."

The more precise the intention, the more effective the healing.

Creating an Energetic Container for Healing

Before beginning a joint-focused Reiki session, the practitioner must create a safe and balanced energetic space. This involves both physical preparation (adjusting the environment) and energetic preparation (grounding and centering).

1. Prepare the Environment

Creating a calm and energetically clear environment enhances the effectiveness of the Reiki session.

- Clean the Space: Remove clutter and ensure the room feels clean and inviting.
- Control Lighting: Use soft, dim lighting or candles to create a calming atmosphere.
- Set the Temperature: Ensure the room is comfortable (neither too hot nor too cold).
- Sound: Play soft music, nature sounds, or Reiki healing tones to create a relaxing background.
- Scent: Use essential oils (such as lavender, frankincense, or sandalwood) to calm the nervous system and support relaxation.

Example:

- If the session is focused on the shoulders (Heart Chakra), rose or bergamot essential oils can help open emotional flow.
- If the session is focused on the knees (Root Chakra), patchouli or cedarwood oils can create a grounding effect.

2. Grounding and Centering the Practitioner

The practitioner's energetic state directly influences the effectiveness of the session. If the practitioner is distracted, ungrounded, or emotionally tense, it will be difficult to direct Reiki energy effectively.

Conscious breathwork and focused mantras help direct and amplify the flow of energy, promotin balance and emotional release.

Grounding Technique:

- Stand with feet shoulder-width apart.
- Breathe deeply and imagine roots extending from the soles of your feet into the earth.
- Draw energy upward from the earth into your body and heart center.

Centering Technique:

- Place one hand on your heart and one hand on your solar plexus.
- Breathe slowly and deeply, focusing your awareness on the center of your body.
- Imagine a golden light filling your body, aligning you with your highest self.

Clearing Technique:

- Sweep your hands through your aura to remove any stagnant energy.
- Visualize white light surrounding your body, forming a protective shield.

Example:

- If the client's joint issue is linked to emotional stress, grounding helps the practitioner remain stable and emotionally present during the session.
- If the client's joint pain reflects instability, centering helps the practitioner create an energetic foundation of strength and calm.

3. Grounding and Centering the Client

Before beginning the session, it's important to help the client relax and align their energy. When the client is calm and energetically receptive, the flow of Reiki energy is enhanced.

Relaxation Technique:

- Ask the client to close their eyes and take slow, deep breaths.
- Guide the client to focus on the sensation of their breath moving in and out of the body.
- Encourage the client to let go of tension with each exhale.

Grounding Technique:

- Direct the client to visualize roots growing from their feet into the earth.
- Encourage them to feel supported and stable.

Set a Shared Intention:

- Ask the client to silently or verbally state their own intention for the session.
- Example: "My intention is to release tension and restore ease of movement in my shoulders."
- Repeat the intention together to align the energy between the practitioner and the client.

Conscious breathwork and focused mantras help direct and amplify the flow of energy, promote balance and emotional release.

Identifying the Emotional and Energetic Pattern

Once the client is relaxed and aligned, the next step is to identify the underlying emotional or energetic pattern connected to the joint.

Ask Open-Ended Questions:

- "When did you first notice discomfort in this joint?"
- "Does this joint pain increase during times of stress or emotional challenge?"
- "How does this joint pain affect your emotional state?"
- "Do you feel any emotional connection to this discomfort?"

Example:

- If the client's knee pain began during a stressful career transition, it reflects a Root Chakra imbalance related to stability and trust.
- If the client's shoulder tension increases during relationship conflict, it reflects a Heart Chakra imbalance related to emotional vulnerability.

Identify Emotional Patterns Linked to the Joint:

Joint	Emotional Pattern	Example
Shoulders	Emotional burden, resistance to vulnerability	Carrying emotional weight from family or work
Hips	Fear of vulnerability, creative blocks	Difficulty expressing creative energy or emotional openness
Knees	Fear of moving forward, lack of confidence	Feeling uncertain about life's path
Wrists	Fear of expression, blocked creativity	Holding back from expressing true thoughts
Ankles	Lack of grounding, emotional instability	Feeling insecure about life's direction
Elbows	Difficulty receiving support	Unwillingness to depend on others

Conscious breathwork and focused mantras help direct and amplify the flow of energy, promote balance and emotional release.

Sample Healing Intentions Based on Joint Location:

- Shoulders: "My intention is to release emotional burdens and open myself to love and connection."
- Hips: "My intention is to release creative blocks and restore emotional flow."
- Knees: "My intention is to release fear and step forward with confidence."
- Wrists: "My intention is to express my creativity and personal truth freely."
- Ankles: "My intention is to feel balanced, supported, and grounded."
- Elbows: "My intention is to remain flexible and open to receiving support."

Creating the Right Emotional State

For the session to be effective, both the practitioner and the client must enter a state of emotional neutrality and energetic receptivity. This allows the Reiki energy to flow without interference from mental or emotional resistance.

- Encourage the client to let go of expectations.
- Encourage the client to trust the healing process.
- Remind the client that Reiki works on the emotional, physical, and spiritual levels simultaneously.

Key Takeaways:

- Intention is the foundation of effective joint healing.
- The practitioner must be grounded and centered before starting the session.
- Creating a calm and balanced environment enhances the flow of Reiki energy.
- Understanding the emotional patterns connected to the joint helps target the healing.
- Setting a shared intention with the client creates alignment and focus.

Conscious breathwork and focused mantras help direct and amplify the flow of energy, promotin *balance and emotional release.*

Identifying Areas of Tension and Energetic Blockages in the Joints

In Reiki practice, identifying areas of tension and energetic blockages in the joints is essential for effective healing. Joints serve as energetic intersections where multiple meridians and chakras meet, creating both a physical and energetic flow point. When energy is flowing smoothly through the joints, the body experiences strength, flexibility, and emotional ease. However, when energy becomes stagnant or misaligned, the result is physical discomfort, limited mobility, and emotional resistance.

Energetic blockages in the joints often reflect unresolved emotional patterns, stress, trauma, or spiritual misalignment. As a Reiki practitioner, your goal is to develop sensitivity to both the physical and energetic cues that reveal where these blockages are located. By identifying the specific areas of tension and stagnation, you can direct Reiki energy more precisely, dissolve blockages, and restore the body's natural state of balance.

Why Joints Are Prone to Energetic Blockages

Joints are structurally and energetically unique because they are high-traffic areas where multiple energy pathways intersect. This makes them more susceptible to tension and energetic stagnation than other parts of the body.

Three Primary Reasons Joints Hold Blockages:

1. Energetic Crossroads
   - Joints are where multiple meridians and energy channels intersect.
   - When the flow of energy becomes restricted, the blockage often settles at the joint because of the complexity of energetic flow at that location.
2. Emotional Storage Points
   - Joints hold unprocessed emotional energy related to life patterns (e.g., fear, insecurity, emotional burdens).
   - Emotional tension translates into physical tension, creating stiffness and discomfort in the joint.
3. Limited Circulation and Structural Misalignment
   - When a joint is misaligned or inflamed, it restricts the flow of energy through the related meridians.
   - Reduced circulation and energy flow create muscle tightness and further energetic imbalance.

For example:

- A person experiencing emotional stress related to fear of change may develop tightness in the hips (Sacral Chakra connection).
- A person carrying emotional burdens may experience tension in the shoulders (Heart Chakra connection).

Conscious breathwork and focused mantras help direct and amplify the flow of energy, promot *balance and emotional release.*

Signs of Energetic Blockages in the Joints

Blockages in the joints create both physical and emotional symptoms. The key to identifying blockages is to observe the combination of physical and emotional patterns linked to each joint.

Physical Signs of Joint Blockages:

- Stiffness and reduced range of motion
- Pain during movement
- Clicking or grinding sensation in the joint
- Inflammation or swelling
- Muscle tightness around the joint
- Instability or weakness

Emotional and Energetic Signs of Joint Blockages:

- Emotional heaviness or resistance
- Feeling "stuck" in life or unable to move forward
- Creative or emotional blocks
- Unprocessed trauma or emotional pain
- Difficulty trusting others or expressing emotions
- Fear or anxiety tied to specific life changes

Example:

- A person with hip tightness may have difficulty expressing creative energy or emotional vulnerability (Sacral Chakra).
- A person with knee stiffness may struggle with trusting life's path or feeling secure in their decisions (Root Chakra).

- A person with shoulder tension may feel emotionally burdened or responsible for others' emotional well-being (Heart Chakra).

Methods for Identifying Energetic Blockages in the Joints

1. Intuitive Scanning

One of the most effective ways to identify blockages is through intuitive scanning. This involves using your hands and intuition to "sense" the flow of energy through the body.

Technique:

- Have the client lie down or sit comfortably.
- Slowly pass your hands over the body, about 2–4 inches above the surface of the skin.
- Focus on the joints and areas where you sense energetic resistance or imbalance.
- Notice any sensations such as:
  - Heat or cold
  - Tingling or buzzing
  - Magnetic pull or resistance
  - Heaviness or density
  - Emotional tension or unease

Interpretation:

- Heat or tingling = Energy is flowing but needs direction or balancing.
- Cold or numbness = Energy is stagnant or blocked.

Conscious breathwork and focused mantras help direct and amplify the flow of energy, promote balance and emotional release.

- Magnetic pull or resistance = Deep energetic blockage or emotional holding pattern.
- Heaviness or density = Suppressed emotional energy.

Example:

- If you feel heat around the knees, it may indicate inflammation or overactivity in the Root Chakra.
- If you feel cold or numbness in the hips, it may reflect creative blocks or emotional stagnation related to the Sacral Chakra.

2. Muscle Testing (Applied Kinesiology)

Muscle testing provides a direct way to identify weakness, misalignment, or energy blocks in the joints.

Technique:

- Have the client extend their arm.
- Apply gentle pressure while asking a direct question (e.g., "Is there a blockage in the left hip?").
- If the muscle weakens, it reflects a blocked or weakened energy flow.

Interpretation:

- Strong response = Energy is flowing properly.
- Weak response = Energetic blockage or emotional resistance.

Example:

- If the knee muscle weakens during testing, it reflects a disruption in the Root Chakra and feelings of insecurity or fear about moving forward.

3. Palpation and Physical Sensation

You can also identify joint blockages through direct physical contact.

Technique:

- Place your hands gently on the joint.
- Feel for muscle tightness, warmth, or uneven energy flow.
- Observe the client's response to pressure or movement.

Interpretation:

- Warmth = Energy congestion or inflammation.
- Coldness = Reduced energy flow or emotional detachment.
- Tenderness or pain = Stored emotional trauma or misalignment.

Example:

- A person with tender shoulders may be holding emotional burdens.
- A person with cold ankles may feel emotionally ungrounded or insecure about life's direction.

Conscious breathwork and focused mantras help direct and amplify the flow of energy, promoting balance and emotional release.

4. Emotional and Verbal Cues

Blocked energy in the joints often reflects emotional patterns. Asking questions and listening to the client's language and emotional tone can reveal underlying energetic patterns.

Questions to Ask:

- "When did you first notice the discomfort?"
- "Does this pain increase when you're stressed?"
- "Do you feel emotionally stuck or uncertain about something in your life?"
- "Have you experienced any recent emotional challenges?"

Example:

- If the client mentions feeling emotionally "stuck," it often reflects blocked energy in the hips (Sacral Chakra).
- If the client feels "weighed down" by responsibility, the blockage may be in the shoulders (Heart Chakra).

How Specific Joints Reflect Energy Blockages

Joint	Energetic Pattern	Sign of Blockage
Shoulders	Emotional burdens, resistance to vulnerability	Tension, heaviness, restricted range of motion
Hips	Fear of change, creative blocks	Tightness, limited movement, emotional resistance
Knees	Trust, moving forward in life	Stiffness, instability, inflammation
Wrists	Communication, creative expression	Weakness, discomfort with movement
Elbows	Flexibility in relationships	Stiffness, resistance to bending or extending
Ankles	Grounding, emotional stability	Weakness, rolling, lack of balance

Conscious breathwork and focused mantras help direct and amplify the flow of energy, promote balance and emotional release.

How Reiki Clears Joint Blockages

Once a blockage is identified, Reiki works to dissolve it by:

- Directing energy into the joint to increase circulation and energy flow.
- Dissolving emotional and energetic knots through the use of Reiki symbols.
- Restoring balance to the meridian and chakra connected to the joint.
- Releasing emotional patterns held within the joint.

Key Takeaways:

- Joints are highly sensitive to energetic blockages due to their role as energy intersections.
- Blocked energy creates both physical and emotional symptoms.
- Reiki practitioners can identify blockages through scanning, muscle testing, and intuition.
- Clearing joint blockages restores the flow of energy through the entire body.
- Balanced joints create greater physical mobility, emotional resilience, and spiritual harmony.

Grounding and Protective Practices Before Starting a Joint-Focused Reiki Session

Grounding and protection are essential steps in any Reiki session, but they are particularly important when working with joints because joints serve as energy crosspoints where multiple meridians and energy channels intersect. This makes them highly sensitive to both positive and negative energetic influences.

When a practitioner is properly grounded and protected, they become a clear channel for Reiki energy. Without proper grounding and protection, the practitioner may:

- Absorb the client's negative or stagnant energy.
- Experience energetic drain or emotional fatigue.
- Feel overwhelmed by the client's emotional state.
- Be less effective in directing Reiki energy where it's needed.

Similarly, grounding and protection help the client feel safe and supported during the session. A grounded client is more receptive to Reiki energy and more able to release emotional and physical resistance. When both the practitioner and client are grounded and protected, the session is more effective, balanced, and energetically stable.

Conscious breathwork and focused mantras help direct and amplify the flow of energy, promote balance and emotional release.

Why Grounding and Protection Are Essential for Reiki Work

Joints hold not only physical tension but also emotional and energetic patterns. These patterns are often tied to past trauma, unresolved emotional conflicts, and blocked life energy. When a Reiki practitioner works on joints, they are directly interacting with these deep-rooted emotional and energetic imprints.

Without grounding and protection, the practitioner may unintentionally:

- Take on the client's emotional energy.
- Become emotionally drained or energetically overloaded.
- Experience difficulty separating their own energy from the client's energy.

Grounding allows the practitioner to remain stable and connected to the earth's energy, creating a steady energetic flow. Protection establishes an energetic boundary, preventing negative or stagnant energy from being absorbed by the practitioner or interfering with the session.

The Three Pillars of Grounding and Protection

1. Grounding – Establishing a strong connection to the earth to create stability and energetic balance.
2. Centering – Focusing your awareness inward to maintain emotional and energetic balance.

3. Protection – Establishing an energetic shield to prevent energetic interference and maintain clarity.

Step 1: Grounding Techniques for the Practitioner

Grounding is the process of connecting your energy to the earth's core energy. This creates stability, clarity, and emotional strength.

1. Rooting into the Earth

- Stand or sit comfortably with your feet flat on the ground.
- Close your eyes and take deep, slow breaths.
- Imagine roots growing from the soles of your feet, extending deep into the earth's core.
- Visualize the earth's energy rising through these roots, filling your legs and lower body with a sense of strength and stability.
- Continue breathing, focusing on the feeling of connection and support from the earth.

This technique strengthens the Root Chakra, helping you feel emotionally and physically stable during the session.

2. Grounding Through Visualization

- Sit or stand with your spine straight.
- Close your eyes and imagine a bright beam of light descending from above your head, passing through your body, and anchoring itself into the earth's core.

Conscious breathwork and focused mantras help direct and amplify the flow of energy, promoting balance and emotional release.

- Imagine this beam of light surrounding your body, connecting you both to the earth and to universal energy.
- Breathe deeply and focus on the sensation of balance between the earth's energy (grounding) and the universal energy (spiritual connection).

This technique balances the Root Chakra and Crown Chakra, allowing energy to flow freely without emotional imbalance or interference.

3. Grounding Through Breath and Body Awareness

- Sit or stand comfortably.
- Inhale deeply, focusing on the sensation of your breath moving through your body.
- As you exhale, imagine any tension or stagnant energy flowing down through your feet and into the earth.
- Repeat this cycle for 1–2 minutes until you feel stable and clear.

This technique enhances body awareness and strengthens the energetic connection to the physical body.

4. Grounding With Nature (Optional)

- If possible, perform the grounding exercise outside or near natural elements like trees, water, or grass.
- Stand barefoot on the ground and feel the connection between your body and the earth.
- Allow the energy of nature to stabilize and strengthen your energy field.

This technique strengthens the Root Chakra and increases the body's natural energetic resilience.

Step 2: Centering Techniques for the Practitioner

Centering is the process of bringing your focus inward and aligning your energy field. Centering ensures that you are emotionally and mentally stable, helping you avoid becoming overwhelmed by the client's energy during the session.

1. Heart-Centered Focus

- Place one hand on your heart and one hand on your solar plexus.
- Breathe deeply, focusing on the rise and fall of your chest.
- Imagine a golden light expanding from your heart, surrounding your body.
- Affirm: *"I am centered. I am balanced. I am aligned."*

This technique stabilizes emotional energy and strengthens the Heart Chakra and Solar Plexus Chakra.

2. Creating an Energetic Core

- Sit or stand comfortably.
- Close your eyes and visualize a column of light running through the center of your body, from the crown of your head to your feet.
- Focus on this central line of energy, feeling it as a strong and steady pillar.

Conscious breathwork and focused mantras help direct and amplify the flow of energy, promote balance and emotional release.

- Imagine this core line connecting you to the earth below and the universe above.
- Affirm: *"I am centered and aligned."*

This technique creates an energetic anchor that allows you to remain emotionally balanced and spiritually connected.

Step 3: Protection Techniques for the Practitioner

Protection establishes a boundary around your energy field, preventing you from absorbing the client's emotional or energetic imbalances.

1. Creating an Energetic Shield

- Visualize a bubble of white or golden light surrounding your body.
- Set the intention that this shield will protect you from absorbing any negative or unwanted energy during the session.
- Affirm: *"I am protected. Only light and healing energy may pass through."*

This technique strengthens the aura and prevents energetic interference.

2. Cutting Energetic Cords (After the Session)

- After the session, visualize any energetic cords connecting you to the client.
- Use your hand to "cut" these cords or visualize them dissolving.
- Affirm: *"I release all energy that is not mine."*

This technique ensures that you do not retain any of the client's emotional or energetic patterns.

3. Creating Sacred Space

- Before the session, call upon a protective force (such as spiritual guides or universal energy).
- Ask for protection for both yourself and the client.
- Set the intention that the healing space will be clear of any negative or interfering energy.
- Use Reiki symbols (e.g., Cho Ku Rei for power and protection) to seal the space.

This technique strengthens the energetic container, ensuring that only positive healing energy is present.

Grounding and Protection for the Client

The client also benefits from being grounded and protected before the session.

Grounding:

- Encourage the client to visualize roots extending from their feet into the earth.
- Guide them to focus on the sensation of stability and support.

Protection:

- Guide the client to visualize a protective bubble of light around their body.

Conscious breathwork and focused mantras help direct and amplify the flow of energy, promote balance and emotional release.

- Set the intention that they will remain energetically balanced and supported during the session.

Emotional Safety:

- Encourage the client to set their own personal intention for the session.
- Remind them that they are in a safe and supportive space.

How Grounding and Protection Influence Joint Healing

- A grounded and protected practitioner is able to channel Reiki energy more effectively.
- Grounding creates a stable foundation, allowing Reiki energy to penetrate deeply into the joints.
- Protection prevents energy transference between the practitioner and client.
- When the client is grounded, they are more receptive to healing and better able to integrate the effects of the session.

Signs That Grounding and Protection Are Complete:

- Practitioner feels calm, focused, and emotionally neutral.
- Client feels relaxed and receptive.
- The healing space feels clear and energetically balanced.
- Reiki energy flows smoothly without resistance.

Key Takeaways:

- Grounding creates stability and balance in the practitioner and client.
- Centering strengthens emotional focus and alignment.
- Protection creates a safe boundary, preventing energy transference.
- Grounding and protection enhance the overall effectiveness of the Reiki session.
- A well-grounded session supports deeper emotional and physical release.

Conscious breathwork and focused mantras help direct and amplify the flow of energy, promoti. balance and emotional release.

Chapter 5: Hand Positions and Techniques for Joint Healing

Grounding and Protective Practices Before Starting a Joint-Focused Reiki Session

Grounding and protection are essential steps in any Reiki session, but they are particularly important when working with joints because joints serve as energy crosspoints where multiple meridians and energy channels intersect. This makes them highly sensitive to both positive and negative energetic influences.

When a practitioner is properly grounded and protected, they become a clear channel for Reiki energy. Without proper grounding and protection, the practitioner may:

- Absorb the client's negative or stagnant energy.
- Experience energetic drain or emotional fatigue.
- Feel overwhelmed by the client's emotional state.
- Be less effective in directing Reiki energy where it's needed.

Similarly, grounding and protection help the client feel safe and supported during the session. A grounded client is more receptive to Reiki energy and more able to release emotional and physical resistance. When both the practitioner and client are grounded and protected, the session is more effective, balanced, and energetically stable.

Why Grounding and Protection Are Essential for Reiki Work

Joints hold not only physical tension but also emotional and energetic patterns. These patterns are often tied to past trauma, unresolved emotional conflicts, and blocked life energy. When a Reiki practitioner works on joints, they are directly interacting with these deep-rooted emotional and energetic imprints.

Without grounding and protection, the practitioner may unintentionally:

- Take on the client's emotional energy.
- Become emotionally drained or energetically overloaded.
- Experience difficulty separating their own energy from the client's energy.

Grounding allows the practitioner to remain stable and connected to the earth's energy, creating a steady energetic flow. Protection establishes an energetic boundary, preventing negative or stagnant energy from being absorbed by the practitioner or interfering with the session.

Conscious breathwork and focused mantras help direct and amplify the flow of energy, promot balance and emotional release.

The Three Pillars of Grounding and Protection

1. Grounding – Establishing a strong connection to the earth to create stability and energetic balance.
2. Centering – Focusing your awareness inward to maintain emotional and energetic balance.
3. Protection – Establishing an energetic shield to prevent energetic interference and maintain clarity.

Step 1: Grounding Techniques for the Practitioner

Grounding is the process of connecting your energy to the earth's core energy. This creates stability, clarity, and emotional strength.

1. Rooting into the Earth

- Stand or sit comfortably with your feet flat on the ground.
- Close your eyes and take deep, slow breaths.
- Imagine roots growing from the soles of your feet, extending deep into the earth's core.
- Visualize the earth's energy rising through these roots, filling your legs and lower body with a sense of strength and stability.
- Continue breathing, focusing on the feeling of connection and support from the earth.

This technique strengthens the Root Chakra, helping you feel emotionally and physically stable during the session.

2. Grounding Through Visualization

- Sit or stand with your spine straight.
- Close your eyes and imagine a bright beam of light descending from above your head, passing through your body, and anchoring itself into the earth's core.
- Imagine this beam of light surrounding your body, connecting you both to the earth and to universal energy.
- Breathe deeply and focus on the sensation of balance between the earth's energy (grounding) and the universal energy (spiritual connection).

This technique balances the Root Chakra and Crown Chakra, allowing energy to flow freely without emotional imbalance or interference.

3. Grounding Through Breath and Body Awareness

- Sit or stand comfortably.
- Inhale deeply, focusing on the sensation of your breath moving through your body.
- As you exhale, imagine any tension or stagnant energy flowing down through your feet and into the earth.
- Repeat this cycle for 1–2 minutes until you feel stable and clear.

This technique enhances body awareness and strengthens the energetic connection to the physical body.

Conscious breathwork and focused mantras help direct and amplify the flow of energy, promote balance and emotional release.

4. Grounding With Nature (Optional)

- If possible, perform the grounding exercise outside or near natural elements like trees, water, or grass.
- Stand barefoot on the ground and feel the connection between your body and the earth.
- Allow the energy of nature to stabilize and strengthen your energy field.

This technique strengthens the Root Chakra and increases the body's natural energetic resilience.

Step 2: Centering Techniques for the Practitioner

Centering is the process of bringing your focus inward and aligning your energy field. Centering ensures that you are emotionally and mentally stable, helping you avoid becoming overwhelmed by the client's energy during the session.

1. Heart-Centered Focus

- Place one hand on your heart and one hand on your solar plexus.
- Breathe deeply, focusing on the rise and fall of your chest.
- Imagine a golden light expanding from your heart, surrounding your body.
- Affirm: *"I am centered. I am balanced. I am aligned."*

This technique stabilizes emotional energy and strengthens the Heart Chakra and Solar Plexus Chakra.

2. Creating an Energetic Core

- Sit or stand comfortably.
- Close your eyes and visualize a column of light running through the center of your body, from the crown of your head to your feet.
- Focus on this central line of energy, feeling it as a strong and steady pillar.
- Imagine this core line connecting you to the earth below and the universe above.
- Affirm: *"I am centered and aligned."*

This technique creates an energetic anchor that allows you to remain emotionally balanced and spiritually connected.

Step 3: Protection Techniques for the Practitioner

Protection establishes a boundary around your energy field, preventing you from absorbing the client's emotional or energetic imbalances.

1. Creating an Energetic Shield

- Visualize a bubble of white or golden light surrounding your body.
- Set the intention that this shield will protect you from absorbing any negative or unwanted energy during the session.
- Affirm: *"I am protected. Only light and healing energy may pass through."*

This technique strengthens the aura and prevents energetic interference.

Conscious breathwork and focused mantras help direct and amplify the flow of energy, promoting balance and emotional release.

2. Cutting Energetic Cords (After the Session)

- After the session, visualize any energetic cords connecting you to the client.
- Use your hand to "cut" these cords or visualize them dissolving.
- Affirm: *"I release all energy that is not mine."*

This technique ensures that you do not retain any of the client's emotional or energetic patterns.

3. Creating Sacred Space

- Before the session, call upon a protective force (such as spiritual guides or universal energy).
- Ask for protection for both yourself and the client.
- Set the intention that the healing space will be clear of any negative or interfering energy.
- Use Reiki symbols (e.g., Cho Ku Rei for power and protection) to seal the space.

This technique strengthens the energetic container, ensuring that only positive healing energy is present.

Grounding and Protection for the Client

The client also benefits from being grounded and protected before the session.

Grounding:

- Encourage the client to visualize roots extending from their feet into the earth.

- Guide them to focus on the sensation of stability and support.

Protection:

- Guide the client to visualize a protective bubble of light around their body.
- Set the intention that they will remain energetically balanced and supported during the session.

Emotional Safety:

- Encourage the client to set their own personal intention for the session.
- Remind them that they are in a safe and supportive space.

How Grounding and Protection Influence Joint Healing

- A grounded and protected practitioner is able to channel Reiki energy more effectively.
- Grounding creates a stable foundation, allowing Reiki energy to penetrate deeply into the joints.
- Protection prevents energy transference between the practitioner and client.
- When the client is grounded, they are more receptive to healing and better able to integrate the effects of the session.

Conscious breathwork and focused mantras help direct and amplify the flow of energy, promote balance and emotional release.

Signs That Grounding and Protection Are Complete:

- Practitioner feels calm, focused, and emotionally neutral.
- Client feels relaxed and receptive.
- The healing space feels clear and energetically balanced.
- Reiki energy flows smoothly without resistance.

Key Takeaways:

- Grounding creates stability and balance in the practitioner and client.
- Centering strengthens emotional focus and alignment.
- Protection creates a safe boundary, preventing energy transference.
- Grounding and protection enhance the overall effectiveness of the Reiki session.
- A well-grounded session supports deeper emotional and physical release.

By grounding and protecting both yourself and the client, you create the ideal energetic foundation for a successful joint-focused Reiki session.

Techniques for Relieving Inflammation, Tension, and Emotional Energy in Joints

Inflammation, tension, and emotional energy are interconnected. When a joint becomes inflamed or tense, it reflects not only physical strain but also underlying emotional and energetic imbalances. In Reiki practice, joints are understood as energy intersections where meridians and chakras meet, making them particularly sensitive to emotional and energetic disruptions.

Blocked or stagnant energy in a joint restricts the natural flow of ki (life force energy), leading to physical discomfort, stiffness, and inflammation. Likewise, unresolved emotional patterns (such as fear, stress, or resentment) can create energetic tension in the joint, reinforcing the physical symptoms.

Reiki works by dissolving these energetic blockages, restoring balance to the related chakras and meridians, and releasing emotional patterns held in the joints. By combining specific Reiki techniques with physical and energetic adjustments, the practitioner can relieve inflammation and tension while supporting emotional release and deeper healing.

Why Joints Hold Inflammation, Tension, and Emotional Energy

Joints are prone to inflammation and tension because they serve as both structural and energetic hubs.

Conscious breathwork and focused mantras help direct and amplify the flow of energy, promote balance and emotional release.

1. Structural Stress

- Joints bear the weight of the body and absorb impact during movement.
- Repeated stress from poor posture, overuse, or injury creates muscle tension and physical misalignment.
- Misalignment creates resistance in the flow of energy through the joint.

2. Emotional Holding Patterns

- Emotional stress and trauma often settle in the joints where energy circulation is slower.
- When emotional energy is not processed, it becomes trapped in the connective tissue and joint space.
- Emotional tension creates muscle stiffness and joint misalignment, reinforcing the physical blockage.

3. Energetic Blockages

- When energy becomes stagnant in the meridians connected to the joint, it creates an energetic knot.
- Stagnant energy disrupts both physical and emotional balance.
- Over time, blocked energy weakens the joint and increases inflammation.

Example:

- A person carrying emotional burdens from childhood may develop chronic tension in the shoulders.
- A person who struggles with trust and fear of vulnerability may experience stiffness and inflammation in the hips (linked to the Sacral Chakra).
- A person feeling uncertain or fearful about life's direction may develop knee pain (connected to the Root Chakra).

Reiki Techniques for Relieving Inflammation, Tension, and Emotional Energy

Reiki is uniquely effective for joint healing because it addresses the energetic, emotional, and physical layers simultaneously. When the practitioner directs Reiki energy to a joint, it works to:

- Dissolve energetic blockages.
- Restore circulation and energy flow through the joint.
- Relax the surrounding muscles and connective tissue.
- Release stored emotional energy and trauma.
- Reduce inflammation and pain by restoring energetic harmony.

Conscious breathwork and focused mantras help direct and amplify the flow of energy, promoting balance and emotional release.

1. Direct Hand Placement on Joints

Direct hand placement is one of the most effective methods for relieving joint-related discomfort because it delivers Reiki energy directly to the site of tension and inflammation.

Technique:

- Have the client sit or lie down in a comfortable position.
- Place both hands directly on or around the joint.
- Use the Cho Ku Rei (Power Symbol) to increase the flow of energy into the joint.
- Hold the position for 3–5 minutes, or until you feel the energy shift.
- Visualize golden or white light flowing into the joint, dissolving any tension or inflammation.
- Encourage the client to breathe deeply and release any emotional resistance.

Direct hand placement is especially effective for reducing inflammation and relieving joint stiffness.

2. Pulsing Technique for Reducing Inflammation

Pulsing is a dynamic Reiki technique that helps stimulate energy movement and reduce swelling or heat in an inflamed joint.

Technique:

- Place your hands on or around the joint.
- Imagine the Reiki energy "pulsing" into the joint, like waves of light.
- Slowly increase and decrease the intensity of the energy pulse.
- Visualize the heat and inflammation dissolving with each pulse.
- Use the Sei He Ki (Emotional Healing Symbol) to release emotional patterns contributing to the inflammation.
- Repeat the pulsing for 3–5 minutes, or until you sense the energy shift.

Pulsing stimulates lymphatic drainage, reduces swelling, and restores energetic flow through the joint.

3. Reiki Breathwork for Joint Tension

Breathwork helps synchronize the client's energy field with the flow of Reiki energy, facilitating deeper release of tension.

Technique:

- Place your hands directly on the joint or hold them just above the joint.
- Ask the client to take slow, deep breaths.
- On each inhale, visualize Reiki energy flowing into the joint.
- On each exhale, visualize tension and inflammation leaving the joint as dark or gray smoke.

Conscious breathwork and focused mantras help direct and amplify the flow of energy, promote balance and emotional release.

- Continue for 5–7 minutes, encouraging the client to relax with each breath.

Breathwork releases emotional resistance and enhances the flow of Reiki energy into the joint.

4. Chakra Balancing Through the Joint

When a joint becomes inflamed or tense, it reflects an imbalance in the corresponding chakra. Balancing the chakra restores energetic harmony, reducing both physical and emotional symptoms.

Technique:

- Identify the chakra linked to the joint (e.g., hips = Sacral Chakra, knees = Root Chakra).
- Place one hand on the joint and the other on the corresponding chakra.
- Use the Cho Ku Rei symbol to strengthen the energetic connection.
- Imagine the energy flowing from the chakra into the joint, dissolving blockages and restoring balance.
- Continue until you feel the energy become steady and balanced.

Chakra balancing strengthens the energetic flow through the joint and improves emotional alignment.

5. Cross-Body Connection for Joint Flexibility

Joints work in pairs and often reflect cross-body imbalances. For example, tension in the left knee may reflect an emotional or energetic imbalance in the right shoulder.

Technique:

- Place one hand on the affected joint and the other on the opposite joint or shoulder.
- Channel Reiki energy between the two points, visualizing a line of light connecting them.
- Use the Sei He Ki symbol to release emotional tension between the joints.
- Visualize the connection becoming balanced and harmonious.

This technique harmonizes the body's energy flow and improves cross-body flexibility.

6. Circular Motion Technique for Joint Mobility

This technique helps stimulate energy flow and increase the range of motion in a stiff joint.

Technique:

- Place your hands on either side of the joint.
- Direct Reiki energy in a circular motion around the joint.
- Visualize the joint opening and becoming more fluid.

Conscious breathwork and focused mantras help direct and amplify the flow of energy, promote balance and emotional release.

- Use the Cho Ku Rei symbol to increase the strength of the energy flow.
- Continue until you feel the joint "soften" or release tension.

The circular motion mimics the natural movement of the joint, encouraging energy flow and improving mobility.

7. Emotional Release Technique

Stored emotional energy creates tension and inflammation in the joints. This technique helps dissolve the emotional pattern connected to the joint.

Technique:

- Place your hands directly on the joint.
- Use the Sei He Ki symbol to release emotional energy.
- Ask the client to silently name the emotion connected to the discomfort (e.g., fear, grief, resentment).
- Encourage the client to breathe deeply and imagine the emotion dissolving with each exhale.
- Continue until the energy becomes lighter or more expansive.

Emotional release restores energetic flow and reduces physical tension.

How to Tell When a Blockage Is Released

During a Reiki session, you may notice signs that the blockage or tension has been released:

- Warmth or tingling in the joint.
- The joint feels more flexible or "looser."
- The client may sigh, cry, or experience emotional relief.
- The client reports feeling lighter or more relaxed.
- Muscle tension in the surrounding area begins to soften.

Key Takeaways:

- Joint tension reflects both physical and emotional imbalances.
- Reiki dissolves blockages, restores energy flow, and reduces inflammation.
- Direct hand placement, breathwork, and pulsing are effective for reducing inflammation.
- Chakra balancing and emotional release techniques restore energetic harmony.
- Healing joints creates a ripple effect, improving emotional and physical health.

By combining these Reiki techniques, you can restore flow, ease tension, and dissolve emotional patterns stored in the joints — creating lasting physical and emotional balance.

Conscious breathwork and focused mantras help direct and amplify the flow of energy, promoting balance and emotional release.

Combining Reiki with Breathwork and Visualization for Enhanced Joint Healing

Breathwork and visualization are powerful tools that, when combined with Reiki, enhance the flow of energy through the body, deepen the healing process, and strengthen the mind-body connection. Working on joints requires more than simply addressing physical discomfort — it involves dissolving energetic blockages and releasing emotional patterns stored in the joint.

Breathwork and visualization complement Reiki by:

- Opening energy channels in the body.
- Releasing stored tension and emotional resistance.
- Increasing the client's receptivity to Reiki energy.
- Helping the practitioner direct and amplify Reiki energy.
- Restoring the flow of ki (life force energy) through the chakras and meridians.

Joints serve as energetic gateways where multiple meridians and chakras meet, making them ideal targets for combined Reiki, breathwork, and visualization techniques. Breathwork and visualization help the client consciously engage with the healing process, while Reiki works at the deeper energetic level to dissolve blockages and restore balance.

Why Breathwork and Visualization Enhance Reiki's Effectiveness

Reiki energy is directed by conscious intention. When a client's breath and mental focus are aligned with the Reiki energy, it creates a powerful synergy that enhances the flow of healing energy.

1. Breathwork Enhances Energy Flow

- Breath serves as a bridge between the physical body and the energetic body.
- Conscious breath increases oxygenation, which improves circulation and muscle relaxation.
- The rhythmic flow of breath mimics the natural flow of energy through the meridians, encouraging energetic alignment.

2. Visualization Directs Reiki Energy

- The mind cannot differentiate between imagined and real experiences — visualization activates the same neurological pathways as physical sensation.
- When the client visualizes the joint healing, it creates an energetic blueprint for Reiki energy to follow.
- Focused visualization enhances the strength and precision of the Reiki flow.

Conscious breathwork and focused mantras help direct and amplify the flow of energy, promot balance and emotional release.

Example:

- A person with knee stiffness due to emotional resistance to change can use breathwork to release physical tension and visualization to create a sense of movement and confidence.
- A person with shoulder tightness from emotional burden can use breathwork to open the Heart Chakra and visualization to release emotional weight and restore balance.

Breathwork Techniques for Joint Healing

Breathwork activates the parasympathetic nervous system, helping the body shift from a state of stress to relaxation. This allows Reiki energy to flow more effectively through the body's energy channels.

1. Deep Diaphragmatic Breathing (Grounding and Relaxation)

Deep, slow breathing into the diaphragm creates a sense of safety and calm, allowing the body to become more receptive to Reiki energy.

Technique:

- Have the client lie down or sit comfortably.
- Place your hands on the joint you are working on.
- Instruct the client to breathe in slowly through the nose, expanding the belly.
- Have them exhale slowly through the mouth, releasing tension with each breath.

- Synchronize your Reiki flow with the client's breath — visualize the Reiki energy flowing into the joint with each inhale and the tension releasing with each exhale.

Benefits:

- Activates the parasympathetic nervous system.
- Reduces muscle tension and emotional resistance.
- Improves circulation to the joint.

2. Breath Focus on the Joint (Directing Energy to the Joint)

This technique helps the client consciously direct breath and energy toward the affected joint, increasing the Reiki flow and deepening the healing.

Technique:

- Place your hands on the joint.
- Have the client close their eyes and breathe deeply.
- Instruct them to imagine the breath flowing directly into the joint as they inhale.
- As they exhale, have them visualize any tension or blocked energy leaving the joint.
- Continue for 5–7 minutes until you feel the energy shift.

Benefits:

- Improves focus and energetic flow.
- Releases physical and emotional tension.
- Deepens the client's connection to their body.

Conscious breathwork and focused mantras help direct and amplify the flow of energy, promote balance and emotional release.

3. Rhythmic Breathing with Reiki Pulsing (Balancing and Aligning Energy)

Rhythmic breathing combined with pulsing Reiki energy helps reset the natural flow of energy through the meridians and joints.

Technique:

- Place your hands on the joint.
- Instruct the client to breathe in for a count of four, hold for four counts, and exhale for four counts.
- As the client breathes in, direct Reiki energy into the joint with a pulsing sensation (imagine the energy flowing in waves).
- On the exhale, visualize the joint softening and expanding.
- Repeat for 5–7 minutes.

Benefits:

- Regulates the nervous system.
- Balances the energy flow through the joint.
- Creates a calming effect on the mind and body.

4. Alternate Nostril Breathing (Nadi Shodhana) (Rebalancing Masculine and Feminine Energy)

This technique helps balance the flow of energy through the left and right sides of the body, which reflects the balance of the masculine and feminine energies (yin and yang).

Technique:

- Have the client sit comfortably.
- Instruct them to close their right nostril with their thumb and inhale through the left nostril.
- Close the left nostril with the ring finger, open the right nostril, and exhale through the right nostril.
- Inhale through the right nostril, close it, and exhale through the left nostril.
- Continue for 3–5 minutes while directing Reiki to the affected joint.

Benefits:

- Balances the energy flow through the meridians.
- Reduces stress and emotional imbalance.
- Improves mental clarity and emotional regulation.

Visualization Techniques for Joint Healing

Visualization activates the body's natural ability to heal by creating a mental image of health and balance. When combined with Reiki, visualization enhances the energetic flow and strengthens the connection between mind, body, and spirit.

1. Golden Light Visualization (Strengthening and Restoring the Joint)

Technique:

- Place your hands on the joint.

Conscious breathwork and focused mantras help direct and amplify the flow of energy, promoting balance and emotional release.

- Instruct the client to close their eyes and visualize a warm golden light surrounding the joint.
- Have them imagine the golden light penetrating into the joint, dissolving any darkness, tension, or stagnation.
- Visualize the joint becoming strong, flexible, and pain-free.
- Continue for 5–7 minutes or until the joint feels lighter.

Benefits:

- Restores strength and flexibility.
- Dissolves emotional and physical tension.
- Rebalances energy flow.

2. Water Flow Visualization (Releasing Stagnant Energy)

Technique:

- Place your hands on the joint.
- Instruct the client to imagine a stream of clear, flowing water moving through the joint.
- Encourage them to visualize the water washing away any tension, inflammation, or negative energy.
- Imagine the water carrying the stagnant energy away from the body.
- Continue until the energy feels clear and light.

Benefits:

- Clears stagnant energy.

- Reduces inflammation.
- Improves energy circulation.

3. Expansion and Opening Visualization (Increasing Mobility and Flexibility)

Technique:

- Place your hands on the joint.
- Instruct the client to visualize the joint opening and expanding with each inhale.
- On each exhale, have them visualize any resistance or tightness leaving the joint.
- Continue until the joint feels relaxed and more mobile.

Benefits:

- Increases range of motion.
- Reduces stiffness and tension.
- Improves flexibility and ease of movement.

Combining Breathwork, Visualization, and Reiki

1. Start with deep diaphragmatic breathing to calm the nervous system.
2. Guide the client through a visualization based on their specific joint issue.
3. Direct Reiki energy into the joint using the Cho Ku Rei symbol to increase power and focus.
4. Encourage the client to sync their breath with the Reiki flow.

Conscious breathwork and focused mantras help direct and amplify the flow of energy, promote balance and emotional release.

5. Conclude with a closing visualization of the joint being surrounded by light and fully restored.

Key Takeaways:

- Breathwork opens energy channels and deepens Reiki flow.
- Visualization creates an energetic blueprint for healing.
- Directing breath and Reiki into the joint dissolves physical and emotional resistance.
- Combining all three techniques increases flexibility, reduces inflammation, and restores balance.
- The mind-body connection is strengthened, leading to deeper and more lasting healing.

By combining Reiki with breathwork and visualization, you create a powerful healing process that restores both physical and energetic alignment within the joints and the whole body.

Chapter 6: Working with Specific Joints

Shoulders: Carrying Burdens, Responsibility, and Self-Expression

The shoulders serve as a powerful energetic and physical center for carrying responsibility and expressing emotional energy. In both physical and energetic terms, the shoulders are designed to bear weight — they support the arms and facilitate a wide range of motion that allows us to reach out into the world. However, when emotional stress, responsibility, or unexpressed feelings accumulate, the energy becomes trapped in the shoulder joints, leading to tension, stiffness, and discomfort.

In Reiki practice, the shoulders are energetically linked to the Heart Chakra (Anahata) and the Throat Chakra (Vishuddha), which govern emotional openness, connection, and self-expression. When the energy in the shoulders becomes blocked or misaligned, it reflects emotional burdens, communication issues, and difficulties with vulnerability or self-expression.

By directing Reiki energy to the shoulders, you can release the physical tension and emotional patterns held there,

Conscious breathwork and focused mantras help direct and amplify the flow of energy, promote balance and emotional release.

restoring balance to the heart and throat energy pathways. This helps the client not only regain physical ease but also open up emotionally and express themselves with greater confidence and authenticity.

The Physical and Energetic Role of the Shoulders

The shoulders are complex anatomical structures that are designed for strength, stability, and flexibility. Each shoulder joint is made up of bones, muscles, tendons, and ligaments that work together to allow a wide range of motion.

However, the shoulders are more than just mechanical joints — they are also energetic hubs where emotional and spiritual patterns are stored.

Anatomical Role of the Shoulders:

- Support the weight of the arms and upper body.
- Allow for a wide range of motion, including rotation, flexion, and extension.
- Act as stabilizers for the spine and upper body.
- Connect the arms to the heart center and facilitate reaching outward (both physically and emotionally).

Energetic Role of the Shoulders:

- Act as a bridge between the Heart Chakra and the Throat Chakra.
- Store emotional tension and responsibility.

- Reflect emotional patterns related to love, connection, and communication.
- Influence the ability to give and receive emotional support.

The Shoulder-Heart-Throat Chakra Connection:

1. Heart Chakra (Anahata) – Governs love, emotional openness, and compassion.
   - When the shoulders are tense or painful, it often reflects difficulty with emotional openness or vulnerability.
   - Carrying emotional burdens may create tension in the shoulders, restricting the flow of love and emotional connection.
2. Throat Chakra (Vishuddha) – Governs communication and self-expression.
   - When the shoulders are tense, it reflects difficulty expressing thoughts or emotions openly.
   - Blocked energy in the Throat Chakra creates tension in the upper back, neck, and shoulders.
3. Solar Plexus Chakra (Manipura) – Governs personal power and confidence.
   - Misalignment in the Solar Plexus Chakra can reflect a feeling of being overburdened by responsibility or lacking control over one's life.
   - Overwhelm and tension in the shoulders may stem from suppressed feelings of inadequacy or disempowerment.

Conscious breathwork and focused mantras help direct and amplify the flow of energy, promoti
balance and emotional release.

Emotional and Spiritual Patterns Stored in the Shoulders

Tension and pain in the shoulders often reflect unresolved emotional patterns and life challenges. Reiki practitioners can use these patterns as energetic clues to direct healing and restore balance.

1. Carrying Emotional Burdens

The shoulders reflect the emotional weight of life's responsibilities and expectations.

- Taking on too much responsibility for others.
- Feeling obligated to care for others at the expense of one's own well-being.
- Holding onto guilt, shame, or emotional stress from the past.

Example:

- A person with constant shoulder tightness may feel weighed down by work and family obligations.
- Reiki directed to the shoulders and Heart Chakra can help release this emotional weight and restore balance.

2. Difficulty in Giving and Receiving Support

The shoulders reflect the balance between giving and receiving emotional support.

- Tension in the shoulders may reflect a resistance to asking for help or receiving emotional support.
- Overworking the shoulders reflects overextension and an imbalance in personal boundaries.

Example:

- A person who struggles to ask for help may experience shoulder stiffness and pain.
- Reiki directed to the shoulders and Heart Chakra helps release resistance and restore openness to receiving support.

3. Resistance to Emotional Vulnerability

The shoulders reflect emotional protection and defensiveness.

- Tight or guarded shoulders may reflect a fear of emotional rejection.
- Difficulty relaxing the shoulders may reflect fear of letting one's guard down.

Example:

- A person with chronic shoulder tension may feel emotionally guarded or fearful of intimacy.
- Reiki directed to the shoulders and Throat Chakra can help soften emotional defenses and encourage openness.

Conscious breathwork and focused mantras help direct and amplify the flow of energy, promote balance and emotional release.

4. Unexpressed or Suppressed Communication

Blocked energy in the shoulders often reflects difficulty expressing emotions or personal truth.

- Difficulty expressing one's needs or desires.
- Holding back emotional truth for fear of judgment or rejection.
- Feeling emotionally "choked" or silenced.

Example:

- A person with tension in the shoulders and neck may feel frustrated or unable to speak up.
- Reiki directed to the shoulders and Throat Chakra helps clear the block and restore open communication.

How Reiki Relieves Shoulder Tension and Restores Balance

Reiki dissolves blocked energy in the shoulders by restoring the flow of ki through the chakras and meridians connected to the shoulder joint. When the energetic flow is restored, physical and emotional tension naturally begin to release.

1. Direct Hand Placement on the Shoulders

- Place both hands directly on the shoulders or hover just above the surface of the skin.
- Use the Cho Ku Rei (Power Symbol) to increase the flow of Reiki energy.

- Visualize warm, golden light flowing into the shoulder joint, dissolving tension and resistance.
- Continue for 3–5 minutes or until you feel the energy shift.

Direct hand placement strengthens the energetic connection and increases physical and emotional release.

2. Shoulder Cradling Technique (Emotional Reassurance)

- Have the client lie down or sit comfortably.
- Cradle the client's shoulders gently with both hands.
- Breathe deeply and focus on creating a feeling of emotional safety.
- Use the Sei He Ki (Emotional Healing Symbol) to dissolve emotional resistance.
- Encourage the client to release any emotional weight.

This technique helps the client feel emotionally supported and reassured.

3. Cross-Body Shoulder Technique (Balancing Left and Right Energies)

- Place one hand on the left shoulder and the other hand on the right hip (or vice versa).
- Direct Reiki energy between these two points, balancing the flow of energy through the body's energy field.
- Visualize a line of light connecting the left and right sides of the body.

Conscious breathwork and focused mantras help direct and amplify the flow of energy, promote balance and emotional release.

- Hold for 3–5 minutes until you feel the energy settle.

This technique balances the masculine (right) and feminine (left) energy channels.

4. Shoulder Circulation Technique (Increasing Flexibility)

- Place both hands on the shoulder joint.
- Direct Reiki energy in a circular motion around the joint.
- Imagine the shoulder joint expanding and becoming more fluid.
- Hold until you feel the tension release.

This technique increases range of motion and flexibility.

5. Affirmation and Breath Technique (Releasing Emotional Burdens)

- Place hands on the shoulders.
- Ask the client to take deep breaths.
- Have the client silently or verbally repeat affirmations such as:
    - *"I release the weight of responsibility."*
    - *"I am supported."*
    - *"It is safe to express my truth."*
- Continue until you feel the energy shift.

Affirmations align the client's consciousness with the flow of Reiki energy.

Key Takeaways:

- Shoulder tension reflects emotional and energetic burdens.
- Reiki releases both physical and emotional resistance in the shoulders.
- The Heart and Throat Chakras are directly connected to the shoulders.
- Restoring flow in the shoulders increases emotional openness and self-expression.
- When the shoulders are balanced, the client feels emotionally lighter, more confident, and more open to support.

By working on the shoulders with Reiki, you help the client release emotional weight and restore the ability to give and receive love freely.

Elbows: Flexibility in Giving and Receiving

The elbows serve as both physical and energetic hinges that reflect the body's ability to move, bend, and adapt to life's changing circumstances. In Reiki practice, the elbows are not just mechanical joints — they hold deep energetic and emotional patterns related to giving, receiving, and adaptability.

Energetically, the elbows are connected to the Heart Chakra (Anahata) and the Solar Plexus Chakra (Manipura), which govern emotional openness, personal boundaries, and self-worth. The way we hold, extend, or restrict movement through the elbows reflects how open or resistant we are to the flow of energy, relationships, and opportunities in our lives.

Tension or discomfort in the elbows often reflects emotional or energetic resistance to receiving help, offering support, or trusting life's natural flow. Reiki works to dissolve these energetic blockages, restoring ease of movement and emotional balance in the process.

The Physical and Energetic Role of the Elbows

The elbows are designed to provide both strength and flexibility. They allow us to extend and bend the arms, offering a balance between reaching out (giving) and drawing in (receiving).

Anatomical Role of the Elbows:

- Act as a hinge joint, allowing the arm to bend and extend.
- Provide structural support for the arms and hands.
- Enable controlled movement and strength for lifting, pushing, and pulling.
- Absorb pressure and shock during movement.

Energetic Role of the Elbows:

- Reflect the balance between giving and receiving energy.
- Represent emotional and physical flexibility.
- Store emotional resistance or difficulty accepting help.
- Reflect how we manage personal boundaries in relationships.

Chakra Connection to the Elbows

The elbows are directly linked to the Heart Chakra and Solar Plexus Chakra, which influence emotional receptivity, self-worth, and personal power.

1. Heart Chakra (Anahata) – Governs Love and Emotional Openness

- The elbows reflect the ability to open the heart and extend emotional support.
- When the elbows are tense or blocked, it often reflects emotional defensiveness or hesitation to give love freely.

Conscious breathwork and focused mantras help direct and amplify the flow of energy, promote balance and emotional release.

- Pain or stiffness in the elbows may reflect a fear of emotional vulnerability or rejection.

Example:

- A person who struggles to express love or offer emotional support to others may experience elbow stiffness or weakness.

2. Solar Plexus Chakra (Manipura) – Governs Confidence and Personal Power

- The elbows reflect how much control and personal power a person feels when interacting with others.
- Tension or discomfort in the elbows reflects difficulty establishing healthy boundaries in relationships.
- Pain in the elbows may reflect an imbalance of control — either giving too much or refusing to accept help.

Example:

- A person who feels obligated to help others at their own expense may develop chronic elbow pain due to weakened personal boundaries.

Emotional and Spiritual Patterns Stored in the Elbows

The energetic patterns held in the elbows reflect how a person manages the flow of energy in relationships and life circumstances. Tightness, pain, or restricted movement in the elbows often reflects underlying emotional and spiritual resistance.

1. Flexibility and Adaptability

The elbows reflect the ability to bend and adjust to life's changes.

- Flexible, pain-free elbows reflect emotional adaptability and openness.
- Stiffness or pain in the elbows reflects resistance to change or difficulty adapting to new circumstances.
- The inability to "bend" reflects emotional or spiritual inflexibility.

Example:

- A person going through a career or relationship transition may develop elbow pain due to underlying fear or resistance to change.
- Reiki directed to the elbows and Solar Plexus Chakra can help release resistance and restore confidence.

2. Giving and Offering Support

The elbows reflect how easily a person offers emotional or physical support to others.

- Strong, open elbows reflect a balanced ability to give love and support.
- Pain or discomfort in the elbows reflects emotional withholding or guardedness.

Conscious breathwork and focused mantras help direct and amplify the flow of energy, promote balance and emotional release.

- Overuse of the elbows reflects overextension —
  giving too much to others at one's own expense.

Example:

- A person who feels emotionally drained from
  caring for others may develop tension or
  inflammation in the elbows.
- Reiki directed to the elbows and Heart Chakra can
  help restore balance and emotional boundaries.

3. Receiving and Allowing Support

The elbows reflect how receptive a person is to receiving
emotional or physical support.

- Open elbows reflect the ability to trust others and
  receive love freely.
- Tension or pain in the elbows reflects difficulty
  accepting help or emotional vulnerability.
- Emotional self-sufficiency and fear of dependence
  often show up as blocked elbow energy.

Example:

- A person who feels unworthy of emotional support
  may experience chronic tension in the elbows.
- Reiki directed to the elbows and Solar Plexus
  Chakra can help dissolve this resistance and
  encourage openness.

4. Establishing Personal Boundaries

The elbows reflect the energetic balance between giving and protecting oneself.

- Strong, healthy elbows reflect balanced personal boundaries.
- Weakness or tension in the elbows reflects difficulty setting limits or feeling overextended.
- Misalignment in the elbows reflects a power struggle between emotional openness and self-protection.

Example:

- A person who feels emotionally manipulated may develop elbow weakness or joint instability.
- Reiki directed to the elbows and Solar Plexus Chakra helps strengthen personal boundaries and restore confidence.

Reiki Techniques for Healing the Elbows

Reiki restores the natural balance between giving and receiving by dissolving energetic blockages in the elbows. When energy flows freely through the elbow joints, emotional flexibility, strength, and confidence are restored.

Conscious breathwork and focused mantras help direct and amplify the flow of energy, promoting balance and emotional release.

1. Direct Hand Placement on the Elbows

- Have the client sit comfortably with their arms relaxed.
- Place your hands on the inside and outside of the elbow joint.
- Use the Cho Ku Rei (Power Symbol) to increase the flow of Reiki energy into the joint.
- Hold for 3–5 minutes or until you feel the energy shift.
- Visualize golden light flowing into the elbow, softening tension and increasing flexibility.

This technique releases energetic and physical tension in the joint.

2. Cross-Body Elbow Technique (Balancing Opposing Energies)

- Place one hand on the left elbow and the other on the right knee (or vice versa).
- Channel Reiki energy between the two points.
- Visualize a line of light connecting the elbow and knee, restoring energetic balance between giving and receiving.
- Use the Sei He Ki symbol to dissolve emotional resistance.
- Hold until the energy becomes balanced.

This technique balances masculine and feminine energy, improving emotional and physical flexibility.

3. Elbow Rotation Technique (Restoring Flexibility)

- Place one hand on the upper arm and the other on the forearm.
- Slowly guide the arm through a gentle range of motion.
- Visualize white light moving through the joint, restoring smooth and balanced movement.
- Use the Cho Ku Rei symbol to increase energy flow through the joint.
- Continue until you feel the energy release.

This technique improves mobility and reduces stiffness.

4. Emotional Release Technique (Letting Go of Burdens)

- Place both hands on the elbow.
- Ask the client to take slow, deep breaths.
- Guide the client to silently or verbally state:
  - *"I release the burden of responsibility."*
  - *"It is safe to receive support."*
  - *"I trust in the flow of life."*
- Use the Sei He Ki symbol to dissolve emotional resistance.
- Hold until you feel the energy lighten.

This technique helps release emotional tension and strengthens receptivity.

5. Visualization Technique for Flexibility

- Place both hands on the elbow.

Conscious breathwork and focused mantras help direct and amplify the flow of energy, promot balance and emotional release.

- Have the client close their eyes and visualize the elbow joint expanding and becoming more fluid.
- Encourage them to imagine golden light moving through the joint.
- Visualize the elbow becoming soft, strong, and balanced.
- Hold until you feel the energy stabilize.

This technique restores flexibility and emotional openness.

Key Takeaways:

- The elbows reflect the balance between giving and receiving.
- Reiki releases emotional and physical tension in the elbows.
- The Heart and Solar Plexus Chakras govern the energy flow through the elbows.
- Healing the elbows improves emotional flexibility and strength.
- Balanced elbow energy strengthens emotional boundaries and increases confidence in giving and receiving.

By working on the elbows with Reiki, you help the client restore the natural balance between offering support and allowing themselves to receive love and care.

Wrists: Trust and Communication

The wrists are more than just physical joints that allow movement of the hands — they serve as energetic gateways that reflect a person's ability to trust themselves and others, and to express themselves openly and authentically. In Reiki practice, the wrists are closely connected to the Throat Chakra (Vishuddha) and the Heart Chakra (Anahata), which govern communication, emotional openness, and the ability to trust life's flow.

Physically, the wrists allow flexibility and dexterity in the hands, which are tools for both creation and connection. Energetically, the wrists reflect the balance between offering and receiving, as well as how easily a person expresses their inner truth. Tension or discomfort in the wrists reflects emotional or spiritual patterns related to communication, trust, and emotional vulnerability.

When Reiki is applied to the wrists, it not only relieves physical discomfort but also works to restore the energetic balance between trust and expression. By clearing energetic blockages in the wrists, the client may experience greater ease in communicating, trusting others, and creatively expressing themselves.

The Physical and Energetic Role of the Wrists

The wrists serve as both a mechanical joint and an energetic bridge between the arms and the hands. Their structural design allows strength and flexibility, while their

Conscious breathwork and focused mantras help direct and amplify the flow of energy, promote balance and emotional release.

energetic role reflects the balance between control and surrender in life.

Anatomical Role of the Wrists:

- The wrist is composed of eight small carpal bones, connecting the hand to the forearm.
- The tendons and ligaments surrounding the wrist allow strength, flexibility, and precise hand movements.
- The wrists support the hands during movement, bearing weight and facilitating dexterity.
- Healthy wrist movement allows for fluid, controlled motion in the hands and fingers.

Energetic Role of the Wrists:

- The wrists reflect trust in life's process — how easily a person lets go of control and trusts the flow of life.
- The wrists reflect communication — how freely a person expresses themselves emotionally and verbally.
- Tension in the wrists reflects emotional hesitation, guardedness, or fear of vulnerability.
- Open, fluid wrist movement reflects emotional openness, creative flow, and balanced communication.

Chakra Connection to the Wrists

The energetic health of the wrists is directly linked to the Throat Chakra (communication) and the Heart Chakra (emotional openness). The flow of energy through these chakras influences how a person interacts with others and expresses their truth.

1. Throat Chakra (Vishuddha) – Governs Communication and Self-Expression

- The wrists reflect how easily a person expresses their truth and communicates openly.
- Tension in the wrists may reflect fear of speaking out or holding back emotional truth.
- Weak or painful wrists may reflect insecurity about one's creative abilities or personal voice.
- Blocked wrist energy may reflect difficulty expressing emotions verbally.

Example:

- A person who feels they can't express themselves authentically at work or in a relationship may develop wrist stiffness or pain.

2. Heart Chakra (Anahata) – Governs Emotional Trust and Openness

- The wrists reflect emotional receptivity and the ability to trust others.
- Tension in the wrists reflects guardedness or fear of emotional vulnerability.

Conscious breathwork and focused mantras help direct and amplify the flow of energy, promoti. balance and emotional release.

- If the Heart Chakra is blocked, the person may experience wrist pain when trying to engage emotionally or creatively.

Example:

- A person who has experienced betrayal or emotional hurt may develop wrist tension as a form of emotional self-protection.

Emotional and Spiritual Patterns Stored in the Wrists

Tension, stiffness, or weakness in the wrists often reflects deeper emotional patterns related to trust, self-expression, and creative flow.

1. Trust and Surrender

The wrists reflect the ability to let go of control and trust life's unfolding.

- Open, relaxed wrists reflect a sense of trust and emotional surrender.
- Stiffness or pain in the wrists reflects difficulty letting go or trusting others.
- Weakness in the wrists reflects insecurity or lack of confidence in life's path.

Example:

- A person who feels the need to control every aspect of life may experience chronic wrist tension or pain.

- Reiki directed to the wrists and Heart Chakra helps dissolve this resistance and restore trust.

2. Fear of Emotional or Creative Vulnerability

The wrists reflect emotional and creative openness.

- Pain or tightness in the wrists reflects a fear of emotional or creative expression.
- Guarded wrists reflect fear of rejection or judgment.
- Weak or unstable wrists reflect emotional self-protection and hesitation.

Example:

- A person who struggles with creative expression may experience weakness or discomfort in the wrists when trying to engage in creative work.
- Reiki directed to the wrists and Throat Chakra encourages emotional and creative flow.

3. Blocked Communication

The wrists reflect the ability to communicate one's truth with ease and confidence.

- Tension in the wrists reflects hesitation or fear of speaking out.
- Pain in the wrists reflects feeling unheard or emotionally stifled.
- Guarded wrists reflect a pattern of emotional suppression.

Conscious breathwork and focused mantras help direct and amplify the flow of energy, promot balance and emotional release.

Example:

- A person who feels that their opinions or emotions are not valued may develop chronic wrist pain.
- Reiki directed to the wrists and Throat Chakra helps clear blocked communication.

4. Overextension or Over-Giving

The wrists reflect the energetic balance between giving and receiving.

- Tight, strained wrists reflect over-giving or emotional overextension.
- Weak wrists reflect emotional exhaustion or depletion.
- Painful wrists reflect difficulty setting emotional boundaries.

Example:

- A person who constantly gives emotional support to others but struggles to receive support may experience wrist tightness or weakness.
- Reiki directed to the wrists and Heart Chakra helps restore balance and reinforce healthy boundaries.

Reiki Techniques for Healing the Wrists

Reiki restores the natural balance between trust, communication, and creative flow by dissolving blockages and increasing the flow of energy through the wrists.

1. Direct Hand Placement on the Wrists

- Have the client sit or lie down in a comfortable position.
- Place both hands gently on the wrists, or hold the wrists between your palms.
- Use the Cho Ku Rei (Power Symbol) to increase the flow of Reiki energy into the joint.
- Hold for 3–5 minutes or until you feel the energy shift.
- Visualize the wrists softening and becoming more flexible.

This technique reduces physical stiffness and opens the energy flow through the wrists.

2. Wrist Rotation Technique (Restoring Flexibility)

- Place one hand on the wrist and the other on the hand.
- Slowly and gently rotate the wrist in a circular motion.
- Direct Reiki energy through the wrist as you rotate.
- Use the Sei He Ki symbol to dissolve emotional resistance.
- Continue until the joint feels more open and relaxed.

Conscious breathwork and focused mantras help direct and amplify the flow of energy, promote balance and emotional release.

This technique increases range of motion and restores emotional ease.

3. Cross-Body Wrist Technique (Balancing Masculine and Feminine Energies)

- Place one hand on the left wrist and the other on the right hip (or vice versa).
- Channel Reiki energy between the two points.
- Visualize a line of light connecting the wrist and hip.
- Hold until you feel the energy stabilize.

This technique balances emotional and creative flow between the left and right sides of the body.

4. Emotional Release Technique (Restoring Trust)

- Place both hands on the wrist.
- Ask the client to take slow, deep breaths.
- Guide the client to silently or verbally state:
    - *"I release my fear of trusting."*
    - *"It is safe to communicate my truth."*
    - *"I trust life's flow."*
- Use the Sei He Ki symbol to dissolve emotional resistance.
- Hold until you feel the energy soften.

This technique helps dissolve emotional and creative blocks.

5. Visualization Technique (Opening the Energy Flow)

- Place both hands on the wrist.

- Have the client close their eyes and visualize a stream of blue light (Throat Chakra color) flowing through the wrist.
- Encourage the client to imagine this light dissolving any tightness or tension.
- Hold until you feel the energy stabilize.

This technique strengthens communication and trust.

Key Takeaways:

- The wrists reflect trust, communication, and creative expression.
- Tension in the wrists reflects emotional resistance or guardedness.
- Reiki dissolves physical and energetic blockages, restoring emotional flow.
- Open wrists reflect emotional and creative confidence.
- Healing the wrists strengthens the client's ability to trust and express themselves.

By working on the wrists with Reiki, you help the client restore confidence in communication and trust in the natural flow of life.

Conscious breathwork and focused mantras help direct and amplify the flow of energy, promoti *balance and emotional release.*

Hips: Emotional Movement and Creative Energy

The hips are among the most emotionally charged and energetically sensitive areas of the body. They represent the body's center of gravity and are deeply connected to emotional flow, creative energy, and personal power. In Reiki practice, the hips are closely tied to the Sacral Chakra (Swadhisthana) and the Root Chakra (Muladhara), which govern creativity, emotional balance, sensuality, security, and groundedness.

The hips provide physical support and flexibility for movement, but they also act as an energetic reservoir where emotional experiences, especially those related to relationships, self-expression, creativity, and vulnerability, are stored. When energy becomes blocked or stagnant in the hips, it often reflects emotional holding patterns such as fear, creative suppression, unresolved trauma, or difficulty trusting life's flow.

Blocked energy in the hips can manifest as physical tension, reduced range of motion, or chronic discomfort. Emotionally, it may show up as creative stagnation, emotional numbness, fear of intimacy, or resistance to change. Reiki directed to the hips helps release these patterns, restoring emotional freedom, creative flow, and physical ease.

The Physical and Energetic Role of the Hips

The hips play a dual role — they provide strength and support while also allowing for flexibility and freedom of movement. This reflects their energetic function as centers for balancing strength with emotional flow and creative expression.

Anatomical Role of the Hips:

- The hip joint is a ball-and-socket joint, providing a wide range of motion.
- The hips support the body's weight and maintain balance during movement.
- The surrounding muscles (hip flexors, gluteal muscles, and psoas) help control the body's posture and alignment.
- The hips absorb physical stress and tension from walking, running, and standing.

Energetic Role of the Hips:

- The hips serve as energetic "containers" for emotional and creative energy.
- They reflect how well a person flows with life's changes.
- Open hips reflect emotional and creative flow; tight hips reflect emotional and creative resistance.
- The hips reflect the balance between stability (Root Chakra) and creative flow (Sacral Chakra).

Conscious breathwork and focused mantras help direct and amplify the flow of energy, promote balance and emotional release.

Chakra Connection to the Hips

The energetic health of the hips is directly linked to the Sacral Chakra and the Root Chakra. These chakras govern emotional health, creative expression, and feelings of safety and stability.

1. Sacral Chakra (Swadhisthana) – Governs Creativity and Emotional Flow

- The Sacral Chakra is located just below the navel and governs emotions, sensuality, and creativity.
- Blocked Sacral Chakra energy manifests as creative stagnation, emotional numbness, or difficulty in relationships.
- Open Sacral Chakra energy allows for emotional flow, creative inspiration, and pleasure.
- Tight or painful hips often reflect suppressed creative energy or unresolved emotional experiences.

Example:

- A person who feels creatively blocked or emotionally shut down may experience tightness in the hips.
- Reiki directed to the hips and Sacral Chakra helps release this blocked energy, restoring emotional and creative flow.

2. Root Chakra (Muladhara) – Governs Stability and Security

- The Root Chakra is located at the base of the spine and governs feelings of safety, security, and groundedness.
- Blocked Root Chakra energy reflects fear of instability, financial insecurity, or lack of emotional support.
- Open Root Chakra energy allows a person to feel safe, confident, and connected to the earth.
- Pain or weakness in the hips reflects a lack of emotional or physical stability.

Example:

- A person experiencing fear about financial security or emotional instability may have weak or painful hips.
- Reiki directed to the hips and Root Chakra helps restore a sense of grounding and strength.

Emotional and Spiritual Patterns Stored in the Hips

The hips act as energetic "storage centers" for deep emotional patterns and creative energy. Reiki practitioners often find that tension in the hips reflects unresolved emotional issues and suppressed creative impulses.

1. Emotional Flow and Resistance

The hips reflect the balance between emotional flow and emotional resistance.

Conscious breathwork and focused mantras help direct and amplify the flow of energy, promote balance and emotional release.

- Open hips reflect emotional receptivity and the ability to process feelings with ease.
- Tight or painful hips reflect emotional holding patterns and unresolved emotional pain.
- Difficulty moving the hips reflects resistance to emotional or personal change.

Example:

- A person going through a difficult breakup may experience tightness in the hips due to emotional resistance and fear of vulnerability.
- Reiki directed to the hips and Sacral Chakra helps dissolve this resistance and restore emotional flow.

2. Creative Expression and Stagnation

The hips are linked to creative energy and self-expression.

- Open hips reflect creative flow and the ability to express oneself freely.
- Stiffness or weakness in the hips reflects creative stagnation or fear of creative failure.
- Pain in the hips reflects blocked creative energy and difficulty accessing inspiration.

Example:

- A person who feels creatively blocked in their career or personal life may develop tightness or discomfort in the hips.
- Reiki directed to the hips and Sacral Chakra helps release creative blocks and restore inspiration.

3. Sexual and Sensual Energy

The Sacral Chakra governs sexual energy and intimacy.

- Open hips reflect comfort with intimacy and emotional closeness.
- Tight or painful hips reflect fear of intimacy, shame, or sexual trauma.
- Difficulty in hip movement reflects emotional discomfort with vulnerability.

Example:

- A person with a history of emotional or sexual trauma may experience tight hips or pelvic misalignment.
- Reiki directed to the hips and Sacral Chakra helps dissolve emotional trauma and restore comfort with intimacy.

4. Fear of Change and Life Transitions

The hips reflect how well a person adapts to life's changes and transitions.

- Open hips reflect emotional flexibility and confidence in life's path.
- Stiff or weak hips reflect fear of the unknown or resistance to change.
- Hip instability reflects uncertainty and lack of emotional grounding.

Conscious breathwork and focused mantras help direct and amplify the flow of energy, promote balance and emotional release.

Example:

- A person going through a major life transition (divorce, career change) may experience hip weakness or pain.
- Reiki directed to the hips and Root Chakra helps strengthen emotional resilience and trust.

Reiki Techniques for Healing the Hips

Reiki works to dissolve energetic blockages in the hips by restoring the natural flow of ki (life force energy) through the Sacral and Root Chakras. When the energy flow is restored, emotional openness, creative flow, and physical mobility are enhanced.

1. Direct Hand Placement on the Hips

- Have the client lie down comfortably.
- Place both hands on the hip joints.
- Use the Cho Ku Rei (Power Symbol) to increase the flow of Reiki energy into the joint.
- Hold for 3–5 minutes or until you feel the energy shift.
- Visualize the hips softening and becoming more flexible.

This technique helps dissolve physical and emotional tension.

2. Hip Cradling Technique (Emotional Reassurance)

- Have the client lie on their side.
- Gently cradle the hip with both hands.
- Use the Sei He Ki (Emotional Healing Symbol) to release emotional trauma stored in the hip.
- Encourage the client to breathe deeply as you hold the position.

This technique creates emotional safety and reassurance.

3. Hip Rotation Technique (Restoring Flexibility)

- Place one hand on the hip and the other on the opposite knee.
- Gently rotate the leg through a comfortable range of motion.
- Direct Reiki energy into the joint as you rotate.
- Visualize golden light flowing through the hip, restoring mobility.

This technique improves range of motion and restores energetic flow.

4. Emotional Release Technique (Letting Go of Fear and Creative Resistance)

- Place both hands on the hip.
- Ask the client to silently or verbally state:
    - *"I release fear of change."*
    - *"I allow creative flow."*
    - *"I trust life's unfolding."*

*Conscious breathwork and focused mantras help direct and amplify the flow of energy, promot
balance and emotional release.*

- Use the Sei He Ki symbol to dissolve emotional resistance.

This technique restores emotional and creative freedom.

Key Takeaways:

- The hips reflect emotional movement and creative energy.
- Tension in the hips reflects emotional holding patterns and creative blocks.
- Reiki directed to the hips restores emotional and physical balance.
- Open hips reflect emotional flexibility, creative flow, and strength.
- Healing the hips enhances personal confidence and emotional openness.

By working on the hips with Reiki, you help the client reclaim emotional freedom, creative flow, and confidence in life's unfolding.

Knees: Humility, Adaptability, and Trust in Life's Path

The knees play a vital role in both physical movement and spiritual surrender. They symbolize a person's relationship with life's path — their willingness to adapt, trust, and surrender to the unfolding of life's events. In Reiki practice, the knees are linked to the Root Chakra (Muladhara) and the Sacral Chakra (Swadhisthana), which govern security, stability, adaptability, and emotional flow.

The knees act as shock absorbers for the body, bearing weight and allowing for movement, bending, and balance. Energetically, the knees reflect how well a person navigates change and how much they trust the path that life presents. Tension, weakness, or pain in the knees often reflects difficulty with surrender, fear of change, emotional rigidity, or a struggle to find stability and confidence in life.

When Reiki energy is directed to the knees, it works to dissolve emotional and energetic resistance, restore physical and emotional balance, and strengthen the client's ability to trust in life's unfolding.

The Physical and Energetic Role of the Knees

The knees serve as a structural and energetic hinge between strength and flexibility. They allow the body to remain upright and balanced while also permitting fluid and controlled movement. This reflects the deeper

Conscious breathwork and focused mantras help direct and amplify the flow of energy, promote balance and emotional release.

energetic balance between personal strength and emotional surrender.

Anatomical Role of the Knees:

- The knee is a hinge joint that connects the femur (thigh bone), tibia (shin bone), and patella (kneecap).
- The knee joint is supported by ligaments and tendons that provide strength and stability.
- The knee absorbs impact during walking, running, jumping, and bending.
- Healthy knees provide strength and flexibility, allowing the body to move through different planes of motion.

Energetic Role of the Knees:

- The knees reflect humility — the ability to bend, surrender, and trust.
- They reflect adaptability — the ability to respond to life's changes with flexibility and ease.
- The knees reflect trust — the confidence to step forward on life's path.
- Tension or discomfort in the knees reflects emotional rigidity or fear of moving forward.

Chakra Connection to the Knees

The knees are primarily governed by the Root Chakra and Sacral Chakra. These chakras influence emotional security, adaptability, and personal confidence in life's path.

1. Root Chakra (Muladhara) – Governs Security and Grounding

- The Root Chakra is located at the base of the spine and governs feelings of safety, stability, and connection to the earth.
- Healthy knee function reflects a balanced Root Chakra, where the person feels stable and grounded in life.
- Knee pain or weakness reflects insecurity, lack of trust, or instability in life's foundation.
- Fear of stepping forward, both physically and emotionally, reflects a blocked Root Chakra.

Example:

- A person going through a financial or emotional crisis may experience knee pain due to feelings of instability and insecurity.
- Reiki directed to the knees and Root Chakra helps restore emotional and physical stability.

2. Sacral Chakra (Swadhisthana) – Governs Emotional Flow and Adaptability

- The Sacral Chakra is located below the navel and governs emotional flexibility, creativity, and relationships.
- Healthy knee function reflects emotional flexibility and the ability to move through life's changes.
- Knee stiffness reflects emotional resistance, fear of change, or difficulty trusting life's flow.

Conscious breathwork and focused mantras help direct and amplify the flow of energy, promoting balance and emotional release.

- Emotional patterns related to control or rigidity often manifest as knee tension or inflammation.

Example:

- A person struggling to adapt to a major life change (e.g., divorce, career shift) may experience knee stiffness or weakness.
- Reiki directed to the knees and Sacral Chakra helps dissolve emotional resistance and restore adaptability.

Emotional and Spiritual Patterns Stored in the Knees

The knees are energetic containers for fear, trust, adaptability, and surrender. Reiki practitioners often find that knee tension or discomfort reflects patterns of emotional resistance, fear of vulnerability, and difficulty in trusting life's natural flow.

1. Humility and Emotional Surrender

The ability to bend the knees reflects humility and emotional surrender.

- Open, flexible knees reflect the ability to trust life and surrender to its unfolding.
- Stiff or painful knees reflect resistance to letting go of control.
- Difficulty bending the knees reflects emotional or spiritual rigidity.

Example:

- A person struggling to accept help or emotional support may experience stiffness in the knees.
- Reiki directed to the knees and Root Chakra helps restore humility and emotional openness.

2. Fear of Moving Forward

The knees reflect emotional and spiritual confidence in stepping forward in life.

- Strong, balanced knees reflect emotional security and confidence.
- Weak or painful knees reflect fear of taking the next step or uncertainty about life's path.
- Knee misalignment reflects emotional indecision or spiritual imbalance.

Example:

- A person feeling stuck in their career or relationship may experience knee weakness or pain when walking.
- Reiki directed to the knees and Root Chakra helps dissolve fear and restore confidence.

3. Resistance to Change

The knees reflect emotional adaptability and the ability to flow with life's changes.

Conscious breathwork and focused mantras help direct and amplify the flow of energy, promote balance and emotional release.

- Flexible knees reflect emotional openness and adaptability.
- Stiff or painful knees reflect fear of change or emotional resistance.
- Inflamed knees reflect frustration or inner conflict about life's direction.

Example:

- A person struggling to let go of the past may experience knee stiffness or inflammation.
- Reiki directed to the knees and Sacral Chakra helps release resistance and restore emotional flexibility.

4. Lack of Trust in Life's Path

The knees reflect spiritual trust and confidence in life's unfolding.

- Strong knees reflect inner trust and a sense of purpose.
- Weak or unstable knees reflect insecurity or fear of the unknown.
- Hyperextension or misalignment reflects emotional instability or a lack of direction.

Example:

- A person experiencing doubt about their life path may experience weak or misaligned knees.
- Reiki directed to the knees and Root Chakra helps restore trust and emotional stability.

Reiki Techniques for Healing the Knees

Reiki works to dissolve energetic blockages in the knees by restoring the natural flow of ki (life force energy) through the Root and Sacral Chakras. When the energy flow is restored, emotional strength, physical flexibility, and spiritual trust are enhanced.

1. Direct Hand Placement on the Knees

- Have the client lie down comfortably.
- Place both hands on the knees.
- Use the Cho Ku Rei (Power Symbol) to increase the flow of Reiki energy into the joint.
- Visualize golden light flowing into the knees, dissolving resistance and restoring strength.
- Hold for 3–5 minutes or until you feel the energy shift.

This technique restores physical and energetic balance.

2. Knee Cradling Technique (Restoring Emotional Safety)

- Have the client lie down with knees bent.
- Gently cradle the knee with both hands.
- Use the Sei He Ki (Emotional Healing Symbol) to release emotional fear and resistance.
- Encourage the client to take deep, calming breaths.

This technique creates emotional safety and encourages trust.

Conscious breathwork and focused mantras help direct and amplify the flow of energy, promot. balance and emotional release.

3. Emotional Release Technique (Letting Go of Fear)

- Place both hands on the knee.
- Ask the client to silently or verbally state:
  - *"I release my fear of change."*
  - *"I trust life's unfolding."*
  - *"It is safe to move forward."*
- Use the Sei He Ki symbol to dissolve emotional resistance.

This technique helps the client release emotional fear and restore trust.

4. Cross-Body Knee Technique (Balancing Masculine and Feminine Energies)

- Place one hand on the left knee and the other on the right hip (or vice versa).
- Direct Reiki energy between the two points.
- Visualize a line of light connecting the knee and hip.

This technique balances masculine and feminine energy.

Key Takeaways:

- The knees reflect humility, adaptability, and trust in life's path.
- Reiki restores emotional and physical balance in the knees.
- Open knees reflect emotional and spiritual trust.
- Healing the knees helps clients embrace change with confidence and ease.

Ankles: Balance, Grounding, and Stability

The ankles are the foundation of movement and balance, both physically and energetically. In Reiki practice, the ankles represent the body's connection to grounding, stability, and energetic balance. They reflect a person's ability to stay emotionally and spiritually grounded while navigating life's changes.

Physically, the ankles provide flexibility and strength, supporting the body's weight and facilitating movement. Energetically, the ankles are linked to the Root Chakra (Muladhara) and the Earth Star Chakra (below the feet), which govern feelings of safety, stability, and connection to the earth.

When energy becomes blocked or stagnant in the ankles, it often reflects emotional instability, fear of the unknown, or difficulty trusting life's unfolding. Reiki directed to the ankles helps to release this stagnant energy, restore physical and emotional balance, and strengthen the client's sense of connection and stability.

The Physical and Energetic Role of the Ankles

The ankles serve as both a structural joint and an energetic connector between the body and the earth. Their ability to provide both strength and flexibility reflects the deeper spiritual balance between groundedness and freedom of movement.

Conscious breathwork and focused mantras help direct and amplify the flow of energy, promoti. balance and emotional release.

Anatomical Role of the Ankles:

- The ankle is a hinge joint formed by the tibia (shin bone), fibula (calf bone), and talus (foot bone).
- Ligaments and tendons support the ankle, allowing for dorsiflexion (lifting the foot) and plantar flexion (pointing the foot).
- The ankle bears the body's weight and stabilizes the body during walking, running, and standing.
- Healthy ankle function allows for strength, flexibility, and shock absorption.

Energetic Role of the Ankles:

- The ankles represent grounding — the ability to feel stable and secure in life.
- They reflect balance — the ability to adjust to life's challenges and remain centered.
- The ankles reflect trust — the ability to stand confidently on one's path.
- When ankle energy is blocked, it reflects emotional imbalance, instability, and lack of direction.

Chakra Connection to the Ankles

The ankles are primarily connected to the Root Chakra and the Earth Star Chakra. These chakras influence physical stability, emotional balance, and spiritual connection to the earth.

1. Root Chakra (Muladhara) – Governs Safety and Stability

- The Root Chakra is located at the base of the spine and governs feelings of safety, stability, and survival.
- Open Root Chakra energy allows a person to feel emotionally stable and physically balanced.
- Blocked Root Chakra energy creates emotional instability, physical weakness, and insecurity.
- Ankle pain or instability reflects a weakened Root Chakra or lack of emotional security.

Example:

- A person feeling anxious about financial or emotional security may experience ankle weakness or pain.
- Reiki directed to the ankles and Root Chakra helps restore stability and security.

2. Earth Star Chakra – Governs Grounding and Earth Connection

- The Earth Star Chakra is located approximately 12–18 inches below the feet and governs grounding to the earth's energy.
- Open Earth Star Chakra energy allows a person to feel rooted and secure in life's flow.
- Blocked Earth Star Chakra energy creates a sense of feeling "disconnected" from life or ungrounded.
- Weak or unstable ankles reflect an energetic disconnection from the earth.

Conscious breathwork and focused mantras help direct and amplify the flow of energy, promote balance and emotional release.

Example:

- A person who feels disconnected from their purpose or path may experience ankle instability.
- Reiki directed to the ankles and Earth Star Chakra helps strengthen the client's sense of connection and direction.

Emotional and Spiritual Patterns Stored in the Ankles

The ankles are energetic containers for balance, stability, and trust. Reiki practitioners often find that ankle pain or instability reflects emotional patterns related to fear, instability, and resistance to life's unfolding.

1. Emotional and Spiritual Balance

The ankles reflect the balance between emotional stability and personal freedom.

- Strong, flexible ankles reflect emotional and spiritual balance.
- Weak or unstable ankles reflect emotional instability or lack of confidence.
- Stiff or painful ankles reflect resistance to emotional flow and change.

Example:

- A person who feels emotionally overwhelmed or unstable may experience ankle stiffness or weakness.

- Reiki directed to the ankles and Root Chakra helps restore emotional balance and stability.

2. Fear of Moving Forward

The ankles reflect a person's emotional confidence in taking the next step in life.

- Open, strong ankles reflect trust and emotional readiness to move forward.
- Weak or painful ankles reflect fear of the unknown or lack of direction.
- Ankle instability reflects uncertainty about life's path.

Example:

- A person afraid of starting a new career or relationship may experience ankle weakness or sprains.
- Reiki directed to the ankles and Root Chakra helps dissolve fear and restore emotional confidence.

3. Resistance to Change

The ankles reflect a person's ability to adapt and adjust to life's changes.

- Flexible ankles reflect emotional openness and adaptability.
- Stiff or misaligned ankles reflect emotional rigidity and resistance to change.

Conscious breathwork and focused mantras help direct and amplify the flow of energy, promote balance and emotional release.

- Ankle tension reflects fear of stepping into the unknown.

Example:

- A person going through a major life transition may experience ankle stiffness or inflammation.
- Reiki directed to the ankles and Root Chakra helps release resistance and restore emotional flexibility.

4. Lack of Trust in Life's Path

The ankles reflect spiritual confidence and emotional trust in life's unfolding.

- Strong ankles reflect inner trust and security.
- Weak or unstable ankles reflect fear of failure or emotional insecurity.
- Ankle misalignment reflects difficulty trusting oneself or life's path.

Example:

- A person who feels unsupported in life may experience weak or misaligned ankles.
- Reiki directed to the ankles and Root Chakra helps restore emotional confidence and trust.

Reiki Techniques for Healing the Ankles

Reiki restores the natural balance between stability and movement by dissolving blockages and strengthening the energetic connection to the Root and Earth Star Chakras.

When energy flows freely through the ankles, emotional and physical balance are restored.

1. Direct Hand Placement on the Ankles

- Have the client lie down comfortably.
- Place both hands on the inside and outside of the ankle.
- Use the Cho Ku Rei (Power Symbol) to increase the flow of Reiki energy into the joint.
- Hold for 3–5 minutes or until you feel the energy shift.
- Visualize golden light flowing into the ankle, dissolving resistance and restoring strength.

This technique restores physical and energetic stability.

2. Ankle Rotation Technique (Restoring Flexibility)

- Place one hand on the ankle and the other on the sole of the foot.
- Gently rotate the ankle through a comfortable range of motion.
- Direct Reiki energy into the joint as you rotate.
- Visualize white light flowing through the ankle, increasing flexibility and strength.

This technique improves mobility and restores energetic flow.

Conscious breathwork and focused mantras help direct and amplify the flow of energy, promoting balance and emotional release.

3. Cross-Body Ankle Technique (Balancing Opposing Energies)

- Place one hand on the left ankle and the other on the right knee (or vice versa).
- Direct Reiki energy between the two points.
- Visualize a line of light connecting the ankle and knee.
- Hold until you feel the energy stabilize.

This technique balances masculine and feminine energy.

4. Emotional Release Technique (Letting Go of Fear and Instability)

- Place both hands on the ankle.
- Ask the client to silently or verbally state:
    - *"I release my fear of instability."*
    - *"I am supported by the earth."*
    - *"It is safe to move forward."*
- Use the Sei He Ki symbol to dissolve emotional resistance.

This technique restores emotional confidence and grounding.

5. Visualization Technique (Strengthening Grounding and Trust)

- Place both hands on the ankle.
- Have the client close their eyes and visualize a stream of red light (Root Chakra color) flowing through the ankle.

- Encourage the client to imagine this light dissolving any tightness or tension.
- Hold until you feel the energy stabilize.

This technique strengthens the connection between emotional stability and physical strength.

Key Takeaways:

- The ankles reflect balance, grounding, and emotional trust.
- Reiki restores emotional and physical stability in the ankles.
- Open, strong ankles reflect emotional confidence and adaptability.
- Healing the ankles helps the client feel grounded and supported in life's unfolding.

By working on the ankles with Reiki, you help the client restore emotional and physical balance, trust in life's process, and confidence in moving forward.

Conscious breathwork and focused mantras help direct and amplify the flow of energy, promote balance and emotional release.

Fingers and Toes: Precision and Action

The fingers and toes represent the body's ability to engage with the world in a precise, deliberate, and balanced way. In Reiki practice, the fingers and toes reflect the energetic balance between intentional action and spiritual alignment. While the larger joints (such as the hips and shoulders) reflect broader emotional patterns, the fingers and toes govern the finer details of how a person interacts with their environment — physically, emotionally, and energetically.

The fingers and toes are connected to the Root Chakra (for grounding and stability) and the Crown Chakra (for spiritual alignment and purpose). They reflect how well a person is able to align spiritual insight with physical action, representing the integration of thought and action — or, more spiritually, the connection between divine guidance and earthly execution.

Blocked or tense energy in the fingers or toes reflects difficulty with control, precision, creative flow, or alignment between spiritual purpose and physical expression. Reiki helps dissolve these energetic blockages, restore fluidity and balance, and improve a person's confidence in taking aligned action in their life.

The Physical and Energetic Role of the Fingers and Toes

The fingers and toes serve as fine-tuned instruments for interacting with the world. Their role extends beyond physical function to emotional, energetic, and spiritual alignment.

Anatomical Role of the Fingers and Toes:

- The fingers are composed of 14 phalanges (bones), connected by tendons and ligaments.
- The toes are composed of similar structures and play a key role in balance and grounding.
- Fingers allow for precision, grip, and dexterity in physical actions.
- Toes provide stability and balance for movement and grounding.
- The hands and feet are richly supplied with nerve endings, making them sensitive to physical and energetic input.

Energetic Role of the Fingers and Toes:

- Fingers represent precision — the ability to act with intention and control.
- Toes represent balance — the ability to remain stable while moving through life.
- Energetic imbalances in the fingers reflect indecision, creative stagnation, or lack of confidence in one's ability to act.
- Imbalances in the toes reflect instability, fear of missteps, or difficulty grounding one's actions.

Chakra Connection to the Fingers and Toes

The fingers and toes are connected to both the Root Chakra (for grounding and balance) and the Crown Chakra

Conscious breathwork and focused mantras help direct and amplify the flow of energy, promote balance and emotional release.

(for spiritual guidance). The balance between these two chakras reflects the ability to align spiritual insight with practical action.

1. Root Chakra (Muladhara) – Governs Grounding and Stability

- The Root Chakra governs physical and emotional security.
- Open Root Chakra energy allows a person to feel balanced, supported, and stable.
- Blocked Root Chakra energy creates fear of action or hesitation in movement.
- Weak or painful toes reflect a lack of confidence or emotional security in taking the next step.

Example:

- A person feeling emotionally or financially insecure may experience toe pain or difficulty balancing.
- Reiki directed to the toes and Root Chakra helps restore emotional and physical balance.

2. Crown Chakra (Sahasrara) – Governs Spiritual Alignment and Insight

- The Crown Chakra governs spiritual connection and purpose.
- Open Crown Chakra energy allows a person to receive divine guidance and act with confidence.
- Blocked Crown Chakra energy creates confusion, indecision, and lack of clarity in action.

- Stiffness in the fingers reflects difficulty bringing spiritual insight into practical action.

Example:

- A person feeling creatively blocked or spiritually disconnected may experience stiffness in the fingers.
- Reiki directed to the fingers and Crown Chakra helps reconnect spiritual inspiration with practical execution.

3. Heart Chakra (Anahata) – Governs Connection and Emotional Precision

- The Heart Chakra governs love, connection, and emotional expression.
- The fingers, especially the thumbs and index fingers, reflect how comfortably a person connects with others through touch and emotional presence.
- Open Heart Chakra energy allows for precise and loving interaction with the world.
- Tension in the fingers reflects guardedness or emotional withdrawal.

Example:

- A person who struggles to express affection physically may experience tension or numbness in the fingers.
- Reiki directed to the fingers and Heart Chakra helps restore emotional openness and connection.

Conscious breathwork and focused mantras help direct and amplify the flow of energy, promote balance and emotional release.

Emotional and Spiritual Patterns Stored in the Fingers and Toes

Tension, stiffness, or weakness in the fingers and toes reflects emotional or spiritual imbalances in how a person approaches life's finer details — including creative expression, emotional connection, and practical action.

1. Precision and Control

The fingers reflect the ability to take focused and intentional action.

- Open, flexible fingers reflect confidence and creative flow.
- Stiffness or tension in the fingers reflects fear of failure or perfectionism.
- Weakness in the fingers reflects indecision or lack of creative confidence.

Example:

- A person struggling with creative work or decision-making may experience finger stiffness or weakness.
- Reiki directed to the fingers and Crown Chakra helps restore creative flow and confidence.

2. Emotional and Physical Balance

The toes reflect the balance between emotional stability and physical grounding.

- Strong, stable toes reflect emotional and physical balance.
- Weak or painful toes reflect emotional instability or lack of direction.
- Overly sensitive toes reflect emotional vulnerability or fear of missteps.

Example:

- A person feeling emotionally off-balance or uncertain about their life path may experience toe pain or weakness.
- Reiki directed to the toes and Root Chakra helps restore balance and emotional grounding.

3. Taking Aligned Action

The fingers and toes reflect how comfortably a person translates spiritual guidance into practical action.

- Open, relaxed fingers and toes reflect ease in taking inspired action.
- Tension or discomfort reflects hesitation, self-doubt, or creative stagnation.
- Stiff fingers reflect difficulty turning ideas into action.

Example:

- A person with a creative vision but fear of executing it may experience finger tension or weakness.

Conscious breathwork and focused mantras help direct and amplify the flow of energy, promote balance and emotional release.

- Reiki directed to the fingers and Crown Chakra helps dissolve this hesitation and increase creative confidence.

4. Fear of Moving Forward

The toes reflect how confidently a person steps forward in life.

- Strong, stable toes reflect trust and confidence.
- Weak or painful toes reflect insecurity and fear of making the wrong decision.
- Misaligned toes reflect internal conflict or a feeling of being "off track."

Example:

- A person hesitant to make a big life decision may experience pain or imbalance in the toes.
- Reiki directed to the toes and Root Chakra helps restore emotional security and trust in life's path.

Reiki Techniques for Healing the Fingers and Toes

Reiki works to dissolve energetic blockages and restore balance between spiritual guidance and physical action. When the energy flow is restored through the fingers and toes, confidence, precision, and emotional alignment are enhanced.

1. Direct Hand Placement on Fingers and Toes

- Have the client sit or lie down comfortably.
- Place your hands on the fingers or toes.
- Use the Cho Ku Rei (Power Symbol) to increase the flow of Reiki energy.
- Visualize light flowing into the fingers or toes, softening tension and increasing strength.

This technique restores confidence and alignment.

2. Finger and Toe Massage Technique (Restoring Flexibility)

- Gently massage each finger or toe while directing Reiki energy.
- Rotate the fingers or toes to release tension.
- Visualize the light restoring balance and flow through the joints.

This technique improves flexibility and energetic balance.

3. Cross-Body Finger and Toe Technique (Balancing Opposing Energies)

- Place one hand on the left hand or foot and the other on the right hip or shoulder.
- Direct Reiki energy between the two points.
- Visualize a line of light connecting the two sides of the body.

This technique restores masculine and feminine balance.

Conscious breathwork and focused mantras help direct and amplify the flow of energy, promote balance and emotional release.

4. Emotional Release Technique (Letting Go of Hesitation)

- Place both hands on the fingers or toes.
- Ask the client to silently or verbally state:
    - *"I trust my path."*
    - *"It is safe to act on my inspiration."*
    - *"I release fear of failure."*

This technique increases creative confidence and trust.

Key Takeaways:

- The fingers and toes reflect precision, balance, and aligned action.
- Reiki restores confidence and emotional balance through the fingers and toes.
- Open, flexible fingers and toes reflect confidence and alignment.
- Healing the fingers and toes strengthens emotional clarity and action.

By working on the fingers and toes with Reiki, you help the client translate spiritual guidance into confident, aligned action.

Chapter 7: Releasing Emotional Trauma Stored

How to Identify Emotional Imprints

The body serves as a living record of emotional and energetic experiences. Emotional trauma, whether from past injuries, stress, emotional wounds, or unresolved conflict, is often stored in the body's joints. The joints act as energetic storage centers where emotional energy becomes imprinted and held, particularly when the trauma is not fully processed or released. This stored energy can create physical discomfort, stiffness, inflammation, and reduced mobility — all of which are signs that emotional healing is needed.

Reiki practice teaches that trauma is not purely psychological — it also embeds itself in the physical and energetic layers of the body. The joints, being the points where multiple meridians intersect and where physical movement occurs, are particularly prone to holding these imprints. When emotional trauma becomes trapped in the joints, it disrupts the natural flow of ki (life force energy), leading to stagnation, tension, and recurring pain.

Conscious breathwork and focused mantras help direct and amplify the flow of energy, promoti
balance and emotional release.

Identifying these emotional imprints is the first step in releasing them. Reiki practitioners are trained to sense blocked energy in the body and interpret the emotional patterns linked to specific joints. By working with the energetic and emotional layers of the joint, Reiki helps to dissolve these imprints, restore energetic flow, and release the emotional weight that has been held in the body.

How Trauma Becomes Stored in the Joints

Emotional trauma can become embedded in the joints due to the body's natural response to stress and emotional conflict. When the body experiences trauma — whether physical, emotional, or spiritual — the nervous system activates a protective response. This creates muscle tension, energetic contraction, and the formation of "energetic knots" within the body's energy system.

When the trauma is not fully processed or resolved, the body "remembers" the experience and stores it in specific energetic and physical points — most often in the joints. This happens for several reasons:

1. Joints as Energy Crossroads

Joints are natural energy intersections where multiple meridians and energy pathways meet. Because of this, they become natural collection points for emotional energy.

- When energy flow through the joints is blocked or stagnant, the emotional trauma remains trapped.

- The body "locks down" the joint as a protective measure, causing stiffness and reduced mobility.
- This stored trauma can lead to chronic discomfort, inflammation, or misalignment.

Example:

- A person who experienced a traumatic fall as a child may develop chronic knee pain as an adult, not because of physical damage, but because the energetic imprint of fear and instability remains trapped in the joint.

2. Muscular and Fascia Memory

The body's fascia (connective tissue) and muscles record emotional experiences. When trauma occurs, the fascia contracts and holds tension as a protective mechanism.

- Over time, this tension becomes habitual, creating muscular imbalances and joint misalignment.
- The joint becomes restricted, and the emotional trauma is "locked in" at the physical and energetic level.
- The fascia and muscles surrounding the joint continue to "hold" the trauma even if the original cause is no longer present.

Example:

- A person who experienced emotional betrayal may unconsciously tense their shoulders and neck,

Conscious breathwork and focused mantras help direct and amplify the flow of energy, promote balance and emotional release.

creating chronic shoulder tightness and restricted mobility.

3. Energetic Blockages in the Meridians and Chakras

Emotional trauma creates blockages in the body's energy system, preventing the natural flow of ki.

- Blocked energy creates pressure and tension within the joint.
- The energy becomes "stuck" and cannot circulate freely.
- This leads to inflammation, stiffness, and chronic discomfort.

Example:

- A person struggling with suppressed grief may experience shoulder and elbow pain due to blocked energy in the Heart Chakra and Lung Meridian.

4. Emotional Self-Protection Mechanism

The body responds to emotional trauma by "locking down" the joint as a form of self-protection.

- If the trauma is related to feeling emotionally unsafe or unstable, the body will create tension in the corresponding joint.
- The locked joint prevents the person from moving forward emotionally or physically.

- The joint essentially becomes "frozen" as a defense mechanism.

Example:

- A person who has experienced abandonment or emotional loss may develop hip stiffness, reflecting the body's resistance to moving forward emotionally.

Signs of Emotional Trauma Stored in the Joints

Recognizing the signs of emotional trauma stored in the joints allows the Reiki practitioner to identify and target the areas needing energetic release. These signs can appear as physical, emotional, or energetic imbalances.

1. Chronic Pain or Stiffness Without Physical Cause

- Pain that persists despite medical treatment or physical therapy often reflects an emotional or energetic blockage.
- The pain may appear or intensify during periods of emotional stress.
- The location of the pain may correlate with unresolved emotional patterns.

Conscious breathwork and focused mantras help direct and amplify the flow of energy, promote balance and emotional release.

Example:

- A person who experiences ongoing shoulder pain despite no physical injury may be holding unresolved emotional burdens.

2. Reduced Range of Motion

- Joints that feel "stuck" or difficult to move often reflect emotional resistance.
- The restricted mobility mirrors emotional inflexibility or a fear of moving forward.
- The affected joint may feel stiff or misaligned even when physically rested.

Example:

- A person going through a divorce may experience hip tightness and reduced mobility due to emotional resistance to change.

3. Sharp or Burning Sensations

- Sharp or burning pain in the joints reflects blocked emotional energy or unresolved anger.
- The sensation may come and go based on emotional or environmental triggers.
- The pain may intensify when the person is emotionally triggered.

Example:

- A person who suppresses resentment may experience burning sensations in their wrists or elbows.

4. Swelling or Inflammation Without Physical Injury

- Swelling or inflammation in the joints reflects emotional stagnation and energetic pressure.
- The body's inflammatory response reflects the body's attempt to protect the joint from emotional overload.
- The inflammation may decrease after emotional release through Reiki or other forms of healing.

Example:

- A person holding onto emotional grief may experience swollen knees or ankles.

5. Numbness or Tingling

- Numbness or tingling in the joints reflects emotional disconnection or suppressed feelings.
- The person may feel emotionally "cut off" or unable to express themselves.
- The joint's sensitivity returns once the emotional blockage is released.

Conscious breathwork and focused mantras help direct and amplify the flow of energy, promoti. balance and emotional release.

Example:

- A person who suppresses their creative energy may experience numbness in the fingers.

6. Weakness or Instability

- Weak or unstable joints reflect a lack of emotional security or confidence.
- The person may feel uncertain about their life path or emotionally unsupported.
- The joint's strength returns once emotional security is restored.

Example:

- A person feeling unsure about a career change may experience weakness in the knees or ankles.

How to Identify Emotional Imprints During a Reiki Session

Reiki practitioners can identify emotional imprints by tuning into the body's energetic patterns and physical sensations.

Emotional imprints are stored patterns of unresolved emotions, trauma, and stress that become embedded in the body's energetic field. During a Reiki session, practitioners can identify these imprints by tuning into the body's energetic flow and paying attention to areas of stagnation, resistance, or discomfort. A blocked joint, for example, may feel unusually heavy, warm, cold, or tense when Reiki energy is directed toward it. Practitioners may also sense emotional cues such as sadness, fear, or anxiety arising during the session, which are often linked to the emotional memory stored within the joint or energy center. By holding space and maintaining a neutral, compassionate presence, the practitioner allows these imprints to surface and be released, restoring the natural flow of energy through the body's chakras, meridians, and nadis.

1. Scanning the Energy Field

- Begin the session by scanning the body's energy field with your hands.
- Pay attention to areas where you feel heat, coolness, heaviness, or energetic "pulling."
- These sensations indicate areas of energetic stagnation or emotional trauma.

2. Feeling for Resistance or Tension

- Place your hands on the joint and feel for resistance or tightness.
- If the energy feels "sticky" or blocked, this indicates emotional resistance.
- Resistance may feel like a "pulling" or "pushing" sensation in your hands.

3. Emotional or Physical Reactions from the Client

- The client may experience spontaneous emotional release during the session.

Conscious breathwork and focused mantras help direct and amplify the flow of energy, promote balance and emotional release.

- Tears, shaking, or changes in breathing reflect the body's release of stored trauma.
- Encourage the client to allow the emotions to surface without judgment.

4. Intuitive Messages or Visions

- Reiki energy often provides intuitive guidance about the emotional source of the blockage.
- You may "see" or "sense" the emotional memory behind the trauma.
- Trust your intuition and allow the energy to guide the healing process.

Key Takeaways:

- Emotional trauma is often stored in the joints due to the body's protective response to stress and unresolved conflict.
- Reiki practitioners can identify emotional imprints by sensing blocked or stagnant energy.
- Signs of emotional trauma include chronic pain, reduced mobility, inflammation, numbness, and emotional triggers.
- Releasing these patterns restores physical and emotional balance, allowing the client to move forward with greater ease and confidence.

By identifying emotional imprints in the joints, Reiki practitioners can guide clients through emotional release, restoring both physical and emotional harmony.

Techniques to Clear Emotional Trauma from the Joints

Emotional trauma stored in the joints creates energetic blockages that disrupt the flow of ki (life force energy) and restrict both physical and emotional movement. Reiki offers a powerful method for clearing these blockages by restoring the natural flow of energy through the body's chakras, meridians, and energetic pathways.

When trauma becomes trapped in the joints, it reflects deeper emotional patterns such as fear, guilt, shame, grief, and resistance to change. The body stores these unresolved emotional experiences in the joints because they serve as energy crossroads — where multiple meridians intersect and energetic flow is naturally concentrated. Clearing emotional trauma from the joints not only restores physical flexibility and comfort but also helps the client release emotional patterns and restore emotional balance.

Reiki techniques for joint healing involve a combination of direct energy work, symbol activation, breathwork, and visualization. The goal is to dissolve the energetic knots, release emotional imprints, and restore smooth, balanced energy flow.

Conscious breathwork and focused mantras help direct and amplify the flow of energy, promot balance and emotional release.

Step 1: Preparing the Client for Emotional Release

Before starting the session, you must create a safe, supportive environment for the client. Emotional trauma release can bring up suppressed memories and feelings, so the client needs to feel emotionally and physically secure.

1. Set the Intention

- Explain to the client that the goal of the session is to release emotional patterns stored in the joints.
- Encourage the client to approach the session with an open mind and heart.
- Ask the client to silently or verbally state:
  - *"I am ready to release what no longer serves me."*
  - *"It is safe for me to let go of past emotional pain."*

2. Grounding Technique (Rooting the Client's Energy)

- Place your hands on the client's ankles or feet.
- Visualize a red light flowing from the Root Chakra down through the legs and into the earth.
- Imagine energetic "roots" extending from the feet into the ground.
- Hold this position for 2–3 minutes until the client feels grounded.

Grounding helps create emotional stability and provides a safe foundation for releasing deeper emotional trauma.

3. Body Scan and Energy Reading (Identifying Trauma Points)

- Begin the session by scanning the client's energy field with your hands.
- Slowly move your hands over the body without touching it.
- Pay attention to areas where you feel:
  - Heat or coolness (indicates energetic imbalance)
  - Heaviness or pressure (indicates blocked emotional energy)
  - Tingling or magnetic pull (indicates energetic stagnation)

Take note of these areas — they are likely the joints holding emotional trauma.

Step 2: Direct Techniques for Clearing Emotional Trauma from Joints

The following Reiki techniques are designed to target blocked energy in the joints, release emotional trauma, and restore balance.

1. Direct Hand Placement on the Joint (Opening the Energy Pathway)

- Place your hands directly on the joint where trauma is held (e.g., knees, hips, shoulders).
- Use the Cho Ku Rei (Power Symbol) to open the energetic flow in the joint.
  - Draw the Cho Ku Rei symbol over the joint.

Conscious breathwork and focused mantras help direct and amplify the flow of energy, promoti balance and emotional release.

- o Silently repeat the name of the symbol three times.
- Direct Reiki energy into the joint.
- Hold for 3–5 minutes or until you feel the energy shift.

This technique opens the energetic pathway and increases the flow of ki into the joint.

2. Sei He Ki Symbol for Emotional Release (Releasing Emotional Imprints)

- Place one hand on the joint and the other on the related chakra (e.g., knee and Root Chakra).
- Draw the Sei He Ki (Emotional Healing Symbol) over the joint.
    - o Silently repeat the name of the symbol three times.
- Visualize a wave of golden light flowing into the joint.
- Imagine the light dissolving any emotional knots or trauma stored in the joint.
- Encourage the client to take deep, slow breaths.
- Hold until you feel the energy shift or lighten.

Sei He Ki works to dissolve emotional trauma at the subconscious and cellular levels.

3. Cross-Body Healing Technique (Balancing Opposing Energies)

- Place one hand on the affected joint and the other hand on the opposite side of the body (e.g., left shoulder and right hip).
- Direct Reiki energy between these two points.
- Visualize a line of light connecting both sides of the body.
- Imagine energy moving back and forth between the two points, creating balance and flow.
- Use the Cho Ku Rei symbol to strengthen the connection.
- Hold for 3–5 minutes or until you feel the energy balance.

This technique harmonizes the left and right sides of the body, restoring physical and emotional balance.

4. Emotional Release Through Breathwork (Activating the Parasympathetic Nervous System)

- Place both hands on the affected joint.
- Ask the client to take a deep breath and imagine pulling energy into the joint.
- As they exhale, guide them to imagine the trauma being released through the breath.
- Repeat for 3–5 breaths.
- If the client becomes emotionally overwhelmed, return to grounding.

Conscious breathwork and focused mantras help direct and amplify the flow of energy, promot balance and emotional release.

This technique helps the client engage the parasympathetic nervous system, signaling the body to release stored emotional tension.

5. Spiral Motion Technique (Restoring Flexibility and Flow)

- Place your hands over the joint.
- Move your hands in a gentle spiral or circular motion.
- Imagine the joint softening and opening.
- Direct Reiki energy into the joint.
- Use the Sei He Ki symbol to release emotional blockages.
- Hold until the energy feels soft and balanced.

This technique restores physical and emotional flexibility in the joint.

6. Muscle and Fascia Release Technique (Clearing Physical Tension)

- Place one hand on the joint and the other on the surrounding muscle or fascia.
- Direct Reiki energy into both the joint and muscle.
- Slowly move your hand along the muscle, releasing tension.
- Use the Cho Ku Rei symbol to strengthen the energy flow.
- Hold until the muscle tension releases.

This technique releases physical tension connected to emotional trauma.

7. Light and Vibration Technique (Dissolving Deep Emotional Trauma)

- Place your hands directly on the joint.
- Visualize the joint filling with white or golden light.
- Imagine the light vibrating through the joint, breaking up any stuck energy.
- Hold for 3–5 minutes or until you feel the energy release.
- Seal the healing with the Cho Ku Rei symbol.

This technique clears deep-seated emotional patterns and restores energetic flow.

Step 3: Emotional Integration and Closing the Session

After clearing emotional trauma from the joints, you must help the client stabilize and integrate the healing.

1. Ground the Client's Energy

- Place your hands on the client's feet.
- Visualize a red light flowing from the Root Chakra into the earth.
- Hold for 2–3 minutes until you feel the energy settle.

2. Affirmations for Emotional Release

Ask the client to repeat affirmations such as:

- *"I am free from emotional pain."*
- *"It is safe for me to move forward."*

Conscious breathwork and focused mantras help direct and amplify the flow of energy, promote balance and emotional release.

- *"I trust the unfolding of life."*
- *"I release the past and embrace the future with confidence."*

3. Seal the Energy Field

- Draw the Cho Ku Rei symbol over the client's entire energy field to seal the healing.
- Encourage the client to stay hydrated and rest after the session.

Key Takeaways:

- Reiki dissolves emotional trauma stored in the joints by restoring energetic flow.
- Techniques such as direct hand placement, spiral motion, and cross-body healing work to release emotional imprints.
- Symbols like Sei He Ki and Cho Ku Rei strengthen emotional healing and restore balance.
- Emotional release may lead to temporary emotional sensitivity — encourage the client to rest and reflect.

By using these Reiki techniques, you empower the client to release long-held emotional trauma, restore physical and emotional flexibility, and regain confidence in moving forward with life.

Affirmations and Guided Meditation for Emotional Release

Affirmations and guided meditation are powerful tools for releasing emotional trauma stored in the joints. While Reiki works to dissolve energetic blockages and restore the natural flow of ki (life force energy), affirmations and meditation help to reprogram the subconscious mind and strengthen emotional resilience.

Emotional trauma stored in the joints often reflects deeper patterns of fear, self-doubt, guilt, or emotional resistance. Affirmations work by replacing these limiting beliefs with empowering thoughts, while guided meditation helps the client reconnect with their body and mind in a safe and supportive way.

When combined with Reiki, affirmations and meditation work synergistically to release emotional tension, promote healing, and create a state of balance and openness.

How Affirmations Work

Affirmations are positive statements that help shift the client's emotional and energetic patterns by replacing negative thought patterns with empowering beliefs.

1. Reprogramming the Subconscious Mind

- Emotional trauma creates subconscious patterns of fear, guilt, and self-doubt.

Conscious breathwork and focused mantras help direct and amplify the flow of energy, promoti balance and emotional release.

- Affirmations help replace these negative patterns with positive thoughts.
- Regular use of affirmations strengthens the new belief system and supports emotional release.

2. Aligning Thoughts with Energy Flow

- When affirmations are combined with Reiki, the positive thought patterns align with the body's energy flow.
- This creates a state of emotional and physical harmony.
- The new thought patterns reinforce the energetic release created by Reiki.

3. Overcoming Resistance to Emotional Healing

- Emotional trauma often creates resistance to letting go.
- Affirmations provide emotional reassurance and security.
- They help the client feel safe and supported while releasing emotional tension.

Affirmations for Joint Healing

The following affirmations target emotional trauma and energetic blockages stored in the joints. They are designed to address patterns of fear, resistance, guilt, and emotional vulnerability.

General Affirmations for Joint Health and Emotional Balance

- *"I release all resistance to healing."*
- *"It is safe for me to move forward."*
- *"My body is strong, flexible, and balanced."*
- *"I release all emotional pain stored in my joints."*
- *"My body and mind are in perfect harmony."*
- *"I trust the process of life."*
- *"It is safe for me to let go."*
- *"I am supported and grounded in every step I take."*

Knees (Humility, Trust, and Adaptability)

- *"I trust the path that is unfolding before me."*
- *"It is safe for me to move forward."*
- *"I release fear and embrace confidence."*
- *"I am grounded and stable."*

Hips (Emotional and Creative Flow)

- *"I release all emotional blocks stored in my hips."*
- *"It is safe for me to express my creativity."*
- *"I flow with the rhythm of life."*
- *"I am emotionally open and free."*

Shoulders (Emotional Burdens and Self-Expression)

- *"I release all burdens I have been carrying."*
- *"I allow others to support me."*
- *"I express my truth with confidence and ease."*
- *"My shoulders are relaxed and free of tension."*

Conscious breathwork and focused mantras help direct and amplify the flow of energy, promote balance and emotional release.

Elbows (Flexibility in Giving and Receiving)

- *"I release the need to control outcomes."*
- *"It is safe for me to give and receive support."*
- *"I welcome new opportunities with flexibility and ease."*
- *"I trust life's flow."*

Wrists (Trust and Communication)

- *"I release all fear of expressing my truth."*
- *"It is safe for me to communicate openly."*
- *"I trust my creative abilities."*
- *"I receive support and guidance with ease."*

Ankles (Balance, Grounding, and Stability)

- *"I am grounded and balanced in all areas of my life."*
- *"I trust life's unfolding path."*
- *"It is safe for me to step forward with confidence."*
- *"I feel supported and secure in every step I take."*

Fingers and Toes (Precision and Action)

- *"I release all hesitation and trust my actions."*
- *"It is safe for me to take the next step."*
- *"I express myself clearly and confidently."*
- *"I act with precision and confidence."*

How to Use Affirmations in a Reiki Session

Affirmations work best when paired with Reiki energy to strengthen their emotional and energetic impact.

1. Direct Hand Placement with Affirmations

- Place your hands on the affected joint.
- Ask the client to silently or verbally repeat the affirmation.
- Channel Reiki energy into the joint while holding the intention of the affirmation.
- Repeat until you feel the energy shift or lighten.

2. Breath-Activated Affirmations

- Ask the client to take a deep breath while repeating the affirmation.
- As they exhale, guide them to imagine the energy of the affirmation moving through the joint.
- Encourage them to release any tension or emotional resistance as they breathe out.

3. Affirmation During Visualization

- While performing a Reiki technique (such as spiral motion or direct placement), guide the client through a visualization.
- Ask the client to repeat the affirmation as they visualize the joint filling with healing light.
- Encourage them to see the joint softening and opening as they repeat the affirmation.

Conscious breathwork and focused mantras help direct and amplify the flow of energy, promote balance and emotional release.

Guided Meditation for Emotional Release

A guided meditation helps deepen the emotional release by allowing the client to engage their subconscious mind while aligning with the body's energetic flow. This creates a powerful state of relaxation and emotional receptivity.

Guided Meditation Script (For Emotional Release in the Joints)

(1) Centering and Relaxation:

- Begin by having the client lie down in a comfortable position.
- Ask them to close their eyes and take three slow, deep breaths.
- Guide them to release any tension in their body with each exhale.

(2) Grounding:

- "Feel the weight of your body sinking into the surface beneath you."
- "Imagine a warm, red light flowing from the base of your spine down through your legs and into the earth."
- "Feel yourself becoming connected to the earth — stable, grounded, and supported."

(3) Focusing on the Joints:

- "Bring your attention to your joints — your shoulders, elbows, hips, knees, ankles, wrists, fingers, and toes."
- "Feel a warm golden light flowing into each joint."
- "Imagine the light softening any tension or discomfort."

(4) Emotional Release:

- "As the light flows into your joints, imagine it dissolving any emotional knots or tension."
- "Release any fear, guilt, shame, or doubt."
- "Let it all melt away with each breath."
- "It is safe to let go."

(5) Releasing Resistance:

- "If you feel any tightness or resistance, breathe into it."
- "With each exhale, allow the resistance to dissolve."
- "Let go of the need to control — trust in the flow of life."

(6) Affirmation Integration:

- "Repeat to yourself: 'I am strong, I am balanced, I am whole.'"
- "Feel the truth of these words resonating through your body."

Conscious breathwork and focused mantras help direct and amplify the flow of energy, promoti balance and emotional release.

(7) Closing and Grounding:

- "Feel the golden light retreating from the joints, leaving you feeling light and free."
- "Take three deep breaths."
- "When you are ready, open your eyes and return to the present moment."

How to Guide the Client After the Session

- Encourage the client to repeat affirmations daily to reinforce the energetic release.
- Suggest that the client drink water and rest after the session.
- Emotional release can continue over the next 24–48 hours — encourage the client to journal any emotions or insights that surface.

Key Takeaways:

- Affirmations and guided meditation strengthen emotional release by reprogramming subconscious patterns.
- Affirmations help shift negative thought patterns to positive beliefs.
- Guided meditation allows deeper emotional integration and alignment.
- Reiki enhances the power of affirmations and meditation by opening the energy flow.

By combining Reiki, affirmations, and meditation, you create a powerful method for clearing emotional trauma and restoring emotional and physical balance.

PART 3:
ADVANCED JOINT
HEALING WITH REIKI

Chapter 8: Combining Reiki with Other Modalities

Combining Reiki with Other Modalities

Using Reiki Alongside Reflexology, Acupressure, and Massage

Reiki is a versatile healing modality that can be combined effectively with other bodywork techniques such as reflexology, acupressure, and massage. While Reiki works on the energetic level by restoring the flow of ki (life force energy), reflexology, acupressure, and massage work more directly on the physical body by targeting muscles, pressure points, and connective tissues.

When these modalities are combined, they create a synergistic effect — where the benefits of each approach are amplified. Reiki helps to dissolve energetic blockages and enhance the body's natural healing ability, while reflexology, acupressure, and massage help to release physical tension, improve circulation, and restore muscular balance. The result is a more profound and integrated healing experience for the client — physically, emotionally, and spiritually.

Why Reiki Works Well with Other Modalities

Reiki works on the energetic level — addressing the flow of life force energy through the chakras, meridians, and aura. Reflexology, acupressure, and massage work on the structural and muscular levels — improving circulation, reducing tension, and increasing mobility.

When combined, Reiki and bodywork complement each other in several key ways:

1. Enhances Energy Flow and Relaxation

- Reiki relaxes the nervous system and activates the parasympathetic (rest-and-digest) response.
- This allows the body to respond more deeply to physical manipulation and muscle release.
- The client becomes more receptive to both energetic and physical healing.

2. Addresses the Root Cause of Tension

- Massage, reflexology, and acupressure release physical tension, but Reiki addresses the energetic and emotional root of that tension.
- Emotional trauma stored in muscles and joints often resurfaces during bodywork.
- Reiki helps process and release these emotional patterns, leading to long-term healing.

Just for today, I will let go of worry and trust the flow of life.

3. Strengthens the Mind-Body Connection

- Reiki helps the client become more aware of their body and emotional state.
- When combined with bodywork, this enhances the client's ability to recognize where they hold tension and emotional resistance.
- The client develops greater sensitivity to their body's needs and responses.

4. Supports Deeper Muscle and Tissue Release

- Reiki softens and relaxes the muscles on an energetic level.
- This allows the physical manipulation of reflexology, acupressure, or massage to work more effectively.
- Muscles release tension more easily when the body is energetically open and relaxed.

5. Creates a Holistic Healing Experience

- Reiki works on the emotional and spiritual layers of healing.
- Reflexology, acupressure, and massage work on the physical layer of healing.
- Combining both approaches creates a more integrated and complete healing experience.

1. Combining Reiki with Reflexology

Reflexology is based on the principle that specific points on the feet, hands, and ears correspond to different organs and systems in the body. By stimulating these points, reflexology encourages the body's natural healing process.

When Reiki is added to reflexology, the energy flow to these reflex points becomes more balanced and aligned. Reiki enhances the overall effect by clearing energetic blockages in the corresponding organs and systems.

How to Combine Reiki with Reflexology

1. Begin with Reiki Grounding:

- Place your hands on the client's feet or ankles.
- Channel Reiki energy into the Earth Star Chakra to strengthen grounding and balance.

2. Activate Reflex Points with Reiki Support:

- As you apply pressure to reflex points on the feet or hands, channel Reiki through your hands.
- Use the Cho Ku Rei (Power Symbol) to increase energy flow into the reflex points.
- If you feel resistance or energetic stagnation, apply the Sei He Ki symbol to dissolve the blockage.

Just for today, I will let go of worry and trust the flow of life.

3. Release and Balance:

- After stimulating the reflex point, hold your hands over the area and allow Reiki to flow.
- This helps integrate the physical release with energetic balance.

Example:

- If a client's digestive system is sluggish, stimulate the digestive reflex point on the sole of the foot while using Reiki to send healing energy to the Solar Plexus Chakra.
- This creates a connection between the physical reflex point and the energetic center governing digestion and personal power.

Benefits:

- Enhances the effect of reflexology by increasing energy flow.
- Strengthens the mind-body connection.
- Balances the corresponding organ system energetically and physically.

2. Combining Reiki with Acupressure

Acupressure is based on the concept of balancing the body's meridians (energy channels) by applying pressure to specific points along these channels. The goal is to release blocked energy and restore balance in the body's flow of qi (chi).

When Reiki is combined with acupressure, the energetic flow through the meridians becomes more responsive. Reiki helps to soften the energetic resistance, allowing acupressure to be more effective.

How to Combine Reiki with Acupressure

1. Begin with Reiki Scanning:

- Use Reiki to scan the body and identify blocked or tense areas.
- Pay attention to areas that feel "dense" or "stuck."

2. Activate Acupressure Points with Reiki:

- As you apply pressure to the acupressure point, channel Reiki into the area.
- Use the Cho Ku Rei symbol to strengthen the energy flow through the meridian.
- If you sense emotional resistance, use Sei He Ki to dissolve emotional blockages.

Just for today, I will let go of worry and trust the flow of life.

3. Hold and Release:

- Once you feel the energy beginning to shift, hold the acupressure point for an additional 10–20 seconds.
- Allow Reiki to complete the energy release and restore balance.

Example:

- If a client has tight shoulders, apply acupressure to the Gallbladder 21 (GB21) point while sending Reiki to the Heart Chakra and Throat Chakra.
- This helps release physical tension while restoring emotional openness and communication.

Benefits:

- Increases the effectiveness of acupressure by dissolving energetic resistance.
- Promotes faster release of muscle and joint tension.
- Balances both the physical and energetic body.

3. Combining Reiki with Massage

Massage works on the muscles, fascia, and connective tissue to release physical tension, improve circulation, and promote relaxation. While massage primarily addresses physical imbalances, Reiki helps release the emotional and energetic patterns held in the muscles and joints.

How to Combine Reiki with Massage

1. Begin with Reiki Relaxation:

    - Start the session by placing your hands on the client's back or shoulders.
    - Channel Reiki to relax the nervous system and increase receptivity to touch.

2. Infuse Reiki Into Massage Strokes:

    - As you apply massage strokes, allow Reiki energy to flow through your hands.
    - Imagine the muscles softening and the energy blockages dissolving with each stroke.

3. Use Symbols to Target Specific Areas:

    - Use Cho Ku Rei to increase energy flow into tight or painful muscles.
    - Use Sei He Ki to dissolve emotional tension stored in the muscle tissue.

4. Seal the Healing with Reiki:

Just for today, I will let go of worry and trust the flow of life.

- After finishing the massage, place your hands on the feet or head.
- Allow Reiki energy to flow and balance the client's energy field.

Example:

- If a client has tightness in the hips due to emotional holding, apply deep tissue massage to the hip flexors while using Reiki to release emotional resistance in the Sacral Chakra.

Benefits:

- Enhances muscle relaxation and recovery.
- Encourages emotional release during bodywork.
- Aligns the energetic and physical body.

Key Takeaways:

- Reiki amplifies the benefits of reflexology, acupressure, and massage by increasing energetic flow and emotional release.
- Reiki helps address the emotional and spiritual root of physical tension.
- Combining Reiki with other bodywork techniques creates a more complete healing experience.
- The use of Reiki symbols (Cho Ku Rei, Sei He Ki) strengthens the effect of physical manipulation.

How Sound Healing and Tuning Forks Can Enhance Joint Release

Sound healing and tuning forks work on the principle that everything in the universe, including the human body, vibrates at a specific frequency. When the body's natural vibratory state becomes disrupted due to stress, trauma, or energetic blockages, it can lead to physical discomfort, emotional imbalance, and reduced energetic flow. Joints, being key energetic crossroads where multiple meridians and chakras intersect, are especially vulnerable to these vibrational imbalances.

Reiki works to restore the natural flow of ki (life force energy) through the body's energetic system. When combined with sound healing and tuning forks, the effect is amplified. The sound frequencies emitted by tuning forks resonate with the body's cells and energy field, helping to release energetic blockages, restore vibrational harmony, and enhance the body's natural healing process.

Tuning forks and sound healing work particularly well with joints because joints are dense, structural areas where energy can easily become trapped. The vibrational resonance of sound waves helps to penetrate this dense tissue, breaking up stagnant energy and restoring flexibility and flow.

Just for today, I will let go of worry and trust the flow of life.

The Science Behind Sound Healing and Vibrational Therapy

Sound healing is based on the principle of resonance and entrainment — the idea that the body and mind naturally adjust their vibratory state to match external sound frequencies.

1. Resonance

- Every organ, tissue, and joint in the body has a specific vibratory frequency.
- When the body is exposed to a sound frequency that matches its natural resonance, it begins to "sync" with that vibration.
- If a joint is out of balance or holding emotional trauma, sound helps it return to its natural vibrational state.

2. Entrainment

- The body naturally aligns with external rhythmic patterns.
- When a tuning fork is struck and held near a joint, the body's natural energetic field starts to "follow" the vibration of the tuning fork.
- This helps dissolve energetic knots, increase circulation, and release stored emotional energy.

3. Cymatics and Cellular Response

- Studies on cymatics (how sound shapes physical matter) have shown that sound waves create geometric patterns in water and cells.
- The body is made up of approximately 70% water, which makes it highly responsive to sound.
- The sound frequencies from tuning forks create harmonious patterns in the body's cellular and energetic structure, helping to "reset" the vibrational field.

4. Nervous System Activation

- Sound stimulates the vagus nerve and activates the parasympathetic nervous system (the relaxation response).
- This allows the body to release tension and heal on a deeper level.
- The calming effect of sound allows Reiki to flow more smoothly through the body's energy channels.

Why Sound Healing and Tuning Forks Are Effective for Joints

Joints are natural energy reservoirs where tension and emotional trauma are often stored. Because sound penetrates deeply into bone and connective tissue, it helps release stagnant energy and improve the flow of ki through the body's meridians and chakras.

1. Bone Conduction

- Bones are excellent conductors of sound.
- When a tuning fork is placed on or near a joint, the vibration travels through the bone and surrounding tissue.
- This creates a deep release of stored tension and blocked energy.

2. Fascia and Connective Tissue Release

- Fascia (the connective tissue surrounding muscles and joints) holds emotional trauma and physical tension.
- Sound vibrations penetrate the fascia, helping to soften and release these energetic knots.
- This allows the joint to regain flexibility and mobility.

3. Balancing the Meridian and Chakra Systems

- Each joint is connected to specific meridians and chakras.
- Tuning forks emit frequencies that resonate with these energetic pathways.
- When sound waves stimulate the meridians, it restores the natural energetic flow.

4. Emotional Release Through Sound

- Emotional trauma stored in the joints often remains hidden until it is activated through bodywork or energetic release.
- Sound vibrations reach the emotional layers of trauma, helping to dissolve fear, guilt, shame, and grief.
- This allows the client to release emotional blockages on a subconscious level.

Best Tuning Forks and Frequencies for Joint Healing

Different tuning forks and sound frequencies resonate with different joints, chakras, and emotional states. When selecting tuning forks for joint healing, consider the following key frequencies:

1. 128 Hz (Root Chakra and Bone Resonance)

- The 128 Hz tuning fork resonates with the body's natural bone frequency.
- It penetrates deeply into the joints, muscles, and bones.
- Best for knees, hips, ankles, and spinal alignment.

2. 136.1 Hz (OM Frequency)

- The OM frequency resonates with the Earth's natural vibratory rate.
- It promotes grounding, balance, and emotional release.
- Best for balancing the Root and Sacral Chakras.

Just for today, I will let go of worry and trust the flow of life.

- Effective for relieving hip, knee, and ankle tension.

3. 256 Hz and 512 Hz (Cellular Regeneration)

- These frequencies stimulate cellular healing and tissue repair.
- Best for reducing inflammation and joint swelling.
- Effective for arthritis and chronic joint pain.

4. 432 Hz (Heart Chakra Frequency)

- 432 Hz resonates with the natural frequency of the universe.
- Promotes emotional release and spiritual balance.
- Best for shoulder, elbow, and wrist release.

5. 528 Hz (DNA Repair Frequency)

- Known as the "miracle tone."
- Stimulates deep healing at the cellular and energetic level.
- Best for clearing deep emotional trauma stored in the joints.

Techniques for Using Tuning Forks in Reiki Sessions

Combining tuning forks with Reiki creates a powerful healing experience by balancing both the energetic and physical layers of the body.

1. Direct Application on the Joint (For Deep Release)

- Strike the tuning fork and place the stem directly on the joint.
- Channel Reiki energy into the joint while the tuning fork is vibrating.
- Hold until the vibration fades.
- Repeat 2–3 times.

This technique restores balance and increases mobility.

2. Hovering Technique (For Energetic Flow)

- Strike the tuning fork and hold it 1–2 inches above the joint.
- Move the tuning fork in a circular motion around the joint.
- Channel Reiki energy through your hands as you move the tuning fork.
- This technique clears energetic stagnation and restores flow.

This technique helps with inflammation and stiffness.

3. Cross-Body Balancing (For Emotional and Energetic Alignment)

- Place one tuning fork on the left hip and one on the right knee (or vice versa).
- Strike both tuning forks simultaneously.
- Hold for 20–30 seconds.
- Channel Reiki energy between the two points.

Just for today, I will let go of worry and trust the flow of life.

This technique balances left and right sides of the body.

4. Chakra Resonance Technique (For Emotional Trauma Release)

- Strike the tuning fork and place it on the corresponding chakra associated with the joint.
- Channel Reiki energy into the chakra while the tuning fork vibrates.
- Visualize the chakra opening and balancing.

This technique helps release emotional trauma stored in the joints.

5. Vocal Toning Technique (Enhancing Vibrational Alignment)

- While holding a tuning fork over the joint, use vocal toning (e.g., chanting "OM" or humming).
- The vibration of the voice enhances the effect of the tuning fork.
- This creates a deep release of emotional and physical tension.

This technique combines sound healing with Reiki and breathwork for a multidimensional effect.

Key Takeaways:

- Sound healing and tuning forks enhance Reiki's effect by restoring vibrational balance.
- Joints respond well to sound because of their dense structure and connection to meridians.
- Frequencies like 128 Hz, 432 Hz, and 528 Hz are especially effective for joint healing.
- Techniques such as direct application, hovering, and cross-body balancing promote emotional and physical release.
- The combination of sound and Reiki creates a profound mind-body-spirit connection.

By combining Reiki with sound healing and tuning forks, you create a powerful healing experience that addresses physical, emotional, and energetic imbalances at a deep level.

Just for today, I will let go of worry and trust the flow of life.

Crystal Healing and Essential Oils for Joint-Related Issues

Crystal healing and essential oils complement Reiki by working on both the energetic and physical levels of healing. While Reiki restores the flow of ki (life force energy) through the body's meridians and chakras, crystals and essential oils enhance the process by aligning vibrational energy and stimulating the body's natural healing response.

Joints are particularly receptive to crystal healing and essential oils because they are dense structural areas where energy tends to accumulate and stagnate. The vibrational frequency of crystals and the aromatic compounds in essential oils work to dissolve this stagnation, release emotional trauma, and restore both physical and energetic mobility.

By combining Reiki with crystal healing and essential oils, you create a multilayered healing experience that addresses physical discomfort, emotional patterns, and energetic blockages simultaneously.

Why Crystal Healing and Essential Oils Are Effective for Joints

Crystals and essential oils operate on different but complementary levels of healing:

1. Vibrational Resonance (Crystals)

- Crystals emit specific vibrational frequencies that align with the body's chakras and meridians.
- When a crystal's vibration matches the natural frequency of a joint, it helps dissolve energetic resistance and restore balance.
- Crystals act as amplifiers of Reiki energy, strengthening the flow of ki through the joint.

2. Aromatic and Chemical Stimulation (Essential Oils)

- Essential oils work through both the olfactory system (smell) and skin absorption.
- The aromatic molecules of essential oils trigger the limbic system (the brain's emotional center), which helps release emotional tension stored in the joints.
- Oils with anti-inflammatory and pain-relieving properties help reduce joint stiffness and swelling.

3. Emotional and Physical Release (Synergy Between Reiki, Crystals, and Oils)

- Crystals and oils address the emotional layer of healing by working on the subtle body.

Just for today, I will let go of worry and trust the flow of life.

- Reiki channels life force energy to dissolve the deeper spiritual and emotional causes of joint discomfort.
- The combined effect promotes physical relaxation and emotional clarity.

Crystals for Joint Healing

Crystals work by absorbing, storing, and transmitting energy. Different crystals correspond to different chakras, emotional patterns, and physical issues. For joint healing, choose crystals that align with the Root Chakra (for grounding), the Sacral Chakra (for emotional flow), and the Heart Chakra (for emotional release).

1. Hematite (Grounding and Strength)

- Associated with the Root Chakra.
- Helps strengthen the connection to the earth and increase physical stability.
- Effective for knee, ankle, and hip issues related to fear or insecurity.

How to Use:

- Place hematite on or near the joint during a Reiki session.
- Direct Reiki energy into the crystal and visualize strength and stability flowing into the joint.

2. Black Tourmaline (Protection and Grounding)

- Associated with the Root Chakra.

- Absorbs negative energy and creates a protective energetic shield.
- Effective for joint issues related to emotional overwhelm or energetic overload.

How to Use:

- Hold black tourmaline over the joint while channeling Reiki.
- Use the Cho Ku Rei symbol to strengthen protection and dissolve negative energy.

3. Carnelian (Creativity and Emotional Flexibility)

- Associated with the Sacral Chakra.
- Stimulates emotional flow and physical movement.
- Effective for hip and sacral joint issues related to emotional stagnation.

How to Use:

- Place carnelian on the hip or sacrum during Reiki.
- Use the Sei He Ki symbol to increase emotional release and restore flexibility.

4. Green Aventurine (Healing and Emotional Release)

- Associated with the Heart Chakra.
- Promotes emotional healing and releases stored emotional tension.
- Effective for shoulders, elbows, and wrists related to emotional burdens.

Just for today, I will let go of worry and trust the flow of life.

How to Use:

- Place green aventurine over the joint or hold it in your palm.
- Direct Reiki into the crystal, visualizing the joint softening and emotional release.

5. Amethyst (Calming and Spiritual Alignment)

- Associated with the Crown Chakra.
- Promotes relaxation and higher spiritual connection.
- Effective for tension and pain in the shoulders, wrists, and fingers related to stress or spiritual imbalance.

How to Use:

- Place amethyst on the joint or under the massage table.
- Use the Sei He Ki symbol to promote emotional calm and spiritual clarity.

6. Clear Quartz (Amplification and Clarity)

- Associated with all chakras.
- Amplifies the effect of Reiki and other crystals.
- Helps align the body's energy field and clear stagnant energy in the joints.

How to Use:

- Place clear quartz near the joint or on top of other crystals.
- Direct Reiki energy into the quartz to increase energetic flow and clarity.

7. Red Jasper (Strength and Grounding)

- Associated with the Root Chakra.
- Strengthens the connection to the earth and increases physical endurance.
- Effective for knees, ankles, and hips when the client feels unstable or insecure.

How to Use:

- Place red jasper on the knee or hip during Reiki.
- Use Cho Ku Rei to increase grounding and strength.

Just for today, I will let go of worry and trust the flow of life.

Essential Oils for Joint Healing

Essential oils work on both the physical and emotional levels by reducing inflammation, improving circulation, and promoting emotional relaxation. For joint healing, choose oils that have both anti-inflammatory and emotional balancing properties.

1. Frankincense (Anti-Inflammatory and Grounding)

- Reduces joint inflammation and swelling.
- Promotes spiritual clarity and emotional grounding.
- Best for knees, hips, and ankles.

How to Use:

- Dilute in a carrier oil and apply to the joint before a Reiki session.
- Channel Reiki energy into the joint as the oil absorbs.

2. Lavender (Calming and Relaxation)

- Relaxes the muscles and soothes the nervous system.
- Reduces joint tension caused by emotional stress.
- Best for shoulder, wrist, and elbow issues.

How to Use:

- Mix with a carrier oil and massage into the joint.
- Combine with Reiki and guided breathing.

3. Ginger (Warming and Pain Relief)

- Increases circulation and reduces joint stiffness.
- Stimulates emotional flow and relieves stagnation.
- Best for hip and knee issues.

How to Use:

- Add to massage oil and apply to the joint.
- Use during a Reiki session with Cho Ku Rei for strength and flow.

4. Eucalyptus (Cooling and Inflammation Relief)

- Reduces swelling and pain.
- Clears mental and emotional fog.
- Best for swollen joints, arthritis, and inflammatory issues.

How to Use:

- Mix with a carrier oil and apply to the joint.
- Direct Reiki into the joint to reduce inflammation.

5. Peppermint (Cooling and Pain Relief)

- Relieves tension and improves circulation.
- Opens emotional flow and increases mental clarity.
- Best for wrist, elbow, and ankle tension.

How to Use:

- Apply directly to the joint (diluted).

Just for today, I will let go of worry and trust the flow of life.

- Combine with Reiki hand placement for enhanced relaxation.

How to Combine Reiki, Crystals, and Essential Oils in a Session

1. Prepare the Joint with Essential Oils

- Massage the affected joint with a blend of essential oils and carrier oil.
- Apply gentle pressure to stimulate circulation.

2. Place Crystals on or Near the Joint

- Select a crystal based on the joint and emotional pattern.
- Channel Reiki energy into the crystal and joint.

3. Direct Reiki into the Joint

- Place your hands on the joint.
- Use Cho Ku Rei for physical balance and strength.
- Use Sei He Ki for emotional release.

4. Hold Until the Energy Shifts

- Hold your hands on the joint until the energy feels lighter or you sense the release.
- Finish with a sealing Cho Ku Rei to stabilize the healing.

Key Takeaways:

- Crystals amplify Reiki's energetic flow and restore vibrational balance.
- Essential oils reduce inflammation and emotional resistance.
- Reiki, crystals, and oils work together to clear trauma and restore mobility.
- Techniques like direct placement, spiral motion, and breathwork enhance healing.

By combining Reiki, crystal healing, and essential oils, you create a multidimensional healing experience that addresses physical, emotional, and energetic imbalances simultaneously.

Just for today, I will let go of worry and trust the flow of life.

Chapter 9: Energy Balancing for Chronic Joint Issues

Arthritis, Inflammation, and Joint Pain from an Energetic Perspective

Arthritis, inflammation, and joint pain are not solely physical conditions — they also have deep emotional and energetic roots. In Reiki and energy medicine, physical discomfort and disease are seen as manifestations of underlying energetic imbalances and emotional blockages. When energy becomes stagnant or misaligned in the joints, it creates friction and tension, which eventually leads to inflammation and discomfort.

Reiki practitioners understand that joints are energetic crossroads where multiple meridians and chakras intersect. When energy is flowing freely through the joints, physical movement is easy and pain-free. However, when energetic flow becomes blocked due to emotional trauma, stress, or spiritual misalignment, the joint becomes a focal point for pain and inflammation.

Arthritis and joint pain often reflect emotional resistance, difficulty adapting to change, and suppressed emotional patterns. Reiki addresses the underlying energetic imbalances by restoring the natural flow of ki (life force energy) through the joints, chakras, and meridians — helping to dissolve inflammation and reduce discomfort at its source.

The Energetic Root of Arthritis and Joint Pain

Arthritis and joint pain often reflect a deeper emotional and energetic conflict. When energy becomes blocked or stagnant in the joints, it reflects resistance to movement on a physical, emotional, or spiritual level.

1. Resistance to Change (Emotional Rigidity)

- Joints reflect the body's ability to adapt and move through life.
- When a person resists change or clings to the past, the energy around the joints becomes stagnant.
- This creates physical stiffness and resistance in the joint, leading to inflammation and discomfort.

Example:

- A person experiencing knee stiffness may subconsciously fear moving forward in life or making important decisions.
- Reiki helps dissolve this fear and restores flow to the joint.

Just for today, I will let go of worry and trust the flow of life.

2. Holding on to Old Emotional Patterns

- The body "remembers" emotional trauma and stores it in the joints.
- Unresolved grief, anger, or shame can create tension and friction in the joint.
- Over time, this tension manifests as chronic pain or inflammation.

Example:

- Shoulder pain may reflect the emotional burden of carrying too much responsibility.
- Reiki helps release the emotional weight and restores flexibility.

3. Loss of Flexibility and Flow

- Joints reflect the balance between strength and flexibility.
- When a person becomes emotionally rigid or resistant to life's flow, the joint reflects this imbalance.
- The result is reduced range of motion, stiffness, and chronic discomfort.

Example:

- Tight hips may reflect emotional stagnation and difficulty expressing creativity or intimacy.
- Reiki helps reopen the emotional flow and restore physical flexibility.

4. Self-Protective Response to Trauma

- After experiencing emotional or physical trauma, the body often "locks down" the affected joint.
- This creates a protective barrier that prevents further emotional pain but also restricts energy flow.
- Over time, this locked state leads to inflammation and discomfort.

Example:

- A person who experienced betrayal may develop hip or knee pain as the body's way of creating emotional and physical resistance to vulnerability.
- Reiki helps dissolve the protective response and restore trust in movement.

5. Emotional and Energetic Imbalances in the Chakras

Each joint corresponds to specific chakras. When these chakras are out of balance, the corresponding joint becomes vulnerable to inflammation and discomfort.

Joint	Associated Chakra	Emotional Pattern
Knees	Root Chakra	Fear of moving forward, insecurity, instability

Just for today, I will let go of worry and trust the flow of life.

Joint	Associated Chakra	Emotional Pattern
Hips	Sacral Chakra	Emotional stagnation, creative block, fear of intimacy
Shoulders	Heart and Throat Chakras	Emotional burden, difficulty expressing feelings
Elbows	Heart and Solar Plexus Chakras	Flexibility in giving and receiving
Wrists	Throat Chakra	Trust and communication issues
Ankles	Root and Sacral Chakras	Fear of change, instability
Fingers	Heart and Throat Chakras	Precision and control
Toes	Root Chakra	Balance and groundedness

Arthritis from an Energetic Perspective

Arthritis is the result of chronic inflammation and joint degeneration. From an energetic standpoint, arthritis reflects deep-seated emotional patterns that have accumulated over time. It indicates a state of long-term resistance to emotional and spiritual growth.

Key Energetic Causes of Arthritis:

1. Resentment – Holding on to anger toward oneself or others.
2. Rigidity – Emotional inflexibility and resistance to change.
3. Self-Judgment – Harsh self-criticism and feelings of inadequacy.
4. Fear of Movement – Fear of stepping into the unknown or embracing change.
5. Feeling Unsupported – Lack of emotional or spiritual support from others or oneself.

Example:

- Arthritis in the knees reflects difficulty trusting life's path and fear of moving forward.
- Reiki helps dissolve the fear and realign the Root Chakra to create emotional and physical stability.

Inflammation from an Energetic Perspective

Inflammation reflects an active state of internal conflict. It occurs when the body's immune system becomes overactive, attacking healthy tissue in response to perceived stress or imbalance.

Key Energetic Causes of Inflammation:

1. Suppressed Anger – Unresolved resentment and frustration create inner conflict.
2. Overwhelm – Feeling emotionally or physically overloaded.

Just for today, I will let go of worry and trust the flow of life.

3. Emotional Misalignment – Living out of alignment with one's authentic self.
4. Lack of Emotional Expression – Suppressing emotional release creates inner heat and pressure.

Example:

- Inflammation in the shoulders may reflect feeling overburdened by responsibilities.
- Reiki helps release emotional pressure and restore energetic balance.

Joint Pain from an Energetic Perspective

Joint pain reflects a disruption in the natural flow of ki through the body's meridians and chakras. Pain is the body's signal that energy is not moving freely and that emotional healing is needed.

Key Energetic Causes of Joint Pain:

1. Emotional Resistance – Fear of emotional vulnerability creates tension and restriction.
2. Energetic Blockage – Stagnant energy creates friction and discomfort in the joint.
3. Fear of Loss – Holding onto emotional pain creates physical contraction.
4. Disconnection from Purpose – Lack of alignment between thoughts and actions creates imbalance.

Example:

- Pain in the elbows may reflect resistance to giving and receiving love or support.
- Reiki helps open the energy flow and restore emotional balance.

Reiki Techniques for Arthritis, Inflammation, and Joint Pain

1. Direct Hand Placement on the Joint (To Restore Energy Flow)

- Place your hands directly on the affected joint.
- Use the Cho Ku Rei symbol to increase the flow of ki.
- Hold until you feel the energy shift.

2. Sei He Ki Symbol for Emotional Release (To Dissolve Emotional Resistance)

- Place one hand on the joint and the other on the corresponding chakra.
- Draw the Sei He Ki symbol over the joint.
- Visualize emotional tension dissolving with each breath.

3. Cross-Body Healing (To Balance Opposing Energies)

- Place one hand on the left side of the body and the other on the right.
- Channel Reiki energy between the two sides.

Just for today, I will let go of worry and trust the flow of life.

- This creates energetic harmony and reduces inflammation.

4. Grounding and Root Chakra Activation (To Restore Stability)

- Place your hands on the knees or ankles.
- Direct Reiki into the Root Chakra.
- Use Cho Ku Rei to increase stability and grounding.

5. Affirmations for Emotional and Physical Flexibility

- *"It is safe for me to move forward."*
- *"I release all emotional resistance."*
- *"My joints are strong, flexible, and balanced."*

Key Takeaways:

- Arthritis, inflammation, and joint pain reflect underlying emotional and energetic imbalances.
- Reiki restores flow through the chakras and meridians, reducing inflammation and pain.
- Emotional resistance and fear of movement are often at the root of joint issues.
- Combining Reiki with sound healing, crystals, and affirmations strengthens the healing process.

By addressing the emotional and energetic root of joint pain, Reiki helps the client restore balance, flexibility, and emotional confidence.

Chakra Imbalances Related to Joint Problems

Chakras are the body's energetic centers that regulate the flow of ki (life force energy) through the body's physical, emotional, and spiritual layers. When the chakras are balanced and open, energy flows freely through the body's meridians and joints, creating a state of physical ease, emotional stability, and spiritual clarity.

However, when a chakra becomes blocked, overactive, or underactive, the corresponding energetic flow to the joints is disrupted. Since joints serve as energetic crossroads where multiple meridians and chakras intersect, imbalances in the chakras often manifest as stiffness, inflammation, restricted movement, or chronic joint pain.

Reiki works to restore balance by dissolving energetic blockages and increasing the flow of ki through the chakras and joints. Understanding which chakras are connected to specific joints allows Reiki practitioners to address not only the physical discomfort but also the emotional and spiritual patterns underlying the imbalance.

Overview of the Chakra System and Joint Connection

There are seven primary chakras aligned along the central axis of the body. Each chakra governs specific emotional, spiritual, and physical functions — including the health and mobility of particular joints. When the chakras are

Just for today, I will let go of worry and trust the flow of life.

balanced, the joints reflect this harmony through strength, flexibility, and pain-free movement.

Chakra	Location	Associated Joints	Energetic Role	Symptoms of Imbalance
Root Chakra (Muladhara)	Base of spine	Knees, hips, ankles	Grounding, stability, security	Knee pain, hip tightness, ankle instability
Sacral Chakra (Swadhisthana)	Lower abdomen	Hips, pelvis	Emotional flow, creativity, pleasure	Hip tension, lower back pain, emotional numbness
Solar Plexus Chakra (Manipura)	Upper abdomen	Elbows, wrists	Personal power, confidence, self-worth	Weak or inflamed elbows and wrists
Heart Chakra (Anahata)	Center of chest	Shoulders, arms	Love, emotional openness, vulnerability	Shoulder tightness, chest restriction

Chakra	Location	Associated Joints	Energetic Role	Symptoms of Imbalance
Throat Chakra (Vishuddha)	Throat	Neck, wrists, fingers	Communication, self-expression	Wrist pain, finger stiffness, throat constriction
Third Eye Chakra (Ajna)	Forehead, between eyes	Head, upper spine	Intuition, insight, perception	Headaches, neck pain, vision issues
Crown Chakra (Sahasrara)	Top of head	Spine, entire skeletal system	Spiritual connection, divine alignment	Chronic pain, lack of alignment, spiritual disconnection

Just for today, I will let go of worry and trust the flow of life.

1. Root Chakra (Muladhara) — Grounding and Stability

The Root Chakra governs the foundation of the body and mind. It represents physical and emotional stability, security, and connection to the Earth. Since the Root Chakra is located at the base of the spine, it influences the strength and mobility of the hips, knees, and ankles.

Signs of Root Chakra Imbalance in Joints:

- Knee pain or weakness reflects a fear of moving forward or feeling unsupported.
- Hip tightness reflects emotional holding patterns and difficulty with personal or creative expression.
- Ankle instability reflects emotional insecurity and fear of change.

Root Chakra Affirmation:

"I am grounded, stable, and supported."

Reiki Technique:

- Place your hands on the hips, knees, and feet.
- Use the Cho Ku Rei symbol to increase grounding and energetic flow.
- Visualize a red light filling the joint and stabilizing the energy flow.

2. Sacral Chakra (Swadhisthana) — Emotional Flow and Creativity

The Sacral Chakra governs the hips, pelvis, and lower back. It regulates emotional flow, creativity, intimacy, and pleasure. When this chakra is blocked, emotional energy becomes trapped in the hips and pelvis, creating stiffness and tension.

Signs of Sacral Chakra Imbalance in Joints:

- Hip tightness reflects difficulty expressing emotions or creative energy.
- Lower back pain reflects emotional stagnation and suppressed sexual or creative energy.
- Inability to engage in intimate relationships or creative expression.

Sacral Chakra Affirmation:

"*I embrace the flow of life with ease and confidence.*"

Reiki Technique:

- Place your hands on the lower abdomen and hips.
- Use the Sei He Ki symbol to dissolve emotional resistance.
- Visualize an orange light flowing into the joint, softening tension and restoring flexibility.

Just for today, I will let go of worry and trust the flow of life.

3. Solar Plexus Chakra (Manipura) — Personal Power and Confidence

The Solar Plexus Chakra governs the elbows and wrists, which reflect a person's ability to take action and express personal power. When this chakra is imbalanced, the person may feel emotionally weak, uncertain, or fearful of asserting themselves.

Signs of Solar Plexus Chakra Imbalance in Joints:

- Elbow pain reflects difficulty giving or receiving support.
- Wrist tension reflects fear of taking action or expressing oneself.
- Weakness in grip or muscle tone reflects low confidence or self-worth.

Solar Plexus Chakra Affirmation:

"I am strong and confident in my actions."

Reiki Technique:

- Place your hands on the elbows and wrists.
- Use the Cho Ku Rei symbol to strengthen and empower the energy flow.
- Visualize a yellow light filling the joint and increasing strength.

4. Heart Chakra (Anahata) — Love and Emotional Openness

The Heart Chakra governs the shoulders and arms, which reflect the ability to give and receive love. When this chakra is blocked, the person may experience emotional heaviness, guardedness, or difficulty trusting others.

Signs of Heart Chakra Imbalance in Joints:

- Shoulder tightness reflects feeling emotionally burdened.
- Arm stiffness reflects difficulty in reaching out or connecting with others.
- Pain in the upper back reflects emotional heartbreak or lack of self-love.

Heart Chakra Affirmation:

"*I give and receive love with ease.*"

Reiki Technique:

- Place your hands on the chest and shoulders.
- Use the Sei He Ki symbol to release emotional tension.
- Visualize a green light filling the joint and heart center.

Just for today, I will let go of worry and trust the flow of life.

5. Throat Chakra (Vishuddha) — Communication and Expression

The Throat Chakra governs the wrists and fingers, which reflect a person's ability to communicate and express themselves.

Signs of Throat Chakra Imbalance in Joints:

- Wrist pain reflects difficulty trusting one's voice.
- Finger stiffness reflects difficulty expressing details or precision in action.
- Chronic throat tightness reflects fear of speaking one's truth.

Throat Chakra Affirmation:

"I express my truth with clarity and confidence."

Reiki Technique:

- Place your hands on the throat and wrists.
- Use the Cho Ku Rei symbol to open the flow of communication.
- Visualize a blue light filling the joint and throat area.

6. Third Eye Chakra (Ajna) — Intuition and Insight

The Third Eye Chakra governs the head, upper spine, and neck. It reflects the ability to perceive clearly and trust one's intuition.

Signs of Third Eye Chakra Imbalance in Joints:

- Headaches and neck pain reflect mental stress and blocked intuition.
- Tension in the cervical spine reflects resistance to spiritual insight.

Third Eye Chakra Affirmation:

"*I trust my inner wisdom.*"

Reiki Technique:

- Place your hands on the forehead and neck.
- Use the Sei He Ki symbol to open intuition and mental clarity.

Just for today, I will let go of worry and trust the flow of life.

7. Crown Chakra (Sahasrara) — Spiritual Alignment

The Crown Chakra governs the entire skeletal structure. When this chakra is blocked, the person may feel disconnected from spiritual guidance.

Signs of Crown Chakra Imbalance in Joints:

- Chronic pain reflects disconnection from spiritual purpose.
- Muscle tension reflects resistance to divine flow.

Crown Chakra Affirmation:

"I am connected to divine wisdom."

Reiki Technique:

- Place your hands on the crown of the head.
- Use the Cho Ku Rei symbol to strengthen spiritual connection.

Key Takeaways:

- Chakra imbalances create joint tension and pain.
- Reiki restores balance by reopening blocked chakras.
- Targeting specific joints helps release emotional resistance and restore flow.
- Affirmations, breathwork, and visualization support long-term healing.

Creating Long-Term Energy Balance Through Consistent Reiki Practice

Reiki is not only a powerful tool for immediate healing — it also serves as a foundation for creating long-term energy balance in the body, mind, and spirit. While a single Reiki session can provide temporary relief from joint pain, stiffness, and emotional tension, true and lasting balance requires a consistent Reiki practice.

Just as physical fitness requires regular exercise to maintain strength and flexibility, the body's energy system requires consistent attention and care to maintain balance and flow. Joints, in particular, serve as energetic crossroads where meridians and chakras intersect. Therefore, keeping the energy flowing freely through the joints is essential for maintaining overall health, emotional balance, and physical mobility.

Reiki works to restore and maintain this balance by continuously aligning the body's energy field, dissolving blockages, and encouraging emotional and spiritual integration. A regular Reiki practice not only prevents future joint issues but also strengthens the body's resilience, increases emotional flexibility, and deepens spiritual awareness.

Just for today, I will let go of worry and trust the flow of life.

Why Consistent Reiki Practice Is Essential

Consistent Reiki practice allows for:

- Ongoing Energy Maintenance – The body's energy field naturally becomes disrupted due to stress, trauma, and environmental factors. Regular Reiki keeps energy flow balanced and prevents stagnation.
- Preventative Healing – Reiki helps dissolve minor energy blockages before they manifest as physical pain or discomfort.
- Emotional Regulation – Emotional patterns often resurface over time. Consistent Reiki helps process and release emotions in real-time, reducing long-term tension and trauma.
- Spiritual Strengthening – Reiki increases the practitioner's sensitivity to energy, enhancing intuition, clarity, and spiritual connection.
- Structural Integrity – Regular Reiki strengthens the energy pathways around the joints, improving joint health and flexibility over time.

How Consistent Reiki Practice Supports Joint Health

1. Strengthens Energy Flow Through the Meridians

- Meridians are the body's energy highways.
- When energy flows freely through the meridians, the joints remain supple and healthy.
- Reiki strengthens and reinforces the meridian pathways by clearing obstructions and increasing the flow of ki.

Example:

- Regular Reiki on the hips improves the flow of energy through the Liver Meridian and Gallbladder Meridian, enhancing flexibility and reducing stiffness.

2. Maintains Chakra Alignment and Balance

- Each joint is connected to specific chakras.
- Consistent Reiki practice keeps the chakras aligned, ensuring smooth energy flow through the joints.
- Balanced chakras promote emotional clarity, physical strength, and spiritual growth.

Example:

- Working regularly on the Root Chakra improves knee health and stability by addressing issues of safety and security.

3. Prevents the Buildup of Emotional and Physical Tension

- Emotional trauma and stress naturally accumulate in the joints over time.
- Consistent Reiki practice releases this tension before it becomes stored as chronic pain or inflammation.
- Regular sessions maintain emotional equilibrium and physical ease.

Just for today, I will let go of worry and trust the flow of life.

Example:

- Weekly Reiki sessions on the shoulders prevent the buildup of tension caused by emotional stress and overwork.

4. Encourages Muscle and Fascia Relaxation

- Reiki relaxes the muscles and fascia surrounding the joints.
- Relaxed fascia allows for greater range of motion and reduced joint stiffness.
- Over time, this leads to improved mobility and reduced risk of injury.

Example:

- Regular Reiki on the knees increases joint flexibility and reduces inflammation by relaxing the surrounding muscles and fascia.

5. Strengthens the Mind-Body Connection

- Consistent Reiki practice heightens body awareness and sensitivity to subtle energy shifts.
- This increased awareness allows for early detection of joint tension or imbalance.
- Practitioners become more attuned to their body's needs and energetic signals.

Example:

- A Reiki practitioner may notice subtle knee tightness before it becomes a serious issue and adjust their practice accordingly.

Long-Term Reiki Techniques for Joint Health and Balance

1. Daily Self-Treatment (15–20 minutes)

Regular self-treatment is the foundation of maintaining long-term energy balance. A simple daily practice of 15–20 minutes can prevent energy stagnation and reduce the accumulation of emotional and physical stress.

Steps:

1. Sit or lie down in a comfortable position.
2. Place your hands on the knees, hips, and shoulders.
3. Channel Reiki using the Cho Ku Rei symbol to strengthen energy flow.
4. Visualize a white or golden light filling the joints and surrounding tissues.
5. Hold each position for 3–5 minutes or until you feel the energy shift.
6. Close the session by visualizing the energy field sealing and stabilizing.

Daily self-treatment maintains joint flexibility and emotional balance.

Just for today, I will let go of worry and trust the flow of life.

2. Weekly Full-Body Reiki Session (60–90 minutes)

A full-body session helps reset the energy field and release any deeper emotional or physical blockages that may have accumulated during the week.

Steps:

1. Begin with a grounding exercise, placing your hands on the feet.
2. Work systematically through the chakras and joints.
3. Focus on areas that feel heavy, resistant, or stagnant.
4. Use the Sei He Ki symbol to release emotional tension.
5. Use the Cho Ku Rei symbol to strengthen and stabilize the energy flow.
6. Seal the energy field with the Cho Ku Rei symbol at the end of the session.

Weekly sessions keep the energetic and physical body aligned and balanced.

3. Monthly Deep Emotional Release Session (90 minutes)

Emotional patterns stored in the joints need deeper attention over time. A monthly deep release session helps dissolve these patterns and prevent emotional or physical stagnation.

Steps:

1. Begin with a body scan to identify emotional blockages.
2. Focus on joints connected to the blocked chakra.
3. Apply direct hand placement on the joint.
4. Use the Sei He Ki symbol to dissolve emotional trauma.
5. Guide the client through a breath-based emotional release.
6. Close the session with the Cho Ku Rei symbol to stabilize the emotional release.

Monthly deep release sessions help prevent chronic joint issues and emotional stagnation.

4. Seasonal Chakra Balancing (4 times per year)

The chakras naturally shift and change with the seasons. A seasonal chakra balancing session helps align the energy system with the Earth's natural rhythms and cycles.

Steps:

1. Focus on the chakras connected to the joints.
2. Use the Cho Ku Rei symbol to strengthen the flow of ki.
3. Use the Sei He Ki symbol to dissolve seasonal emotional patterns (e.g., winter stagnation or summer overactivity).
4. End with grounding and sealing the energy field.

Just for today, I will let go of worry and trust the flow of life.

Seasonal chakra balancing keeps the energetic body aligned with natural cycles.

Reiki Symbols for Long-Term Energy Balance

1. Cho Ku Rei (Power Symbol)

- Use to strengthen and stabilize the energy flow through the joints.
- Enhances physical strength and emotional resilience.
- Ideal for building energetic protection and increasing circulation.

2. Sei He Ki (Emotional Healing Symbol)

- Use to dissolve emotional blockages in the joints.
- Helps release stored trauma and emotional tension.
- Ideal for addressing long-term emotional patterns.

3. Dai Ko Myo (Master Symbol)

- Use for spiritual alignment and deep healing.
- Strengthens the overall energy system.
- Ideal for realigning the body and mind at a spiritual level.

Lifestyle and Supporting Practices for Long-Term Balance

Meditation and Breathwork

- Regular meditation and breathwork enhance Reiki's effect by calming the nervous system and improving energy flow.

Gentle Movement (Yoga, Tai Chi, Qi Gong)

- Gentle physical movement keeps the joints open and energy flowing.
- Movement combined with Reiki improves both physical and energetic flexibility.

Diet and Hydration

- A balanced diet and proper hydration support the body's energy flow and reduce inflammation in the joints.

Key Takeaways:

- Regular Reiki practice maintains joint health and prevents future imbalances.
- Daily self-treatment, weekly sessions, and seasonal balancing create long-term stability.
- Consistent Reiki dissolves emotional and energetic blockages before they manifest as physical issues.
- Combining Reiki with meditation, movement, and diet enhances the healing effect.

Just for today, I will let go of worry and trust the flow of life.

Chapter 10: Self-Treatment and Client Protocols

Step-by-Step Guide for Self-Treatment of Joint Issues

Self-treatment is a foundational practice in Reiki. It empowers the practitioner to take control of their own healing by addressing energetic blockages, releasing emotional patterns, and restoring physical balance. Joint issues, in particular, respond well to consistent self-treatment because joints serve as energetic crossroads where multiple meridians and chakras intersect.

When the flow of ki (life force energy) becomes stagnant or blocked in the joints, it creates stiffness, pain, and reduced mobility. Self-treatment with Reiki allows you to restore this flow by dissolving energetic knots, balancing the chakras, and realigning the meridian system.

The following self-treatment guide provides a structured, step-by-step process for addressing joint issues using Reiki. This practice can be adapted based on the location and nature of the joint discomfort, and it can be performed as part of a daily, weekly, or as-needed self-care routine.

Preparation for Self-Treatment

Set the Intention

Before starting the session, take a moment to clarify your intention. Setting a clear intention directs the flow of Reiki energy and strengthens the healing process.

Example Intentions:

- *"I intend to release pain and restore flexibility in my knee."*
- *"I open myself to emotional healing and physical relaxation."*
- *"I allow the flow of life force energy to move through my body with ease."*

Create a Comfortable Healing Space

- Find a quiet, comfortable place where you won't be disturbed.
- Sit or lie down in a relaxed position with your back supported.
- Keep a glass of water nearby to help ground yourself after the session.
- If desired, you can enhance the healing environment with:
    - Soft music or nature sounds.
    - Essential oils (e.g., lavender for relaxation or eucalyptus for pain relief).
    - Crystals (e.g., amethyst for relaxation, hematite for grounding).

Just for today, I will let go of worry and trust the flow of life.

Ground Yourself Before Beginning

- Close your eyes and take three slow, deep breaths.
- Imagine a red light at the base of your spine, connecting you to the Earth.
- Visualize this light extending down through your legs and into the ground.
- Feel your body becoming stable and supported.

Activate Reiki Energy

- Place your hands together in Gassho (prayer position).
- Silently ask to be a clear channel for Reiki energy.
- Use the Reiki symbols (if you are attuned to them):
  - Draw the Cho Ku Rei symbol to open and increase energy flow.
  - If emotional healing is needed, draw the Sei He Ki symbol.
  - If spiritual alignment is needed, draw the Dai Ko Myo symbol.
- State internally:
  - *"I allow Reiki energy to flow through me for the highest good."*
  - *"I am open to healing."*

Step 1: Full Body Scan to Identify Blockages

The first step is to identify where energy is stagnant or blocked. A body scan helps increase awareness of the joints and reveals where attention is needed.

How to Perform a Reiki Body Scan:

1. Close your eyes and place your hands on your thighs.
2. Slowly move your attention from the top of your head to the tips of your toes.
3. As you focus on each joint, notice any sensations such as:
    o Heat
    o Coldness
    o Tingling
    o Pressure
    o Heaviness
4. Pay attention to any emotional responses that arise as you scan the body.
5. Identify which joints feel tense, tight, or energetically blocked.
6. Focus your self-treatment on these areas.

Example:

- If you feel tension in the knees, it may reflect a blockage in the Root Chakra or emotional insecurity about moving forward.

Just for today, I will let go of worry and trust the flow of life.

Step 2: Direct Reiki to the Joint

Once you've identified the affected joint, begin direct energy work to restore the flow of ki.

How to Direct Reiki to the Joint:

1. Place both hands gently on the joint.
2. Draw the Cho Ku Rei symbol over the joint to open the energy flow.
3. If emotional tension is present, draw the Sei He Ki symbol over the joint.
4. Channel Reiki energy into the joint through your palms.
5. Visualize a warm golden or white light flowing into the joint.
6. Hold this position for 3–5 minutes or until you feel the energy shift.

Example:

- If treating the knee, visualize the knee joint filling with light and softening.
- Imagine energy flowing smoothly through the knee into the surrounding tissue.

Step 3: Spiral Motion Technique (For Flexibility and Flow)

The spiral motion technique helps dissolve energetic stagnation and increases the joint's range of motion.

How to Perform the Spiral Motion Technique:

1. Keep your hands on the joint.
2. Slowly begin to move your hands in a circular motion around the joint.
3. Visualize the energy spiraling through the joint, softening any tension.
4. Use the Cho Ku Rei symbol to strengthen the flow of ki.
5. Continue for 2–3 minutes or until you feel increased warmth and softness.

Example:

- If working on the shoulder, imagine the spiral motion gently expanding the joint's range of motion.

Just for today, I will let go of worry and trust the flow of life.

Step 4: Cross-Body Healing (For Left-Right Balance)

Cross-body healing balances the left and right sides of the body, which helps restore symmetry and stability in the joints.

How to Perform Cross-Body Healing:

1. Place one hand on the affected joint and the other hand on the opposite side of the body.
2. If you are working on the left knee, place the other hand on the right hip.
3. Draw the Cho Ku Rei symbol to strengthen the connection.
4. Visualize energy flowing between the two points.
5. Hold for 3–5 minutes until you feel the energy shift.

Example:

- For knee pain, placing one hand on the left knee and one on the right hip creates energetic symmetry between the left and right sides of the body.

Step 5: Emotional Release with Sei He Ki Symbol

If you sense that emotional trauma or tension is stored in the joint, use the Sei He Ki symbol to promote emotional release.

How to Facilitate Emotional Release:

1. Place one hand on the joint and one hand on the corresponding chakra.
2. Draw the Sei He Ki symbol over both points.
3. Encourage deep breathing — inhaling through the nose and exhaling through the mouth.
4. Ask yourself:
    o *"What emotion is being held here?"*
    o *"What am I ready to release?"*
5. As you breathe out, visualize the emotion dissolving into light.
6. Repeat until you feel emotional relief.

Example:

- If treating tight hips, releasing fear of intimacy or emotional vulnerability may arise.

Just for today, I will let go of worry and trust the flow of life.

Step 6: Seal the Healing with Cho Ku Rei

Sealing the energy helps protect the joint and stabilize the healing process.

How to Seal the Energy Field:

1. Draw the Cho Ku Rei symbol over the joint.
2. Visualize a layer of golden light surrounding the joint.
3. Silently say:
    - *"I seal this healing with love and light."*
4. Take a deep breath and release your hands.

Step 7: Close the Session and Ground the Energy

After completing the session, close the practice with grounding.

How to Ground After Reiki:

1. Place your hands on your knees or feet.
2. Imagine roots extending from the base of your spine into the earth.
3. Breathe deeply and feel the connection to the ground.
4. Take a sip of water to complete the grounding process.

How Often to Perform Self-Treatment

- Daily: For chronic pain or stiffness.
- 2–3 Times per Week: For maintenance and emotional balance.
- As Needed: For acute discomfort or emotional stress.

Key Takeaways:

- Direct hand placement increases energy flow and reduces pain.
- Spiral motion restores flexibility and emotional release.
- Cross-body healing creates energetic balance. Emotional release clears stored trauma from the joint.
- Regular self-treatment strengthens energetic resilience and joint health.

By practicing self-treatment consistently, you maintain flexibility, prevent future discomfort, and build a deeper connection with your body's energy field.

Just for today, I will let go of worry and trust the flow of life.

Structuring a Joint-Focused Reiki Session for Clients

A joint-focused Reiki session follows a structured process designed to target both the physical and energetic layers of the body. Since joints serve as energetic crossroads where multiple meridians and chakras intersect, they are highly sensitive to the flow of ki (life force energy). When energy becomes stagnant or blocked in the joints, it can lead to stiffness, discomfort, inflammation, and emotional imbalance.

A well-structured Reiki session for joint healing addresses the underlying energetic imbalances that contribute to joint issues. By combining direct hand placement, chakra balancing, and emotional release techniques, you help the client restore flexibility, reduce pain, and regain emotional and physical balance.

A typical joint-focused Reiki session lasts between 60 to 90 minutes, depending on the client's condition and goals. It includes preparation, assessment, direct energy work, and closing techniques to seal and stabilize the energy field.

Goals of a Joint-Focused Reiki Session:

- Restore the natural flow of ki through the joints and meridians.
- Dissolve energetic blockages contributing to pain and inflammation.
- Release emotional patterns stored in the joints.
- Improve joint mobility and reduce stiffness.
- Strengthen the body's overall energy system.
- Restore emotional and spiritual alignment.

Session Length:

- Standard Session: 60 minutes
- Extended Session (Deep Release): 90 minutes

Preparation Before the Session

1. Discuss the Client's Concerns

- Begin with a brief conversation to assess the client's physical and emotional condition.
- Ask the client to describe the following:
  - Location and nature of joint pain (e.g., stiffness, sharp pain, swelling).
  - Duration and frequency of the discomfort.
  - Emotional or life circumstances surrounding the onset of joint pain.
  - Previous injuries, surgeries, or trauma related to the joints.

Just for today, I will let go of worry and trust the flow of life.

Example Questions:

- *"How long have you been experiencing this discomfort?"*
- *"Are there particular movements or emotional triggers that make the pain worse?"*
- *"Do you feel emotionally connected to the discomfort in any way?"*

2. Assess the Client's Energy Field (Body Scan)

- Begin with a body scan to detect energetic imbalances and blockages.
- Use your hands to slowly hover over the client's body, moving from head to feet.
- Pay attention to any sensations (e.g., heat, coolness, tingling, heaviness).
- Take note of areas where the energy feels dense or stagnant — these are likely the key points of imbalance.

Example:

- If you sense heaviness around the hips, it may reflect an imbalance in the Sacral Chakra.
- If the shoulders feel cold or blocked, the client may be carrying emotional burdens tied to the Heart Chakra.

3. Set the Intention for Healing

- Setting a clear intention aligns the client's subconscious mind with the healing process and strengthens the flow of Reiki energy.

Example Intentions:

- *"I direct the flow of energy to release tension and pain in the hips."*
- *"I create space for emotional release and physical healing."*
- *"I restore balance and flexibility in the knees and ankles."*

4. Create a Relaxing Environment

- Ensure the room is quiet and comfortable.
- Use soft lighting or candlelight.
- Play calming music or nature sounds.
- Diffuse essential oils (e.g., lavender for relaxation, frankincense for grounding).

Phase 1: Opening and Grounding (5–10 Minutes)

1. Begin with a Grounding Exercise

- Ask the client to close their eyes and take three deep breaths.
- Place your hands on the client's feet or knees.
- Visualize a warm red or golden light flowing from the client's feet into the earth.

Just for today, I will let go of worry and trust the flow of life.

- Draw the Cho Ku Rei symbol over the feet or knees to increase grounding and protection.

Example:

- If the client feels unstable or emotionally overwhelmed, focus more time on grounding through the Root Chakra and legs.

2. Open the Energy Field

- Place your hands at the crown of the head.
- Channel Reiki energy through the crown, visualizing it flowing down through the body.
- Draw the Cho Ku Rei symbol to open the client's energetic field.

Opening the energy field allows Reiki to flow more easily through the joints and meridians.

Phase 2: Direct Reiki for Joint Healing (30–40 Minutes)

1. Direct Hand Placement on Affected Joints

- Start with the joints where the client feels discomfort.
- Place one hand above and one hand below the joint (or on opposite sides).
- Channel Reiki into the joint using the Cho Ku Rei symbol to strengthen energy flow.
- Hold the position for 3–5 minutes or until the energy shifts.

Focus on areas that feel dense or resistant — these are points of energetic blockage.

2. Use the Spiral Motion Technique (For Flexibility and Flow)

- While keeping your hands on the joint, move them in a circular motion.
- Visualize a spiral of golden or white light flowing through the joint.
- This technique helps dissolve blockages and increase joint flexibility.

Use this technique for shoulder, knee, hip, and ankle issues.

3. Cross-Body Healing for Symmetry

- Place one hand on the affected joint and the other hand on the corresponding opposite side of the body.
- For example, if the left knee is being treated, place the other hand on the right hip.
- Channel Reiki energy between the two points to create balance and alignment.

Cross-body healing restores symmetry and balance in the meridians and joints.

4. Emotional Release with Sei He Ki Symbol

- If emotional trauma is stored in the joint, apply the Sei He Ki symbol.

Just for today, I will let go of worry and trust the flow of life.

- Hold one hand on the joint and one on the corresponding chakra.
- Encourage the client to breathe deeply.
- Guide the client to silently repeat an affirmation (e.g., *"It is safe to let go."*).

This technique is especially effective for hips, knees, and shoulders where emotional trauma tends to accumulate.

5. Incorporate Breathwork (Optional)

- Ask the client to inhale deeply into the joint.
- As they exhale, direct Reiki energy into the joint.
- Encourage the client to visualize the joint relaxing and opening.

Breathwork enhances energetic release and increases relaxation.

Phase 3: Chakra Balancing (5–10 Minutes)

- Scan the client's chakras from root to crown.
- Focus on the chakras connected to the affected joints:
    - Root Chakra – Knees, hips, ankles
    - Sacral Chakra – Hips, pelvis
    - Solar Plexus Chakra – Elbows, wrists
    - Heart Chakra – Shoulders, arms
    - Throat Chakra – Wrists, fingers
- Use the Cho Ku Rei symbol to strengthen and balance the chakras.
- Use the Sei He Ki symbol to dissolve emotional patterns.

Balanced chakras support long-term joint health and emotional stability.

Phase 4: Closing and Grounding (5–10 Minutes)

1. Seal the Energy Field

- Draw the Cho Ku Rei symbol over the body to seal the healing.
- Visualize a protective layer of white or gold light surrounding the client.

2. Close with Grounding

- Place your hands on the client's feet or knees.
- Channel Reiki into the feet to reconnect the client to the earth.
- Encourage the client to take deep breaths.

After the Session

- Offer the client a glass of water to help integrate the energy shift.
- Discuss any emotional responses or sensations the client experienced.
- Encourage the client to rest, hydrate, and remain aware of emotional shifts in the coming days.
- If necessary, recommend follow-up sessions.

Advise clients that emotional release may continue for 24–48 hours after the session.

Just for today, I will let go of worry and trust the flow of life.

Key Takeaways:

- Direct hand placement restores energy flow through the joints.
- Cross-body healing creates left-right balance.
- Emotional release techniques dissolve stored trauma.
- Chakra balancing strengthens the body's energetic foundation.
- Consistent sessions create lasting flexibility, strength, and emotional balance.

By structuring the session effectively, you create a comprehensive healing experience that addresses both physical and emotional layers of joint health.

Feedback and Follow-Up Strategies

Effective feedback and follow-up are essential components of a successful Reiki practice, especially when working with joint issues. Since joint problems are often tied to emotional patterns and energetic blockages, the healing process unfolds over time. Consistent feedback allows you to monitor the client's progress, adjust your approach, and strengthen the client's confidence in the healing process.

Many clients experience both physical relief and emotional release after a joint-focused Reiki session. However, healing is not always linear — some clients may experience temporary discomfort or emotional sensitivity as deep-seated trauma surfaces and is released. Thoughtful follow-up helps guide the client through this process and reinforces the benefits of consistent Reiki practice.

Establishing a structured feedback and follow-up process helps to:

- Measure the effectiveness of the session.
- Strengthen the client-practitioner relationship.
- Encourage the client to take an active role in their healing.
- Reinforce the long-term benefits of Reiki.
- Build trust and increase client retention.

Just for today, I will let go of worry and trust the flow of life.

Types of Feedback

1. Immediate Post-Session Feedback (During or After the Session)

Immediate feedback helps you assess how the client's body and mind responded to the session.

Ask Questions Such As:

- *"How do you feel right now?"*
- *"Did you notice any sensations during the session (e.g., warmth, tingling)?"*
- *"Did any emotions or thoughts surface?"*
- *"How does the affected joint feel compared to when you arrived?"*

Why It's Important:

- Helps you identify whether the energy block has been released or if more sessions are needed.
- Reveals whether the client experienced an emotional release or physical improvement.
- Strengthens the client's connection to their body's energetic response.

2. Sensory and Emotional Feedback

Encourage the client to describe any physical or emotional sensations they experienced during the session. This deepens the client's awareness of their body and reinforces the mind-body connection.

Examples:

- Warmth, coolness, tingling, heaviness, or lightness.
- Emotional responses such as sadness, anger, relief, or peace.
- Mental clarity or insights that surfaced during the session.

Example:

- A client with knee pain may feel a sense of warmth or lightness in the joint after the session, indicating improved energy flow.
- A client experiencing hip tightness may feel emotional release connected to relationship patterns.

3. Range of Motion and Physical Response Feedback

If you worked on a joint, assess any improvement in physical function or pain relief.

Ask Questions Such As:

- *"Do you feel more flexibility or less discomfort?"*
- *"Can you move the joint more easily now?"*
- *"On a scale of 1 to 10, how would you rate your pain or discomfort now compared to before the session?"*

Example:

- A client with restricted shoulder movement may be able to lift their arm higher after the session.

Just for today, I will let go of worry and trust the flow of life.

- A client with knee stiffness may feel increased range of motion and reduced swelling.

Immediate improvement reinforces the connection between Reiki and physical healing.

How to Respond to Different Types of Feedback

1. If the Client Experienced Immediate Relief:

- Acknowledge the improvement and explain why it happened.
- Reinforce that Reiki restores energy flow, which naturally leads to physical and emotional relief.
- Encourage the client to continue Reiki practice to maintain long-term balance.

Example:

- *"It's great that you feel more freedom in your knee — the energy was clearly blocked there, and now it's flowing more freely."*

2. If the Client Experienced Emotional Release:

- Explain that emotional release is part of the healing process.
- Encourage the client to allow emotions to surface without judgment.
- Recommend self-care practices (e.g., journaling, gentle movement) to integrate the emotional shift.

Example:

- *"The tears you experienced are a sign that emotional energy was stored in the joint. This is a healthy and necessary release."*

3. If the Client Felt No Immediate Change:

- Explain that healing may take time, especially if the joint issue is chronic.
- Remind the client that Reiki works at both the energetic and cellular level — some benefits may appear in the coming days.
- Encourage consistency with follow-up sessions.

Example:

- *"Even though you don't feel a big difference yet, the energy has already started shifting. Let's give your body time to integrate the changes."*

4. If the Client Felt Worse After the Session:

- Explain that temporary discomfort (known as a healing response) can happen as stagnant energy clears.
- Encourage the client to rest and drink water to help the body process the release.
- Reassure the client that discomfort usually resolves within 24–48 hours.

Just for today, I will let go of worry and trust the flow of life.

Example:

- *"It's not unusual to feel some discomfort as the body releases old patterns. This is a sign that the energy is shifting — it will settle soon."*

Follow-Up Strategies

1. Schedule Follow-Up Sessions

Joint-related issues often require multiple sessions to resolve deep energetic patterns and physical imbalances.

- For chronic pain or stiffness – Recommend weekly sessions for 4–6 weeks.
- For acute issues (recent injury) – Recommend 2–3 sessions within 10 days.
- For maintenance – Recommend biweekly or monthly sessions after the initial series.

Example:

- *"I suggest we schedule weekly sessions for the next month to create consistent energy flow and strengthen the joint's recovery."*

2. Provide Self-Care Recommendations

Encourage the client to support the healing process between sessions through self-care practices.

Examples:

- Daily Reiki self-treatment (teach them hand positions).
- Gentle movement (e.g., yoga, stretching).
- Epsom salt baths to relieve inflammation.
- Breathwork and meditation to support emotional release.
- Affirmations to reinforce positive patterns.

Example:

- *"You may find it helpful to practice self-Reiki on your knees every evening for 5 minutes — this will help maintain the flow of energy."*

3. Suggest Lifestyle Adjustments

Small lifestyle changes can enhance the effectiveness of Reiki and promote long-term joint health.

Examples:

- Increase hydration to reduce joint inflammation.
- Improve sleep quality.
- Avoid inflammatory foods (e.g., processed sugars, excessive alcohol).
- Incorporate grounding exercises (e.g., walking barefoot).

Just for today, I will let go of worry and trust the flow of life.

Example:

- *"Since inflammation can reflect both physical and emotional stress, you might want to explore more grounding practices."*

4. Track Progress Over Time

Maintain a record of the client's progress to monitor patterns and adjust the approach as needed.

Record the Following:

- Pain level before and after sessions.
- Emotional responses and releases.
- Changes in joint mobility and strength.
- Client feedback and insights.

Tracking progress strengthens the client-practitioner relationship and demonstrates the long-term benefits of Reiki.

5. Adjust Techniques Based on Client Response

- If the client responds well to direct hand placement, increase the time spent on that technique.
- If emotional release is more profound, focus more on the Sei He Ki symbol and breathwork.
- If the client reports increased flexibility, incorporate more grounding and stabilization work.

Example:

- *"Since you've had good results with direct hand placement on the knees, let's focus on that in the next session."*

Encouraging Long-Term Commitment

Clients are more likely to commit to consistent Reiki sessions when they see measurable results and understand how the process works.

Key Strategies:

- Explain how consistent Reiki practice creates cumulative benefits.
- Celebrate small improvements — even subtle changes in flexibility or emotional response.
- Reinforce the connection between emotional and physical health.
- Encourage the client to take an active role in their healing.

Key Takeaways:

- Immediate feedback helps measure session effectiveness.
- Emotional release is a sign of deeper healing.
- Follow-up sessions create long-term balance and strength.
- Lifestyle adjustments support ongoing joint health.
- Tracking progress strengthens client trust and retention.

Just for today, I will let go of worry and trust the flow of life.

PART 4: SPIRITUAL AND EMOTIONAL GROWTH THROUGH JOINT HEALING

Just for today, I will let go of worry and trust the flow of life.

Chapter 11: Life Lessons Stored in Joints

How Joint Issues Reflect Emotional and Spiritual Blocks

Joints are more than physical connectors that allow movement — they are also emotional and spiritual storage centers where life lessons, unresolved emotions, and spiritual challenges are held. In Reiki and energy medicine, joint issues are often seen as reflections of deeper emotional and spiritual imbalances. When joints become stiff, inflamed, or painful, it's usually not just a physical problem — it signals a deeper misalignment at the emotional or spiritual level.

Reiki practitioners understand that energy flows through the joints via the meridians and chakras. If the energy flow is disrupted due to emotional trauma, fear, or resistance to change, the affected joint begins to reflect that imbalance through discomfort, tension, or inflammation. By understanding the symbolic meaning of each joint and the energetic lessons connected to it, you can uncover the deeper life patterns and emotional wounds that need healing.

Why Joints Hold Emotional and Spiritual Patterns

Joints are unique because they allow for both movement and flexibility — not just physically, but also emotionally and spiritually. When joint health is compromised, it reflects the body's resistance to movement at some level — whether that's movement through life, emotional growth, or spiritual evolution.

1. Flexibility vs. Rigidity

- Joints represent the ability to move through life with ease.
- When a person is emotionally rigid or spiritually resistant, the joints reflect this through stiffness or limited range of motion.
- Emotional and spiritual flexibility translates into physical flexibility.

2. Emotional Storage in Connective Tissue and Fascia

- Joints are surrounded by connective tissue and fascia — both of which have the ability to store emotional patterns.
- Emotional trauma, stress, and fear create tension in the fascia and connective tissue, which leads to stiffness and inflammation in the joint.
- Reiki works by dissolving these patterns and restoring flow through the joint.

Just for today, I will let go of worry and trust the flow of life.

3. Fear of Change and Uncertainty

- Joints represent transitions and the ability to adapt to life's changes.
- Fear of change or uncertainty often leads to blocked energy in the joints.
- This manifests as joint instability, stiffness, or pain.

4. Protection and Vulnerability

- When a person feels emotionally vulnerable or threatened, the joints often tighten as a protective response.
- This creates muscular tension and restricts joint movement.
- Reiki helps release this protective response and re-establish emotional safety.

5. Life Path and Direction

- Joints (especially the knees, hips, and ankles) reflect how securely a person feels on their life path.
- Difficulty moving forward, lack of trust, or uncertainty about purpose often results in joint-related issues.

The Spiritual and Emotional Meaning of Specific Joints

Each joint in the body corresponds to a specific chakra and reflects a particular emotional or spiritual lesson. Understanding these symbolic connections allows Reiki practitioners to identify the root cause of joint issues and tailor the healing process accordingly.

1. Knees – Trust and Humility (Root Chakra)

The knees represent a person's connection to the Root Chakra — the energy center of stability, survival, and trust. The knees reflect a person's ability to move forward with confidence and trust in life's path.

Emotional and Spiritual Meaning:

- Fear of moving forward.
- Resistance to change.
- Lack of trust in the universe or oneself.
- Humility — difficulty "bending" or surrendering control.
- Feeling unsupported or unstable.

Example:

- A person with chronic knee pain may have difficulty trusting life's direction or feel unsupported by others.
- Reiki on the Root Chakra and knee joint restores grounding and trust.

Lesson: Learning to trust life and surrender control.

Just for today, I will let go of worry and trust the flow of life.

2. Hips – Emotional Flow and Creative Expression (Sacral Chakra)

The hips reflect emotional flow, creativity, and the ability to embrace change. Since the hips are large joints connected to the Sacral Chakra, they store deep emotional patterns related to relationships, intimacy, and personal power.

Emotional and Spiritual Meaning:

- Fear of intimacy or emotional vulnerability.
- Suppression of creative expression.
- Difficulty "going with the flow."
- Fear of losing control.

Example:

- Tight or painful hips may reflect emotional trauma or creative stagnation.
- Reiki helps release these emotional patterns and restore flow.

Lesson: Learning to express emotions and creativity without fear.

3. Shoulders – Carrying Burdens and Emotional Responsibility (Heart and Throat Chakras)

The shoulders reflect a person's ability to carry emotional weight and responsibility. Pain or tension in the shoulders reflects emotional burdens or difficulty expressing vulnerability.

Emotional and Spiritual Meaning:

- Feeling overwhelmed or burdened by responsibility.
- Difficulty asking for help or receiving support.
- Suppressed grief or sadness.
- Feeling "weighed down" emotionally.

Example:

- Shoulder pain may reflect the emotional weight of caring for others without receiving support.
- Reiki on the shoulders and Heart Chakra helps release emotional burdens.

Lesson: Learning to release emotional burdens and accept support.

4. Elbows – Flexibility in Giving and Receiving (Solar Plexus and Heart Chakras)

The elbows reflect how well a person can give and receive emotional and physical support.

Emotional and Spiritual Meaning:

- Resistance to receiving help.
- Difficulty letting go of control.
- Tension in relationships.

Just for today, I will let go of worry and trust the flow of life.

Example:

- Elbow stiffness may reflect emotional defensiveness or a need to protect oneself.
- Reiki helps increase emotional flexibility and openness.

Lesson: Learning to give and receive without fear.

5. Wrists – Trust and Communication (Throat Chakra)

The wrists reflect a person's ability to trust others and express themselves authentically.

Emotional and Spiritual Meaning:

- Fear of self-expression.
- Difficulty trusting others.
- Feeling restricted or silenced.

Example:

- Wrist pain may reflect the fear of speaking up or expressing one's true self.
- Reiki on the wrists and Throat Chakra restores communication and trust.

Lesson: Learning to communicate openly and trust oneself.

6. Ankles – Stability and Balance (Root and Sacral Chakras)

The ankles reflect balance and the ability to adapt to life's changes.

Emotional and Spiritual Meaning:

- Fear of instability.
- Inability to stay grounded.
- Fear of stepping into the unknown.

Example:

- Ankle pain may reflect a fear of losing control or uncertainty about life's direction.
- Reiki on the ankles and Root Chakra restores emotional and physical stability.

Lesson: Learning to trust the journey and remain grounded.

7. Fingers and Toes – Precision and Action (Throat and Root Chakras)

The fingers and toes reflect the ability to take action and follow through with purpose.

Emotional and Spiritual Meaning:

- Fear of failure.
- Overthinking or perfectionism.
- Feeling scattered or unfocused.

Just for today, I will let go of worry and trust the flow of life.

Example:

- Finger stiffness may reflect hesitation or indecision about life choices.
- Reiki on the fingers and Throat Chakra restores clarity and confidence.

Lesson: Learning to take confident action without fear of failure.

Techniques to Release Life Lessons Stored in Joints

1. Sei He Ki Symbol for Emotional Release

- Use the Sei He Ki symbol to dissolve emotional patterns held in the joints.
- Channel Reiki into the joint while holding the Sei He Ki symbol in your mind.

2. Breathwork and Visualization

- Encourage the client to breathe deeply into the joint.
- Visualize emotional tension dissolving with each exhale.

3. Affirmations to Reinforce New Patterns

- Use affirmations to reinforce positive life lessons.
- Example: *"It is safe for me to move forward with confidence."*

4. Emotional Journaling

- Encourage the client to write about emotional patterns connected to joint pain.
- Journaling helps identify and release hidden emotional resistance.

Key Takeaways:

- Joints reflect emotional and spiritual patterns.
- Emotional resistance, fear, and trauma manifest as joint issues.
- Reiki restores emotional flexibility and physical balance.
- Understanding the symbolic meaning of each joint deepens the healing process.
- Releasing stored trauma in the joints allows for greater emotional and spiritual freedom.

By understanding the life lessons stored in the joints, Reiki practitioners can create deeper and more transformative healing experiences.

Just for today, I will let go of worry and trust the flow of life.

Journaling Exercises for Identifying Emotional Patterns Linked to Joint Health

Journaling is a powerful tool for uncovering the emotional and spiritual roots of joint issues. Since joints reflect emotional flexibility, movement through life, and resistance to change, joint pain or stiffness often signals underlying emotional patterns that need to be acknowledged and released.

Reiki practitioners understand that emotional and spiritual patterns are stored in the body, particularly in the connective tissues, fascia, and joints. When a joint becomes stiff or painful, it may reflect unresolved emotional experiences such as fear, grief, anger, or trauma.

Journaling creates a safe space for clients (or yourself) to explore these patterns, uncover their emotional roots, and begin the process of emotional and energetic release. Writing helps to engage the conscious mind and bring hidden emotional patterns into awareness — which allows Reiki to work more effectively in dissolving these patterns at the energetic level.

The following journaling exercises are designed to guide clients through identifying and releasing emotional patterns stored in the joints. These exercises also help clients recognize life lessons connected to joint health and emotional well-being.

How to Introduce Journaling to Clients

- Explain that joints reflect emotional and spiritual flexibility.
- Encourage the client to approach journaling with curiosity and without judgment.
- Let them know that emotional patterns stored in the body are normal — and healing them is part of the Reiki process.
- Suggest that the client write in a quiet, distraction-free environment.
- Encourage clients to write freely and without censoring their thoughts.

Journaling Guidelines:

- Write without judgment — let thoughts flow naturally.
- Be specific about physical sensations and emotional responses.
- Describe life circumstances connected to joint discomfort.
- Acknowledge emotional resistance, but avoid self-criticism.
- If strong emotions arise, pause, breathe, and return when ready.
- Return to the journal exercise after Reiki sessions to monitor progress.

Just for today, I will let go of worry and trust the flow of life.

Journaling Exercises by Joint Type

Each joint reflects a specific emotional or spiritual theme. These exercises target the emotional and spiritual lessons connected to the specific joint, helping clients to uncover hidden patterns.

1. Knee Journaling Exercise – Trust and Moving Forward (Root Chakra)

The knees represent the ability to move forward with trust and stability. Knee pain often reflects fear of moving forward, feeling unsupported, or lack of trust in life's path.

Questions to Explore:

- What is holding me back from moving forward in life?
- Do I trust that life will support me if I take the next step?
- Am I resisting change out of fear of failure?
- Where in my life do I feel unstable or unsupported?
- What would moving forward with confidence feel like?

Example Prompt:
"Write about a time when you hesitated to take a big step forward. What were you afraid of? How did that situation make you feel physically and emotionally?"

2. Hip Journaling Exercise – Emotional Flow and Creative Expression (Sacral Chakra)

The hips reflect emotional flow, creativity, and intimacy. Hip tension often reflects fear of vulnerability, creative blocks, or emotional holding patterns.

Questions to Explore:

- Do I feel comfortable expressing my emotions?
- Am I holding back creatively or sexually?
- Where in my life am I resisting emotional flow?
- How do I feel about intimacy and connection?
- What would emotional and creative freedom feel like?

Example Prompt:
"Describe a time when you held back from expressing yourself creatively or emotionally. What were you protecting yourself from? What emotions did you feel?"

3. Shoulder Journaling Exercise – Emotional Responsibility and Burden (Heart and Throat Chakras)

The shoulders reflect emotional burdens and the weight of responsibility. Shoulder tension often reflects overwhelm, difficulty asking for help, or emotional heaviness.

Questions to Explore:

- What emotional burdens am I carrying that don't belong to me?

Just for today, I will let go of worry and trust the flow of life.

- Do I feel supported, or do I feel like I have to carry everything alone?
- What would it feel like to let go of some of these burdens?
- Am I taking on responsibility for other people's emotions or actions?
- How can I give myself permission to rest?

Example Prompt:
"Write about a situation where you felt emotionally or physically weighed down. What responsibilities were you carrying? How did it affect your body and emotional state?"

4. Elbow Journaling Exercise – Flexibility in Giving and Receiving (Solar Plexus and Heart Chakras)

The elbows reflect the ability to give and receive. Tension in the elbows often reflects resistance to receiving help or difficulty giving without attachment.

Questions to Explore:

- Am I comfortable asking for help?
- Do I feel worthy of receiving support?
- Am I giving too much without feeling appreciated?
- Where in my life am I holding back from extending myself to others?
- How can I open myself to giving and receiving equally?

Example Prompt:
"Write about a time when you felt resistant to asking for or

receiving help. How did that affect your sense of connection and trust?"

5. Wrist Journaling Exercise – Trust and Communication (Throat Chakra)

The wrists reflect trust and communication. Wrist pain often reflects difficulty expressing oneself or fear of vulnerability.

Questions to Explore:

- Do I feel comfortable speaking my truth?
- Am I holding back from expressing how I feel?
- Do I trust others to listen and respect my voice?
- What would it feel like to communicate with confidence?
- How can I practice expressing myself openly?

Example Prompt:
"Write about a time when you felt unable to express yourself. What were you afraid of? How did you feel afterward?"

6. Ankle Journaling Exercise – Balance and Stability (Root and Sacral Chakras)

The ankles reflect balance and grounding. Ankle instability often reflects fear of change, lack of direction, or emotional instability.

Just for today, I will let go of worry and trust the flow of life.

Questions to Explore:

- Do I feel balanced in my life right now?
- What fears are preventing me from feeling grounded and stable?
- Am I afraid of stepping into the unknown?
- How can I create more emotional stability in my life?
- What would emotional and physical balance feel like?

Example Prompt:
"Describe a time when you felt emotionally or spiritually ungrounded. What life circumstances were influencing that feeling?"

7. Finger and Toe Journaling Exercise – Precision and Action (Throat and Root Chakras)

The fingers and toes reflect the ability to take action and follow through with confidence. Pain or tension often reflects indecision, perfectionism, or fear of failure.

Questions to Explore:

- Where in my life am I holding back from taking action?
- Do I feel confident following through with my decisions?
- Am I afraid of making a mistake or failing?
- How can I trust myself more when making decisions?
- What would it feel like to take action without fear?

Example Prompt:
"Write about a time when you hesitated to take action. What were you afraid of? How did that hesitation affect your sense of self-confidence?"

8. Whole Body Journaling Exercise – Overall Flexibility and Trust

This exercise explores the overall connection between emotional and physical flexibility.

Questions to Explore:

- Where in my life am I resistant to change?
- Do I trust myself to handle life's challenges?
- How can I create more flow and ease in my life?
- What emotional patterns keep showing up in my body?
- How can I bring more balance between action and rest?

Example Prompt:
"Describe the last time you felt physically or emotionally stuck. What thoughts and feelings contributed to that state?"

How to Use Journaling with Reiki Sessions:

- Encourage clients to complete journaling exercises before or after Reiki sessions.
- Use the client's responses to guide the focus of future Reiki sessions.

Just for today, I will let go of worry and trust the flow of life.

- Reflect on journaling patterns over time to measure emotional and physical progress.

Key Takeaways:

- Journaling helps identify emotional roots of joint issues.
- Patterns in joint health reflect emotional and spiritual imbalances.
- Regular journaling builds self-awareness and strengthens the mind-body connection.
- Combining journaling with Reiki deepens emotional and physical healing.

By combining Reiki and journaling, clients can uncover hidden emotional patterns and create lasting shifts in both physical and emotional health.

Developing a Spiritual Practice to Maintain Emotional Flexibility and Strength

A consistent spiritual practice is one of the most effective ways to maintain emotional flexibility, inner strength, and energetic balance. Reiki practitioners understand that physical health and emotional well-being are not separate — they are reflections of the body's energetic alignment.

Joints represent the body's ability to move through life with ease and adaptability. When joints become stiff or painful, it often reflects emotional resistance or fear of change. A spiritual practice helps you remain grounded, emotionally open, and energetically aligned — which translates into greater physical flexibility, emotional resilience, and spiritual clarity.

By cultivating a regular spiritual practice, you strengthen your connection to yourself, to universal energy, and to life's natural flow. This creates a sense of inner stability and emotional flexibility, allowing you to move through life's challenges with greater ease and confidence.

Just for today, I will let go of worry and trust the flow of life.

Why Emotional Flexibility and Strength Matter

Emotional flexibility is the ability to:

- Adapt to life's changes without becoming overwhelmed.
- Respond to emotional challenges without shutting down or reacting impulsively.
- Release emotional patterns that no longer serve you.
- Hold space for both positive and difficult emotions without attachment.
- Trust life's unfolding process, even when the path is unclear.

Emotional strength is the ability to:

- Set boundaries without fear of rejection.
- Face life's challenges with courage and inner peace.
- Trust your intuition and make decisions confidently.
- Stay grounded in your values and truth, even under pressure.
- Rebuild emotional balance after setbacks or challenges.

How a Spiritual Practice Supports Emotional Flexibility and Strength

1. Strengthens Your Connection to Universal Energy

Reiki teaches that ki (life force energy) is the foundation of all physical, emotional, and spiritual health.

- When you connect regularly to this universal energy, you feel supported and aligned with life's natural rhythm.
- This connection allows you to move through life with greater ease and trust.
- It creates an inner foundation of peace, even during difficult times.

2. Encourages Emotional Flow and Release

- Spiritual practices like Reiki, meditation, and breathwork help release emotional patterns held in the body's energy field.
- When emotions are processed and released regularly, they don't become stored as tension in the joints.
- Emotional flow creates greater physical ease and flexibility.

3. Increases Inner Stability and Balance

- A regular spiritual practice grounds you, helping you remain calm and centered even when life feels chaotic.
- Spiritual strength comes from knowing that you have the tools to realign and restore balance at any time.
- This creates emotional resilience and confidence in handling life's challenges.

Just for today, I will let go of worry and trust the flow of life.

4. Builds Trust in Life's Process

- A spiritual practice strengthens your connection to life's greater purpose.
- It allows you to trust that even difficult experiences hold lessons and meaning.
- Emotional strength comes from knowing that you are guided and supported.

5. Restores Harmony Between the Body, Mind, and Spirit

- Emotional tension is often reflected physically in the joints and muscles.
- A spiritual practice creates energetic alignment, which translates into emotional balance and physical ease.
- Reiki, in particular, restores balance at all levels — physical, emotional, mental, and spiritual.

Essential Components of a Spiritual Practice

An effective spiritual practice includes physical, mental, emotional, and energetic elements. The goal is to create a well-rounded practice that strengthens both inner flexibility and emotional strength.

1. Reiki Self-Treatment (Daily or Weekly)

Reiki is a powerful tool for maintaining energetic balance and emotional clarity.

- Place your hands on your joints or chakras.

- Use the Cho Ku Rei symbol to strengthen the energy field.
- If emotional resistance arises, use the Sei He Ki symbol to dissolve emotional patterns.
- Visualize the joint or chakra surrounded by white or golden light.
- Hold the position until you feel the energy shift.

Reiki self-treatment prevents emotional and physical tension from accumulating.

2. Grounding Exercises (Daily)

Grounding reconnects you to the Earth and helps stabilize your energy field.

- Walk barefoot on the earth or grass.
- Sit with your hands on your knees and visualize roots growing from your spine into the earth.
- Breathe deeply and visualize energy flowing from the earth into your body.
- Use the Cho Ku Rei symbol to reinforce grounding energy.

Grounding creates emotional stability and strengthens physical balance.

3. Meditation and Breathwork (5–20 minutes daily)

Meditation and breathwork calm the mind and increase emotional awareness.

- Sit in a comfortable position and close your eyes.

Just for today, I will let go of worry and trust the flow of life.

- Focus on your breath — allow it to become deep and natural.
- If thoughts or emotions arise, observe them without judgment.
- Visualize energy flowing through your body, clearing any tension or emotional resistance.

Meditation increases emotional clarity and deepens your connection to universal energy.

4. Affirmations and Intentions (Daily)

Affirmations help reprogram emotional patterns and create new energetic pathways.

- Choose affirmations that reflect emotional strength and flexibility.
- Speak them aloud or silently during Reiki sessions or meditation.

Example Affirmations:

- *"I move through life with ease and confidence."*
- *"I trust life's unfolding process."*
- *"I am emotionally flexible and open to change."*
- *"I release emotional tension with grace and peace."*

Affirmations help integrate new emotional and energetic patterns.

5. Emotional Journaling (Weekly)

Journaling increases self-awareness and helps identify emotional patterns linked to joint issues.

- Write freely about how you're feeling physically and emotionally.
- If a joint feels stiff or painful, explore the emotional meaning behind it.
- Use prompts like:
    - *What emotion am I holding in this joint?*
    - *What would emotional freedom feel like right now?*
    - *What lesson is this discomfort teaching me?*

Journaling helps bring hidden emotional patterns into conscious awareness.

6. Visualization for Emotional Flexibility (As Needed)

Visualization helps reprogram emotional and physical patterns at the subconscious level.

- Visualize yourself moving freely through life with emotional ease and confidence.
- Imagine each joint becoming warm and fluid, releasing any tension.
- See yourself adapting gracefully to life's changes and challenges.
- Use the Cho Ku Rei and Sei He Ki symbols during visualization.

Just for today, I will let go of worry and trust the flow of life.

Visualization strengthens the mind-body connection and enhances emotional flow.

7. Emotional Release Through Movement (Weekly)

Physical movement helps release emotional patterns held in the body.

- Practice yoga, tai chi, or gentle stretching.
- Focus on releasing tension in the hips, shoulders, and knees.
- Use breathwork to guide the release of emotional energy through the joints.
- If emotional resistance arises, place your hands on the affected joint and channel Reiki into it.

Movement helps integrate energetic shifts and restore physical flexibility.

8. Connection to Higher Wisdom (Daily or Weekly)

Developing a spiritual connection increases emotional strength and trust in life's process.

- Meditate on spiritual guidance.
- Ask for insight or clarity from your higher self or spiritual guides.
- Trust your intuitive responses.
- Use the Dai Ko Myo symbol to strengthen spiritual alignment.

Spiritual connection creates a sense of trust and peace, even during challenges.

Sample Daily Spiritual Practice (15–20 Minutes):

1. Grounding – 2 minutes
2. Reiki Self-Treatment – 5–10 minutes
3. Affirmations – 1 minute
4. Meditation/Breathwork – 5 minutes
5. Closing Visualization – 2 minutes

Key Takeaways:

- Emotional flexibility allows you to respond to life with ease.
- Reiki strengthens emotional balance by restoring energetic flow.
- Grounding, meditation, and breathwork increase emotional stability.
- Affirmations and visualization create new emotional patterns.
- Consistency is key — a regular practice creates long-term emotional resilience.

By cultivating a consistent spiritual practice, you create an inner foundation of emotional strength and flexibility — allowing you to face life's challenges with grace and confidence.

Just for today, I will let go of worry and trust the flow of life.

Chapter 12: Integrating Joint Healing into Your Reiki Practice

How to Incorporate Joint Work into Standard Reiki Sessions

Joint work can be seamlessly integrated into a standard Reiki session by focusing on the energetic intersections where joints act as gateways for energy flow. Since joints are where multiple meridians and chakras intersect, they hold both physical and emotional imprints — making them powerful focal points for deeper healing.

Traditional Reiki sessions typically follow a full-body approach, addressing the chakras, energy meridians, and overall energy flow. Incorporating joint work into this structure allows the practitioner to target specific energetic blockages while still maintaining balance within the whole energy system.

Working with the joints enhances the overall effectiveness of a Reiki session by:

- Increasing the flow of ki (life force energy) through the body's natural pathways.
- Releasing stored emotional patterns that have settled in the joints.
- Restoring physical mobility and reducing discomfort.
- Strengthening the connection between the emotional, physical, and spiritual layers of the body.

Why Joint Work Complements a Full-Body Reiki Session

1. Joints represent transitions and the ability to adapt to life's changes — physically and emotionally.
2. Joints are directly linked to specific chakras and meridians — when blocked, they disrupt the entire energy flow of the body.
3. Physical tension in the joints reflects underlying emotional resistance — Reiki helps dissolve both the physical and emotional layers simultaneously.
4. Addressing joints strengthens the foundation of Reiki practice by enhancing the flow of energy through the body's energetic channels.

How to Integrate Joint Work Into a Reiki Session

Joint work can be incorporated at three key points in a standard Reiki session:

Just for today, I will let go of worry and trust the flow of life.

1. Opening Phase – Prepare the client by increasing the flow of ki through the joints.
2. Direct Joint Work – Target specific joints while working on the corresponding chakras and meridians.
3. Closing Phase – Seal the energy and integrate the healing into the whole body.

Step-by-Step Guide to Incorporating Joint Work into a Reiki Session

1. Opening Phase: Grounding and Preparing the Energy Field (5–10 minutes)

The opening phase sets the energetic foundation for the session and increases receptivity to joint healing.

Grounding Exercise:

- Begin by placing your hands on the client's feet or knees.
- Channel Reiki energy through the Root Chakra to establish grounding and stability.
- Draw the Cho Ku Rei symbol over the feet to increase the energy flow through the legs and lower body.

Open the Energy Field:

- Move your hands to the crown of the head.
- Visualize white light flowing through the client's body, preparing the energy system for deeper healing.

- Draw the Cho Ku Rei symbol over the body to open the energy channels.

Body Scan to Identify Blockages:

- Slowly scan the client's body from head to feet with your hands.
- Pay attention to areas of tension, coldness, or heaviness around the joints.
- Mentally note which joints need the most attention during the session.

2. Direct Joint Work: Working with Specific Joints (30–40 minutes)

Direct joint work follows the natural energy flow of the body, beginning at the head and working toward the feet. Focus on the joints where you detected energy stagnation or tension during the body scan.

A. Shoulders – Carrying Burdens and Emotional Responsibility (Heart and Throat Chakras)

- Place one hand on the front of the shoulder and one on the back.
- Channel Reiki into the joint.
- Draw the Cho Ku Rei symbol to strengthen the energy flow.
- If the client expresses emotional tension, use the Sei He Ki symbol to promote emotional release.
- Hold the position until you feel the energy shift (approximately 3–5 minutes).

Just for today, I will let go of worry and trust the flow of life.

Example:

- If the shoulders feel heavy or tense, the client may be carrying emotional burdens.
- Use affirmations like: *"I release all burdens that do not belong to me."*

B. Elbows – Flexibility in Giving and Receiving (Solar Plexus and Heart Chakras)

- Place one hand above the elbow and one hand below the elbow.
- Channel Reiki into the joint using the Cho Ku Rei symbol.
- If the elbow feels tight or resistant, use the Sei He Ki symbol to dissolve emotional resistance.
- Hold for 3–5 minutes or until the energy begins to flow freely.

Example:

- Elbow tension often reflects difficulty in receiving support or asking for help.
- Encourage the client to reflect on where they are resisting emotional support.

C. Wrists – Trust and Communication (Throat Chakra)

- Place one hand on the palm and one on the back of the hand.
- Channel Reiki using the Cho Ku Rei symbol to strengthen the connection between the hands and the throat.

- If trust or communication issues arise, use the Sei He Ki symbol.
- Encourage the client to breathe deeply while the energy is flowing.

Example:

- Wrist tightness may reflect suppressed communication or fear of expressing oneself.
- Use affirmations like: *"I trust myself to express my truth."*

D. Hips – Emotional Flow and Creative Expression (Sacral Chakra)

- Place one hand on the front of the hip and one hand on the back.
- Draw the Cho Ku Rei symbol to increase the flow of energy through the hip joint.
- If emotional tension arises, use the Sei He Ki symbol.
- Visualize the hip softening and expanding.

Example:

- Hip tightness may reflect fear of emotional vulnerability or creative expression.
- Use affirmations like: *"I release all fear surrounding emotional connection."*

Just for today, I will let go of worry and trust the flow of life.

E. Knees – Trust and Stability (Root Chakra)

- Place one hand above the knee and one hand below the knee.
- Channel Reiki into the joint using the Cho Ku Rei symbol.
- If emotional tension or resistance is present, use the Sei He Ki symbol.
- Encourage the client to visualize strength and support flowing through the knee.

Example:

- Knee pain may reflect fear of moving forward or lack of trust in life.
- Use affirmations like: *"I trust life's unfolding process."*

F. Ankles – Grounding and Balance (Root Chakra)

- Place one hand above the ankle and one hand below the ankle.
- Channel Reiki using the Cho Ku Rei symbol to increase grounding.
- If instability or fear is present, use the Sei He Ki symbol.
- Hold until the energy begins to flow freely.

Example:

- Ankle weakness may reflect emotional instability or lack of direction.

- Use affirmations like: *"I am grounded and supported."*

G. Fingers and Toes – Precision and Action (Throat and Root Chakras)

- Place your hands over the fingers or toes.
- Use the Cho Ku Rei symbol to strengthen the flow of energy.
- Encourage the client to visualize energy flowing into the fingers and toes.

Example:

- Tension in the fingers may reflect hesitation in taking action.
- Use affirmations like: *"I trust myself to take the next step."*

3. Closing Phase: Sealing the Energy and Grounding (5–10 minutes)

Balance the Chakras:

- Perform a full chakra balancing from root to crown.
- Draw the Cho Ku Rei symbol over each chakra.

Seal the Energy Field:

- Draw the Cho Ku Rei symbol over the entire body.
- Visualize a protective white or gold light surrounding the client.

Just for today, I will let go of worry and trust the flow of life.

Ground the Client:

- Place your hands on the client's feet.
- Encourage deep breaths and visualization of roots extending into the earth.
- End the session with a brief period of silence.

Post-Session Recommendations:

- Encourage the client to drink water and rest after the session.
- Explain that emotional release may continue for 24–48 hours.
- Suggest self-Reiki techniques for the affected joints.

Key Takeaways:

- Joint work enhances the overall flow of Reiki energy.
- Joints reflect both physical and emotional patterns.
- Combining direct hand placement with chakra work increases effectiveness.
- Balancing the chakras after joint work ensures whole-body harmony.
- Sealing the energy field protects the healing process.

By incorporating joint work into a standard Reiki session, you create deeper emotional, physical, and spiritual alignment for the client.

Teaching Clients About the Emotional and Spiritual Aspects of Joint Health

Educating clients about the emotional and spiritual significance of joint health is a powerful way to deepen their understanding of the mind-body connection and empower them to take an active role in their healing. Reiki practitioners know that physical discomfort, especially in the joints, is rarely just a structural issue — it reflects deeper emotional and spiritual imbalances.

Clients often seek Reiki for physical pain or discomfort, unaware that joint issues are frequently tied to emotional resistance, unresolved trauma, or life patterns. By helping clients understand the deeper meaning behind joint health, you open the door for emotional release, spiritual growth, and lasting physical healing.

Teaching clients about the energetic and emotional connection to joint health gives them the tools to:

- Develop emotional awareness of how life patterns affect the body.
- Recognize and release emotional resistance stored in the joints.
- Align physical movement with emotional flexibility and spiritual growth.
- Take an active role in maintaining joint health through emotional and spiritual balance.

Just for today, I will let go of worry and trust the flow of life.

- View discomfort as a signal for deeper emotional or spiritual work rather than simply a physical problem.

Why Clients Need to Understand the Emotional and Spiritual Side of Joint Health

1. Joints Reflect Flexibility and Adaptability

- Joints allow movement — both physically and emotionally.
- When joints are stiff, painful, or unstable, it often reflects an emotional unwillingness to adapt to change.
- Emotional flexibility is directly linked to physical flexibility — rigid emotional patterns lead to stiff joints.

2. Emotional Patterns Are Stored in the Joints

- Emotions that are not fully processed or released become energetically stored in the body's connective tissues and joints.
- The body remembers emotional trauma, even if the mind has consciously forgotten it.
- Stored emotional patterns create chronic tension and energetic blockages, reducing the body's natural ability to heal.

3. Joint Pain Often Reflects Emotional Resistance

- Physical joint pain signals that an emotional or spiritual lesson is trying to surface.

- Resistance to change, fear of vulnerability, or emotional suppression often shows up as tension or inflammation in the joints.
- By working through the emotional pattern, the physical pain often resolves naturally.

4. Joints Are Gateways for Spiritual Growth

- The joints act as energetic crossroads where multiple meridians and chakras meet.
- When energy flows freely through the joints, the body becomes a more open channel for spiritual alignment and intuitive guidance.
- Releasing tension from the joints increases the flow of life force energy (ki) through the entire energetic field.

How to Educate Clients About the Emotional and Spiritual Connection to Joints

Teaching clients about the mind-body connection requires a gentle and supportive approach. Clients may initially be unaware of the emotional patterns stored in their body or resistant to exploring deeper emotional issues. The key is to build trust and present the information in a way that makes them feel empowered, not judged.

1. Start by Acknowledging Their Physical Discomfort

- Begin by addressing the physical symptoms — clients often seek Reiki for physical relief first.

Just for today, I will let go of worry and trust the flow of life.

- Validate their experience without immediately introducing the emotional connection.
- Establish trust by focusing on physical relaxation and immediate pain relief through Reiki.

Example:
"I can feel some tension in your knee. Let's work on opening up the energy flow there and see how it feels afterward."

2. Introduce the Emotional and Spiritual Connection Gradually

- Once the client feels relaxed and comfortable, introduce the idea that physical discomfort often reflects emotional or spiritual patterns.
- Explain that Reiki works on multiple levels — physical, emotional, and spiritual — which is why the healing often extends beyond the physical body.

Example:
"It's interesting that you're feeling tension in your shoulders — that's often connected to emotional burdens and feeling over-responsible for others."

3. Explain How Joints Reflect Emotional Patterns

Once the client is receptive, explain the specific emotional patterns connected to each joint.

- Keep the language simple and relatable.
- Encourage the client to reflect on their life experiences without pressure.

- Offer examples or metaphors to make the connection clearer.

Example:
"Your knee discomfort may be reflecting a fear of moving forward in life. The knees are closely connected to trust and grounding — when we feel uncertain about the future, it often shows up as stiffness or weakness in the knees."

4. Encourage Reflection Without Judgment

Clients may feel vulnerable when emotional patterns surface. Encourage them to observe these patterns without judgment or resistance.

- Frame emotional patterns as part of the body's natural communication system.
- Reassure the client that becoming aware of these patterns is the first step toward healing.

Example:
"If you notice any emotions coming up during the session, just allow them to surface without trying to stop them. Your body is telling you what it needs to release."

5. Offer Simple Emotional and Spiritual Practices

Once the client understands the emotional link to their joint issues, offer simple tools they can use to maintain emotional flexibility and spiritual balance.

- Self-Reiki techniques for the joints.
- Breathwork and visualization.

Just for today, I will let go of worry and trust the flow of life.

- Affirmations that address emotional resistance.
- Journaling exercises to explore deeper emotional patterns.

Example:
"If you feel tension in your shoulders between sessions, try placing your hands over your heart and channeling Reiki energy there. Breathe deeply and silently repeat, 'I release what I no longer need.'"

Emotional and Spiritual Meaning of Specific Joints

Use the following chart to educate clients about the emotional and spiritual meaning behind specific joint issues:

Joint	Chakra	Emotional/Spiritual Meaning	Suggested Affirmation
Shoulders	Heart, Throat	Carrying burdens, emotional responsibility, fear of vulnerability	*"I release what is not mine to carry."*
Elbows	Solar Plexus, Heart	Flexibility in giving and receiving	*"I give and receive with ease and trust."*
Wrists	Throat	Trust, communication, self-expression	*"It is safe to express my truth."*

Joint	Chakra	Emotional/Spiritual Meaning	Suggested Affirmation
Hips	Sacral	Emotional flow, creativity, intimacy	*"I move through life with ease and confidence."*
Knees	Root	Trust, stability, moving forward	*"I trust the path unfolding before me."*
Ankles	Root, Sacral	Grounding, balance, direction	*"I am balanced and grounded in my path."*
Fingers and Toes	Throat, Root	Precision, action, decision-making	*"I take confident action with ease."*

Encourage Clients to Keep a Healing Journal

- Encourage the client to keep a journal of physical and emotional shifts.
- Suggest they track patterns between emotional experiences and physical joint issues.
- Reflect on progress during follow-up sessions.

Just for today, I will let go of worry and trust the flow of life.

Example:
"You might want to write down any emotions that arise over the next few days. Often, the body continues processing after a Reiki session."

Empower the Client to Trust Their Own Healing Process

- Encourage the client to listen to their body and trust their intuition.
- Reinforce that healing is a process — emotional patterns may take time to shift.
- Let the client know that they are in control of their healing.

Example:
"Your body is incredibly wise. Trust that it knows how to heal — you just need to give it the time and space to realign."

Key Takeaways:

- Physical discomfort in the joints reflects emotional and spiritual patterns.
- Teaching clients the emotional meaning of joint issues empowers them to take an active role in their healing.
- Simple tools like affirmations, breathwork, and self-Reiki support emotional flexibility and strength.
- Healing is a process — awareness of emotional patterns is the first step toward resolution.

- By addressing the emotional and spiritual roots of joint issues, Reiki promotes deeper and more lasting healing.

By educating clients about the emotional and spiritual connection to joint health, you empower them to create deeper and more sustainable healing at every level — physical, emotional, and spiritual.

Building Confidence as a Reiki Practitioner Specializing in Joint Healing

Specializing in joint healing as a Reiki practitioner requires not only technical skill and intuitive awareness but also confidence in your ability to guide clients through physical, emotional, and spiritual transformation. Working with joints involves addressing complex patterns of physical discomfort, emotional resistance, and energetic imbalance — which can initially feel overwhelming or intimidating.

However, confidence as a Reiki practitioner does not come from perfection — it comes from consistent practice, developing deep trust in the Reiki energy, and learning how to hold a safe, supportive space for clients. When you approach joint healing with both skill and confidence, your energy becomes a stabilizing force that enhances the client's healing process.

Confidence in joint healing also allows you to handle difficult cases, guide clients through emotional release, and trust your intuitive responses. The more you deepen your knowledge and refine your technique, the more naturally your confidence will grow — and the more your clients will trust you to facilitate healing at the deepest levels.

Why Confidence Matters in Joint Healing

Confidence is not only about believing in your skills — it's about creating a healing environment where the client feels safe and supported.

- Clients sense the practitioner's confidence — when you are grounded and sure of your abilities, the client feels relaxed and safe, which deepens the healing process.
- Confidence allows you to respond intuitively to the client's energy, even when unexpected emotions or sensations arise during a session.
- When you trust yourself, you give the client permission to trust their own body and healing process.
- Confidence strengthens your ability to establish professional authority — clients are more likely to follow your guidance and return for additional sessions.

Challenges That Can Undermine Confidence

1. Doubting Your Intuitive Responses

- Reiki relies heavily on intuition. If you question your instincts, it can disrupt the flow of energy and reduce your ability to guide the session effectively.
- Confidence grows when you learn to trust the information you receive through sensations, images, or emotional responses.

Just for today, I will let go of worry and trust the flow of life.

2. Overthinking Technique vs. Flow

- While it's important to master hand positions and techniques, focusing too much on "getting it right" can block the natural flow of Reiki energy.
- Confidence comes from balancing technical skill with intuitive flow.

3. Fear of Emotional Release

- Emotional release during joint work can be intense — tears, shaking, or even anger may surface.
- Confidence allows you to hold a stable, grounded space without becoming reactive or anxious.

4. Uncertainty About What to Say

- When clients ask questions about the emotional or spiritual meaning behind their joint issues, uncertainty can undermine your authority.
- Building knowledge about the connection between joint health and emotional patterns increases your ability to respond confidently.

How to Build Confidence as a Reiki Practitioner Specializing in Joint Healing

Confidence develops through a combination of technical mastery, intuitive trust, self-awareness, and client experience. The more you integrate these elements, the stronger your presence becomes — and the more effective your healing work will be.

1. Master the Physical and Energetic Anatomy of Joints

To feel confident working with joints, you need to understand both the physical structure and the energetic function of each joint.

Study the Physical Anatomy of Joints

- Learn the structure and function of key joints (shoulders, elbows, wrists, hips, knees, ankles).
- Understand how muscles, ligaments, and tendons support joint movement.
- Study common joint issues (e.g., arthritis, inflammation, hypermobility).

Example:

- If a client mentions shoulder tension, you'll feel confident knowing that the rotator cuff and deltoid muscle are involved.

Learn the Energetic Role of Joints

- Study the relationship between joints and chakras.
- Understand how meridians flow through the joints and how blockages create tension.
- Master the emotional and spiritual patterns connected to each joint.

Just for today, I will let go of worry and trust the flow of life.

Example:

- Knee pain often reflects Root Chakra imbalances — fear of instability or lack of trust in life's path.
- Hip tension reflects Sacral Chakra issues — fear of emotional vulnerability or creative expression.

2. Develop a Strong Personal Reiki Practice

You cannot hold space for another person's healing if you feel unbalanced yourself. A consistent Reiki practice strengthens your ability to channel energy confidently and hold stable energy during emotionally charged sessions.

Daily Self-Treatment for Grounding and Alignment

- Begin each day with self-Reiki, focusing on your own joints.
- If you feel emotional resistance or tension in your body, use the Sei He Ki symbol to dissolve it.
- Visualize yourself as an open, grounded channel for Reiki energy.

Example:

- Treat your own shoulders and hips before a client session to increase your energetic stability and confidence.

Practice Receiving Reiki from Others

- Experience Reiki from another practitioner to deepen your understanding of how energy feels from the receiving side.
- Notice how emotional and physical shifts occur when the practitioner works on your joints.

Example:

- If you experience emotional release during hip work, you'll have more empathy and insight when guiding a client through a similar experience.

3. Develop Intuitive Confidence

Intuition is one of the most powerful tools in Reiki practice — and one of the hardest to trust at first. Confidence grows when you practice responding to intuitive information without hesitation.

How to Strengthen Intuitive Confidence:

- Close your eyes and place your hands on the client's body.
- Pay attention to any sensations (heat, coolness, tingling).
- Trust the information you receive — even if it doesn't make logical sense.
- If you sense emotional resistance, hold the position longer.
- If an image or message arises, trust that it's part of the healing process.

☑ *Example:*

Just for today, I will let go of worry and trust the flow of life.

- If you sense emotional tension in the knees and the client hasn't mentioned knee pain, trust your instinct and work on the area anyway — the emotional root may surface after the session.

4. Gain Experience Through Case Studies and Feedback

Confidence comes with experience — the more you work with joints, the more patterns and insights will emerge.

Track Case Studies:

- Keep records of the techniques you used and the client's response.
- Track patterns between emotional release and physical relief.
- Reflect on what worked and what could be adjusted.

Example:

- After noticing that hip pain is consistently tied to creative stagnation, you'll feel more confident recognizing and explaining that connection to future clients.

Ask for Client Feedback

- After the session, ask the client how they feel physically and emotionally.
- If a technique worked well, reinforce it in future sessions.

398 DR. CONSTANCE SANTEGO

- If the client didn't notice much change, adjust the approach in the next session.

Example:

- If a client reports increased mobility after spiral motion on the hips, you'll feel more confident using that technique in future sessions.

5. Learn How to Handle Emotional Release

Confidence grows when you know how to respond calmly and effectively to emotional release during a session.

How to Respond to Emotional Release:

- If the client cries or becomes emotional, hold space without judgment.
- Keep your hands steady and continue channeling Reiki.
- If you feel overwhelmed, draw the Cho Ku Rei symbol over your own hands and energy field.
- Reassure the client that emotional release is part of the healing process.

Example:

- If a client experiences deep emotional release in the hips, you might say:
  "It's completely natural to feel emotional release during Reiki — this is a sign that your body is letting go of stored patterns."

Just for today, I will let go of worry and trust the flow of life.

6. Trust the Reiki Energy

Reiki energy is intelligent — you are not "doing" the healing, you are simply facilitating the flow of energy.

- Trust that Reiki knows where to go.
- If you feel uncertain, remind yourself that Reiki energy will find the imbalance and correct it naturally.
- Your role is to remain present and grounded.

Example:

- If you sense resistance in the client's shoulder but don't know why, trust that Reiki will work through it in its own time.

Key Takeaways:

- Master both physical and energetic anatomy.
- Build confidence through case studies and client feedback.
- Trust your intuition and respond calmly to emotional release.
- Keep a consistent personal Reiki practice.
- Trust Reiki's intelligence — you are a facilitator, not the source of healing.

By developing confidence as a Reiki practitioner specializing in joint healing, you become a powerful, grounded channel for transformation — helping clients achieve physical, emotional, and spiritual alignment.

Guided Meditation for Joint Healing

Restoring Flow and Flexibility in the Body

Before you begin, find a quiet, comfortable place where you will not be disturbed. You can sit upright or lie down — whichever position allows you to feel relaxed and supported. If you are sitting, place your feet flat on the floor and let your hands rest gently on your thighs or by your sides.

Take a deep breath in... and slowly exhale.
Take another breath in, feeling the air fill your chest and belly... and release it slowly through your mouth.
With each breath, allow your body to soften and relax.

Now, soften your gaze and allow your awareness to turn inward.

Bring your awareness to your body. Notice any areas of tension or discomfort without judgment — simply observe. Let your breath move through your body, softening and opening any areas that feel tight or restricted.

Just for today, I will let go of worry and trust the flow of life.

Now, place your hands on your knees (or any joint you feel drawn to work on).
Feel the warmth of your hands as Reiki energy begins to flow.

Visualize a soft golden light radiating from your palms, flowing into the joint.
The light is warm and soothing, gently dissolving any tension or stagnation.

As the golden light surrounds the joint, imagine it moving deeper into the tissues, reaching the energetic pathways beneath the surface.

Feel the energy flowing through the joint, clearing away blockages and restoring ease of movement.
With each inhale, you draw in healing energy — with each exhale, you release any tension or resistance.

Notice any sensations that arise — tingling, warmth, heaviness, or lightness.

If you sense emotional resistance or discomfort, simply breathe into it. Allow the energy to soften it without force.

Say silently to yourself:
"I release what no longer serves me. My body moves with ease and grace."

Now, gently shift your focus to the surrounding muscles and ligaments.

Imagine the golden light expanding outward, filling the entire area with warmth and relaxation.

Feel the joint becoming lighter, more fluid, and aligned. Let the breath carry this healing energy through your entire body.

Sit with this sensation for a few more breaths.
Feel the ease and openness within your body.
When you are ready, take a deep breath in... and slowly exhale.

Gently wiggle your fingers and toes, bringing awareness back to your physical body.
When you feel ready, open your eyes.

Take a moment to reflect on how you feel.
Your body is aligned, your energy is flowing, and you are supported.

Repeat this meditation whenever you feel tension or discomfort in your joints — the body knows how to heal when you allow energy to flow.

"I trust the wisdom of my body. My joints are open, strong, and free."

Just for today, I will let go of worry and trust the flow of life.

Specific Joint-Focused Meditations

Targeted Reiki Healing for Individual Joints

The following meditations are designed to target specific joints in the body, helping you to release physical and emotional blockages while restoring balance and flow. Each joint reflects a unique emotional and energetic pattern. By directing Reiki energy to these areas, you not only enhance physical movement and comfort but also resolve deeper emotional and spiritual imbalances.

These meditations combine Reiki hand positions, breathwork, and visualization to create a complete healing experience. As you work through them, pay attention to the sensations that arise — physical warmth or tingling, emotional release, or mental clarity — and allow the energy to move naturally through your body.

1. Healing the Shoulders

Releasing Emotional Burdens and Responsibility

Position: Sit comfortably or lie down. Rest your hands on each shoulder or hover them slightly above.

Intention: Set the intention to release emotional weight and tension stored in the shoulders.

Guidance:
Take a deep breath in... and exhale slowly.
Feel the warmth of your hands as Reiki energy begins to flow into your shoulders.
Imagine a soft golden light radiating from your hands, gently warming the muscles and the joint beneath.
As the light surrounds the joint, feel it dissolving any heaviness or resistance.

Reflect:

- Are you carrying emotional weight that doesn't belong to you?
- Are you holding on to responsibility that needs to be shared or released?
- Are you resisting support from others?

With each exhale, release that weight.
Visualize the light carrying it away, leaving your shoulders open and light.

Just for today, I will let go of worry and trust the flow of life.

"I release the weight of responsibility. I am supported and free."

Stay with this feeling for a few more breaths, then bring your awareness back to the present moment.

2. Healing the Elbows

Flexibility in Giving and Receiving

Position: Sit comfortably with your hands resting on your elbows or hold one elbow at a time.

Intention: Set the intention to restore balance in the flow of giving and receiving.

Guidance:
Breathe in deeply... and exhale fully.
Imagine golden light flowing from your hands into your elbows, softening any tension.
Feel the light filling the joint, encouraging greater flexibility and movement.

Reflect:

- Do you find it easier to give than to receive?
- Are you resisting support or generosity from others?
- Do you struggle with emotional boundaries?

With each exhale, allow any resistance to soften and dissolve.
Feel your elbows becoming more fluid and open.
Visualize the energy flowing freely through your arms.

"I give and receive with ease and grace."

Take a few more breaths, then slowly release your hands.

Just for today, I will let go of worry and trust the flow of life.

3. Healing the Wrists

Trust and Communication

Position: Rest your hands on your wrists or gently hold them between your palms.

Intention: Set the intention to restore trust and open the flow of communication.

Guidance:
Breathe in deeply... and release any tension as you exhale.
Feel Reiki energy flowing through your hands into your wrists.
Visualize golden light wrapping around the joint, softening and strengthening it.

Reflect:

- Do you feel secure expressing yourself?
- Are you holding back communication or creativity?
- Are you struggling to trust the natural flow of life?

With each breath, release hesitation and resistance.
Feel the energy opening the pathway of communication and flow.

"I trust my voice. I express myself with ease and confidence."

Take a few more breaths, feeling the flow of energy through your hands and wrists.

4. Healing the Hips

Emotional Movement and Creative Energy

Position: Place your hands on your hips, palms resting gently on each side.

Intention: Set the intention to release emotional blocks and encourage creative flow.

Guidance:
Breathe deeply... and release any tension with each exhale.
Feel Reiki energy radiating from your hands, flowing into your hips.
Visualize the hips opening, releasing any heaviness or emotional resistance.

Reflect:

- Are you resisting change or movement in your life?
- Are you feeling creatively blocked?
- Do you fear vulnerability or emotional openness?

With each breath, allow emotional weight to dissolve.
Feel the hips becoming more open and fluid.
Sense the golden light flowing down through your legs, grounding you.

"I move through life with grace and creativity."

Take a few more breaths, then slowly release your hands.

Just for today, I will let go of worry and trust the flow of life.

5. Healing the Knees

Humility, Adaptability, and Trust in Life's Path

Position: Rest your hands on each knee or hold them gently.

Intention: Set the intention to release fear and strengthen your trust in life's path.

Guidance:
Inhale deeply... and exhale slowly.
Feel Reiki energy flowing through your knees, soothing the joint.
Visualize golden light filling the area, strengthening and stabilizing it.

Reflect:

- Are you feeling stuck or hesitant about moving forward?
- Are you resisting change or holding on to control?
- Are you struggling to trust the unfolding of life?

With each exhale, release fear and hesitation.
Feel the knees becoming stronger and more stable.
Trust that you are supported on your path.

"I trust life's path. I move forward with strength and grace."

Take a few more breaths, then gently release your hands.

6. Healing the Ankles

Balance, Grounding, and Stability

Position: Rest your hands gently on each ankle or hover above them.

Intention: Set the intention to restore balance and stability.

Guidance:
Breathe in deeply... and exhale fully.
Feel Reiki energy flowing from your hands into your ankles.
Visualize golden light wrapping around the joints, strengthening and balancing them as it gently dissolves any tension or resistance, allowing the energy to flow smoothly and restoring a sense of ease and stability.

Reflect:

- Are you feeling ungrounded or unstable?
- Are you struggling to find your footing in life?
- Are you hesitating to take the next step forward?

With each breath, allow any sense of instability or hesitation to soften.
Imagine the golden light flowing down through your legs, into your ankles, and continuing into the ground beneath you.
See the light forming roots beneath your feet, connecting you to the earth's stabilizing energy.

Just for today, I will let go of worry and trust the flow of life.

Feel the energy strengthening your ankles, providing a sense of confidence and steadiness.

Now, visualize yourself walking forward with ease and confidence.
With each step, feel the support of the earth beneath you.
You are balanced, grounded, and supported by the flow of life.

"I am grounded and balanced. I walk through life with confidence and strength."

Stay with this feeling for a few more breaths.
When you are ready, slowly bring your awareness back to the present moment.
Wiggle your toes, feeling the strength and stability in your body.
Gently release your hands and rest for a moment, absorbing the energy of the practice.

7. Healing the Fingers and Toes

Precision and Action

Position: Hold each finger or toe gently between your hands or place your hands over them.

Intention: Set the intention to enhance precision, focus, and action in your life.

Guidance:
Take a deep breath in... and exhale slowly.
Feel Reiki energy flowing from your hands into your fingers and toes.
Visualize a soft, golden light flowing into each joint — brightening and aligning the energy pathways.
Feel the warmth spreading through the smaller bones and muscles, enhancing flexibility and ease of movement.

Reflect:

- Are you struggling with indecision or hesitation?
- Are you finding it difficult to take action or complete a task?
- Are you feeling scattered or lacking focus?

With each breath, allow any mental clutter or hesitation to soften and dissolve.
Visualize the golden light sharpening your focus and strengthening your intention.
See the light moving through each finger and toe,

Just for today, I will let go of worry and trust the flow of life.

activating the energy of precision and action.
Feel your mind becoming clear and focused.

"I act with precision and confidence. My thoughts and actions are aligned."

Let the energy settle for a few moments.
When you are ready, take a deep breath in... and exhale fully.
Gently move your fingers and toes, feeling the increased sense of clarity and control.
Release your hands and sit quietly for a moment, noticing how your body feels.

8. Healing the Jaw

Expression and Release

Position: Place your hands gently on either side of your jaw or hover your hands a few inches away.

Intention: Set the intention to release tension and open the flow of self-expression.

Guidance:
Breathe in deeply... and exhale slowly.
Feel Reiki energy flowing from your hands into your jaw.
Visualize a soft blue light (the color of the throat chakra) surrounding your jaw, releasing any tightness or tension.

Reflect:

- Are you holding back from expressing your truth?
- Are you clenching your jaw due to stress or suppressed emotion?
- Are you finding it difficult to speak openly and confidently?

With each breath, allow any tightness in the jaw to soften. Visualize the blue light expanding through your throat and jaw, dissolving any resistance or discomfort.
Feel your jaw relaxing and your throat opening — creating space for honest, open communication.
Allow the Reiki energy to fill your throat and mouth, clearing the pathway for self-expression.

Just for today, I will let go of worry and trust the flow of life.

"I express myself with clarity and ease. My truth flows freely and confidently."

Take a few more breaths.
When you are ready, gently release your hands and rest for a moment.
Notice the feeling of openness and ease in your jaw and throat.

9. Healing the Neck

Releasing Stress and Aligning Communication

Position: Place your hands on the sides of your neck or hover them slightly above the area.

Intention: Set the intention to release stress and restore alignment in communication and self-expression.

Guidance:
Breathe deeply... and release tension with each exhale.
Feel Reiki energy flowing from your hands into your neck.
Visualize a soft, flowing blue light moving up and down your neck, clearing any congestion or tightness.

Reflect:

- Are you feeling burdened by unspoken thoughts or emotions?
- Are you struggling to communicate clearly or authentically?
- Are you holding onto tension related to self-expression or fear of being heard?

With each breath, feel the blue light dissolving the tension and opening the energetic pathways through your neck and throat.
Imagine your neck becoming more flexible and aligned.
Feel the energy expanding upward into your throat and downward into your shoulders, creating a clear, open connection.

Just for today, I will let go of worry and trust the flow of life.

"I communicate with ease and confidence. My mind and body are in alignment."

Let the Reiki energy continue to flow through your neck for a few more breaths.
When you feel ready, gently release your hands and return to the present moment.

10. Healing the Lower Back

Support, Safety, and Strength

Position: Place your hands on your lower back or hover them over the area.

Intention: Set the intention to restore a sense of support and inner strength.

Guidance:
Inhale deeply... and exhale fully.
Feel Reiki energy flowing from your hands into your lower back.
Visualize a deep red light (the color of the root chakra) surrounding your lower back, filling it with warmth and strength.

Reflect:

- Are you feeling unsupported or insecure in your life?
- Are you holding onto fear about stability or survival?
- Are you struggling to feel grounded or connected to the earth?

With each breath, feel the red light strengthening the foundation of your body and energy field.
Imagine your spine becoming aligned and stable.
Feel the energy flowing down through your hips, legs, and feet — anchoring you to the earth.

Just for today, I will let go of worry and trust the flow of life.

Allow any sense of fear or insecurity to dissolve as the light expands through your entire lower body.

"I am supported and safe. I trust the foundation of my life."

Stay with this feeling for a few more breaths.
When you are ready, gently release your hands and bring your awareness back to the room.
Feel the sense of strength and grounding in your body.

11. Healing the Pelvis

Creativity, Emotional Flow, and Stability

Position: Rest your hands on your pelvis or hover them over the area.

Intention: Set the intention to restore creative flow and emotional balance.

Guidance:
Take a deep breath in... and release any tension with each exhale.
Feel Reiki energy flowing from your hands into your pelvis.
Visualize a soft orange light (the color of the sacral chakra) radiating through the area.

Reflect:

- Are you feeling creatively blocked or emotionally stagnant?
- Are you struggling with intimacy or vulnerability?
- Are you resisting emotional or physical movement?

With each breath, allow the orange light to dissolve any emotional resistance or creative blockage.
Feel the pelvis becoming more open and aligned.
Imagine the energy flowing freely through your hips and lower abdomen, restoring ease and flow.

"I embrace creative flow. I trust the rhythm of life."

Just for today, I will let go of worry and trust the flow of life.

Sit with this sensation for a few more breaths.
When you are ready, gently release your hands and return to the present moment.
Feel the openness and creative energy flowing through your body.

Closing Reflection

By working with individual joints, you are addressing not only physical tension but also emotional and energetic patterns stored deep within the body.

- Return to these meditations whenever you sense physical discomfort, emotional resistance, or mental fog.
- The more you work with Reiki and the joints, the deeper the connection you will develop between your body and energy system.

Healing begins at the energetic level — and joints are the keys to unlocking that flow.

Quick Reference Guide

Joint-Focused Reiki Techniques and Emotional Patterns

This quick reference guide provides a condensed overview of common joint issues, their associated emotional patterns, and the recommended Reiki symbols and techniques for each joint. Use this section as a tool during Reiki sessions to quickly identify patterns and select the most effective hand placements and techniques for healing.

Common Joint Issues and Recommended Reiki Techniques

Joint	Emotional Pattern	Reiki Symbol	Technique	Hand Placement
Shoulder	Feeling burdened, carrying responsibility	Sei He Ki	Gentle pressure and breathwork	Place hands on top of shoulders or hover above
Elbow	Resistance to giving and receiving	Cho Ku Rei	Circular motion	Place one hand on the inner elbow and the

Just for today, I will let go of worry and trust the flow of life.

Joint	Emotional Pattern	Reiki Symbol	Technique	Hand Placement
			around the joint	other on the outer elbow
Wrist	Difficulty trusting or expressing oneself	Sei He Ki	Hold joint with gentle pressure and use breathwork	Place both hands around the wrist
Hip	Emotional resistance, blocked creative energy	Hon Sha Ze Sho Nen	Visualization of flowing light	Rest hands on the hip or hover over the area
Knee	Fear of moving forward, insecurity	Cho Ku Rei	Circular motion and grounding visualization	Place hands on each side of the knee
Ankle	Lack of stability, ungrounded feelings	Cho Ku Rei	Gentle compression and downward flow	Wrap hands around the ankle

Joint	Emotional Pattern	Reiki Symbol	Technique	Hand Placement
			visualization	
Fingers and Toes	Lack of precision or indecision	Cho Ku Rei	Hold each finger/toe individually	Hold each finger or toe between thumb and forefinger
Jaw	Suppressed emotion, difficulty speaking truth	Sei He Ki	Gentle touch and breathwork	Place hands on both sides of the jaw
Neck	Difficulty in communication, stress	Sei He Ki	Gentle downward stroke and breathwork	Hands on each side of the neck
Lower Back	Lack of support, fear of survival	Dai Ko Myo	Grounding visualization and circular motion	Place hands on the lower back
Pelvis	Creative blockage,	Hon Sha	Visualization of	Rest hands on the pelvis

Just for today, I will let go of worry and trust the flow of life.

Joint	Emotional Pattern	Reiki Symbol	Technique	Hand Placement
	emotional stagnation	Ze Sho Nen	flowing orange light	or hover above
Shoulder Blade	Holding on to emotional pain or feeling unsupported	Sei He Ki	Gentle pressure and release technique	Hands directly on shoulder blades
Big Toe	Feeling stuck, lack of direction	Cho Ku Rei	Hold and rotate toe gently	Wrap fingers around big toe and apply slight pressure
Thumb	Issues with control or letting go	Cho Ku Rei	Gentle hold and breathwork	Hold thumb between thumb and forefinger
Knees and Hips (combined)	Lack of trust in life's path	Cho Ku Rei + Hon Sha Ze Sho Nen	Visualization and circular motion	Hands on knees and hips simultaneously

Joint	Emotional Pattern	Reiki Symbol	Technique	Hand Placement
Ankles and Feet (combined)	Difficulty finding footing in life	Cho Ku Rei	Grounding visualization	Hands on feet or around ankles
Wrists and Elbows (combined)	Tension in communication and action	Sei He Ki	Circular motion and breathwork	Hands on wrist and elbow simultaneously
Jaw and Neck (combined)	Suppressed truth or blocked communication	Sei He Ki	Gentle pressure and breathwork	Hands on jaw and sides of the neck

Best Reiki Symbols for Joint Healing

Symbol	Meaning	Application
Cho Ku Rei (Power Symbol)	"Place the power of the universe here"	Amplify Reiki energy, increase focus, and dissolve physical tension

Just for today, I will let go of worry and trust the flow of life.

Symbol	Meaning	Application
Sei He Ki (Mental/Emotional Symbol)	"God and man become one"	Release emotional resistance, balance mental patterns
Hon Sha Ze Sho Nen (Distance Symbol)	"No past, no present, no future"	Heal emotional patterns connected to past trauma or future anxiety
Dai Ko Myo (Master Symbol)	"The Great Shining Light"	Deep spiritual healing and energetic alignment

Techniques Overview

Technique	Purpose	How to Apply
Circular Motion	Releases stagnant energy and restores flow	Use fingers or palm to create a circular motion over the joint
Direct Pressure	Grounds and stabilizes the energy	Apply gentle pressure directly on or around the joint
Hovering	Directs energy flow without physical touch	Hold hands above the joint, allowing Reiki energy to flow naturally

Technique	Purpose	How to Apply
Breathwork	Enhances the flow of Reiki energy	Encourage deep, steady breathing while directing Reiki
Compression	Grounds and strengthens joint stability	Gently press hands around the joint while visualizing stability
Visualization	Enhances mental focus and energy flow	Imagine light or color flowing through the joint and clearing blockages
Release Technique	Dissolves emotional tension stored in joints	Hold the joint and gently lift or rotate while visualizing emotional release

Emotional Patterns and Joints

- Hips: Reflect emotional movement and creative flow.
- Knees: Represent trust and adaptability — fear of moving forward creates knee tension.
- Shoulders: Carry emotional weight and burdens.
- Elbows: Reflect the balance of giving and receiving.
- Wrists: Reflect trust in communication and flow.
- Ankles: Represent grounding and stability — tension here signals uncertainty or fear of change.

Just for today, I will let go of worry and trust the flow of life.

- Jaw: Reflects suppressed communication and emotional tension.
- Neck: Reflects alignment with truth and expression.
- Lower Back: Reflects support and security — tension signals fear or feeling unsupported.
- Pelvis: Reflects creative and emotional energy — stagnation signals creative blockage.
- Fingers and Toes: Reflect action and precision — hesitation or fear of completion shows up as tightness here.

How to Use This Guide

- Keep this guide accessible during Reiki sessions for quick reference.
- When sensing resistance or tension in a joint, consult the emotional pattern to help guide the session's focus.
- Use the suggested Reiki symbols and techniques to amplify healing and balance.
- Trust your intuition — if you feel drawn to a certain symbol or technique, follow that guidance.

"Healing begins at the joint level — restore flow, restore balance."

Conclusion – Healing from the Inside Out

Joint-focused Reiki is more than just a physical healing practice — it is a powerful tool for aligning the mind, body, and spirit. Joints serve as energetic gateways where emotional patterns, physical health, and spiritual balance intersect. By addressing these energetic crossroads through Reiki, you are not only restoring physical mobility and reducing discomfort — you are also guiding the client toward deeper emotional release and spiritual alignment.

Reiki practitioners often begin their journey focusing on general energy work, but joint healing reveals the profound connection between emotional patterns and physical health. When you work with the joints, you are unlocking stored energy and emotional resistance that have settled in the body over time. This creates space for both physical ease and emotional flexibility, allowing the client to move through life with greater freedom and grace.

Joint issues are rarely isolated physical problems — they reflect deeper imbalances in the body's energy system and emotional state. Through joint-focused Reiki, you are not only relieving discomfort but also helping clients confront and release emotional patterns that may have

Just for today, I will let go of worry and trust the flow of life.

been held in their body for years. This process allows the client to reconnect with their inner strength, deepen their trust in life, and experience greater emotional and physical balance.

How Joint-Focused Reiki Aligns Mind, Body, and Spirit

Healing at the level of the joints creates a ripple effect through the entire energy system.

1. Physical Alignment

- Restoring energy flow through the joints improves physical flexibility and mobility.
- Reducing inflammation and tension increases strength and stability.
- Balanced joints create greater comfort and ease in everyday movement.

2. Emotional Alignment

- Releasing stored emotional patterns in the joints creates greater emotional clarity and freedom.
- Emotional flexibility increases resilience and adaptability.
- Releasing emotional trauma reduces reactive patterns and emotional defensiveness.

3. Spiritual Alignment

- When the joints are open and balanced, energy flows freely through the chakras and meridians.

- The body becomes more receptive to intuitive guidance and spiritual connection.
- Clients feel a greater sense of purpose and inner harmony.

Encouraging Ongoing Practice and Self-Awareness

Healing is not a one-time event — it is a process of continual unfolding and self-discovery. Reiki creates the foundation for healing, but the client's ongoing commitment to self-awareness and emotional balance is essential for lasting results.

As a Reiki practitioner, part of your role is to empower the client to take responsibility for their healing process. Teaching clients to recognize emotional patterns, practice self-care, and maintain consistent energy balance strengthens their ability to sustain the benefits of Reiki between sessions.

1. Encourage Self-Reiki and Reflection

- Teach clients how to practice Reiki on their own joints between sessions.
- Encourage regular journaling to track emotional patterns and physical progress.
- Suggest grounding exercises and breathwork to maintain emotional balance.

Just for today, I will let go of worry and trust the flow of life.

2. Support Emotional and Spiritual Growth

- Encourage clients to reflect on life changes and emotional patterns that surface through joint healing.
- Guide clients toward affirmations and self-care practices that reinforce emotional flexibility.
- Remind clients that emotional release is part of the healing process — it is a sign that deep patterns are shifting.

3. Create a Healing Partnership

- Healing is not something you "do" to a client — it is a co-creative process.
- Encourage the client to view Reiki as a tool they can actively engage with.
- Offer guidance without taking on responsibility for the client's healing.

Empowering Clients to Take an Active Role in Their Healing Journey

True healing occurs when the client becomes an active participant in their own healing process. Reiki practitioners facilitate healing by opening the flow of energy — but it is the client's willingness to integrate that shift into their life that creates long-term change.

Teach the Client to Listen to Their Body

- Explain that joint discomfort is the body's way of communicating deeper emotional or spiritual patterns.
- Encourage clients to tune into these signals without judgment.
- Teach clients to use Reiki, breathwork, and grounding exercises to respond to these signals.

Encourage Emotional and Spiritual Empowerment

- Teach clients that they have the power to release emotional patterns and restore balance.
- Remind clients that healing is not linear — setbacks are part of the process.
- Celebrate small shifts and encourage the client to trust the unfolding process.

Help Clients Build Emotional Resilience

- Emotional and physical flexibility comes from learning how to adapt to life's challenges without resistance.
- Reiki increases the client's ability to remain centered and grounded, even during difficult life transitions.
- The ability to move through life's changes with confidence and ease is one of the greatest gifts of joint-focused Reiki.

Just for today, I will let go of worry and trust the flow of life.

Encouraging Lifelong Healing

Reiki is not just a healing modality — it is a spiritual path that unfolds over time. Joint-focused Reiki strengthens the client's connection to their inner guidance system and increases their ability to handle life's challenges with grace and confidence.

Reiki teaches that healing is not about removing all discomfort — it's about learning to work with the body's natural rhythms, emotions, and energy patterns. Through joint healing, clients discover that they are not powerless in the face of physical or emotional challenges — they have the tools to create balance and alignment from within.

Invite Clients to Stay Connected

- Recommend regular Reiki sessions for maintenance and ongoing alignment.
- Encourage clients to reach out when they feel stuck or emotionally blocked.
- Build long-term relationships with clients based on trust and mutual respect.

Key Takeaways:

- Joint-focused Reiki restores balance at the physical, emotional, and spiritual levels.
- Physical tension in the joints reflects emotional and energetic blockages.
- Releasing stored emotional patterns increases flexibility, both physically and emotionally.

- Teaching clients to engage with their own healing process empowers them to create lasting change.
- Healing is a process of alignment, release, and renewal — it requires patience and self-awareness.

Final Reflection

Joint-focused Reiki is not just about improving physical mobility — it is about restoring the client's ability to move through life with ease and confidence. When energy flows freely through the joints, the body becomes more flexible, the mind more resilient, and the spirit more aligned with life's natural rhythm.

As a Reiki practitioner specializing in joint healing, you have the unique opportunity to guide clients toward deeper physical, emotional, and spiritual integration. You are not simply addressing physical discomfort — you are helping clients reconnect with their inner wisdom, release emotional resistance, and rediscover the joy of moving through life with strength and grace.

When clients experience this level of alignment, they no longer see joint discomfort as a problem — they see it as a signpost guiding them toward deeper healing and self-awareness. That is the true power of joint-focused Reiki — helping clients heal not only from the outside in, but from the inside out.

Just for today, I will let go of worry and trust the flow of life.

Glossary

This glossary provides a quick reference for key terms, concepts, symbols, and techniques used in Reiki practice, including details from all three levels of Reiki (Shoden, Okuden, and Shinpiden). It serves as a comprehensive guide to help you deepen your understanding and apply Reiki principles effectively, particularly when working with joints and energy pathways.

A

Alignment – The balanced flow of energy through the chakras, meridians, and nadis. Proper alignment supports emotional, physical, and spiritual health.

Ajna Chakra – The Third Eye Chakra, located between the eyebrows. Governs intuition, perception, and insight.

Anahata Chakra – The Heart Chakra, located in the center of the chest. Governs love, compassion, and emotional balance.

Attunement – A sacred process in which a Reiki Master transfers the ability to channel Reiki energy to a student. Attunements are given during Reiki Level 1, 2, and 3 training.

Auric Field (Aura) – The energetic field surrounding the body. It consists of multiple layers connected to the chakras and reflects emotional, mental, physical, and spiritual health.

B

Balance – A state where energy flows freely through the body without blockage or resistance. Reiki helps restore balance at the physical, emotional, and spiritual levels.

Breathwork – Techniques that use conscious breathing to direct and enhance the flow of energy through the body.

C

Chakra – Spinning energy centers located along the central axis of the body. There are seven primary chakras and numerous secondary chakras located in the joints and extremities.

Cho Ku Rei – The Power Symbol. Used to increase the flow of Reiki energy, clear blockages, and activate protection.

- Meaning: "Place the power of the universe here."
- Application: Increases power, activates energy flow, and grounds the practitioner.

Cleansing – The process of releasing stagnant or blocked energy from the body or energetic field through Reiki or other energetic practices.

Just for today, I will let go of worry and trust the flow of life.

Conscious Intention – Focusing mental and spiritual energy on a specific outcome or goal during a Reiki session.

Crossroad (Energetic) – A point where multiple energy pathways (chakras, meridians, nadis) intersect. Joints often serve as energetic crossroads.

Crown Chakra (Sahasrara) – The seventh chakra, located at the top of the head. Governs spiritual connection and enlightenment.

D

Dai Ko Myo – The Master Symbol. Used in Reiki Level 3 for spiritual awakening, enlightenment, and deeper healing.

- Meaning: "The Great Shining Light."
- Application: Used to heal the soul and promote spiritual growth.

Distance Healing – Sending Reiki energy to a person, situation, or event across time and space using the symbol Hon Sha Ze Sho Nen.

E

Emotional Blockage – Stored emotional trauma or resistance that restricts the flow of energy through the chakras, nadis, or meridians.

Energy Field – The subtle energetic body surrounding and penetrating the physical body.

Energy Knot – A blockage in the flow of energy through a joint, chakra, or meridian.

F

Flow – The smooth movement of energy through the body's energy channels. Reiki restores flow when energy becomes stagnant.

Flexibility – The ability to adapt emotionally and spiritually, reflected physically in joint mobility.

H

Hand Positions – Specific placements of the hands on or above the body used to channel Reiki energy.

Heart Chakra – See Anahata Chakra

Hon Sha Ze Sho Nen – The Distance Symbol. Used to send Reiki across time and space.

- Meaning: "No past, no present, no future."
- Application: Used for healing events in the past, present, and future; also used for distance healing.

I

Ida Nadi – The left energy channel connected to feminine, cooling, and intuitive energy. Ida is linked to emotional balance and the parasympathetic nervous system.

Just for today, I will let go of worry and trust the flow of life.

Intuitive Reiki – Allowing Reiki to flow based on inner guidance rather than strict hand placements.

J

Joint – A physical and energetic intersection where multiple meridians and nadis meet. Joints store emotional patterns and influence energy flow throughout the body.

K

Ki – Life force energy that flows through the body's meridians and nadis. Reiki channels this energy for healing and balance.

Kundalini – Spiritual energy coiled at the base of the spine. When awakened, it rises through the chakras, leading to enlightenment.

L

Level 1 (Shoden) – The beginner level of Reiki where students learn:

- The history of Reiki.
- Basic hand positions for self-healing and healing others.
- The concept of ki (life force energy).

Level 2 (Okuden) – The practitioner level where students learn:

- Advanced hand positions.

- Emotional and mental healing.
- Reiki symbols (Cho Ku Rei, Sei He Ki, Hon Sha Ze Sho Nen).

Level 3 (Shinpiden) – The Master level where students learn:

- How to perform attunements.
- Spiritual healing and awakening.
- Master symbol (Dai Ko Myo).

M

Meridians – Pathways through which qi (life force energy) flows in the body. Used in Traditional Chinese Medicine and Reiki for energy balancing.

Mind-Body Connection – The relationship between emotional, mental, and physical health. Reiki works on all three levels simultaneously.

N

Nadi – Subtle energy channels through which prana (life force energy) flows. There are thousands of nadis, but the three primary nadis are Ida, Pingala, and Sushumna.

O

Okuden – See Level 2

Just for today, I will let go of worry and trust the flow of life.

P

Pingala Nadi – The right energy channel connected to masculine, heating, and active energy. Pingala is linked to physical energy and the sympathetic nervous system.

Prana – The life force energy that sustains all living beings.

R

Reiki – A Japanese healing technique that channels life force energy through the practitioner's hands into the recipient's body.

- Meaning: "Universal life force energy."

Root Chakra (Muladhara) – The first chakra, located at the base of the spine. Governs security, grounding, and survival.

S

Sahasrara – See Crown Chakra

Sei He Ki – The Emotional Symbol. Used to balance emotional and mental energy.

- Meaning: "God and man become one."
- Application: Used for emotional healing and removing mental patterns.

Shoden – See Level 1

Shinpiden – See Level 3

Solar Plexus Chakra (Manipura) – The third chakra, located at the upper abdomen. Governs confidence, personal power, and digestion.

Sushumna Nadi – The central energy channel that runs through the spine. When open, it allows spiritual awakening and the rise of kundalini energy.

T

Third Eye Chakra (Ajna) – See Ajna Chakra

Tsubo Points – Pressure points along the meridians that serve as access points for energy flow. Similar to secondary chakras.

U

Universal Energy – The source of Reiki energy, believed to be the creative force of the universe.

W

Wisdom Channel – Sushumna Nadi is often called the Wisdom Channel because it governs spiritual awareness and higher consciousness.

Just for today, I will let go of worry and trust the flow of life.

REI (ray)

Universal Life Energy
Spiritual Consciousness
All-Knowing

KI (kee)

Breath
Life Force
Vital Radiant Energy

Chokurei (Show Ku Ray)

Used for Physical Clearing.

Forward 7 is used for general or whole body, backward 7 is used for specific or small areas

Sei He Ki (Say Hey Key)

Used for Emotional Clearing and Mental Clearing

Hon Sha Ze Sho Nen, which is specifically associated with distant healing.

Just for today, I will let go of worry and trust the flow of life.

Companion Books

More is taught about Energy healing, Chakras, and Reiki in my book,

"Secrets of a Healer – Magic of Reiki (Vol X)

Trade paperback ISBN: 978-1-7772220-0-0
eBook ISBN 978-1-7772220-1-7

SECRETS OF A HEALER
VOL. XI
THE REIKI MASTER'S MANUAL

Trade paperback ISBN: 978-1-990062-34-6

eBook ISBN 978-1-990062-35-3

Just for today, I will let go of worry and trust the flow of life.

Angelic Lifestyle A Vibrant Lifestyle from a Grand Reiki Master

Trade paperback ISBN: 978-0-9952112-7-8

Angelic Lifestyle 42-Day Energy Cleanse

Trade paperback ISBN: 978-1-7770818-3-6

eBook ISBN 978-1-7770818-4-3

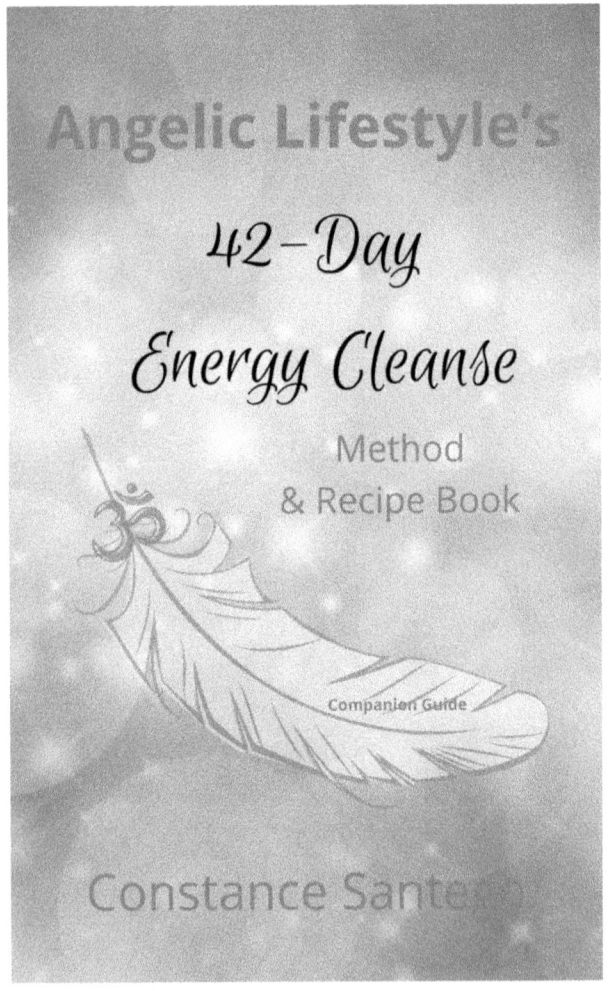

Just for today, I will let go of worry and trust the flow of life.

from my Novel Series,
"The Nine Spiritual Gifts Granted By Spirit"
Vol IV in the series, *"Miracles of a Soul"*

Soft Cover ISBN: 978-1-990062-12-4
eBook ISBN: 978-1-990062-13-1

BASED ON THE NINE SPIRITUAL GIFTS GRANTED BY SPIRIT

MIRACLES *of a* SOUL

A NOVEL
Lexi Constantine's Fifth Adventure
This Time with Archangel Hamied's Help
THE GIFT OF MIRACLES

CONSTANCE SANTEGO

Bibliography

The following sources include foundational texts on Reiki, energy healing, emotional release, joint health, and the connection between mind, body, and spirit. This bibliography reflects a balance of scientific research, spiritual teachings, and practical guides, providing a well-rounded understanding of the material covered in *Reiki and the Power of the Joint Points*.

Reiki and Energy Healing

Arjava Petter, Frank. The Original Reiki Handbook of Dr. Mikao Usui. Tokyo: Lotus Press, 1999.

Rand, William Lee. Reiki: The Healing Touch. Southfield, MI: Vision Publications, 1991.

Stein, Diane. Essential Reiki: A Complete Guide to an Ancient Healing Art. Berkeley, CA: Crossing Press, 1995.

Quest, Eleanor. Reiki Healing for Beginners: Master the Art of Reiki and Increase Your Energy. New York: Harmony Press, 2018.

Tadao, Yamaguchi. Light on the Origins of Reiki: A Handbook for Practicing the Original Japanese Reiki Techniques. Twin Lakes, WI: Lotus Press, 2007.

Just for today, I will let go of worry and trust the flow of life.

Miles, Pamela. Reiki: A Comprehensive Guide. New York: TarcherPerigee, 2006.

Halina, Elizabeth. Reiki for Self-Healing and Transformation. London: Wellbeing Publications, 2019.

Quest, Eleanor. Reiki for Emotional Healing. New York: Harmony Press, 2020.

Joint Health and Physical Healing

Bragg, Patricia. Building Powerful Joints Naturally. Santa Barbara, CA: Health Science Press, 2010.

Letha, Hadady. Asian Health Secrets: The Complete Guide to Asian Herbal Medicine. New York: Crown Publishers, 1996.

McKinnon, Mark. Joint Health and Longevity: A Holistic Guide to Mobility and Flexibility. San Francisco: Natural Health Press, 2018.

Wise, Arthur. Holistic Joint Healing: Restoring Mobility Through Energy and Nutrition. London: Wellbeing Publications, 2017.

Still, Andrew Taylor. The Philosophy of Osteopathy. Kirksville, MO: Published by the Author, 1899.

Thorp, James. Joint Pain Relief: Natural Solutions for Improving Flexibility and Reducing Inflammation. Boulder, CO: Holistic Health Press, 2016.

Weil, Andrew. Spontaneous Healing. New York: Ballantine Books, 1995.

Chakras and Energy Anatomy

Judith, Anodea. Wheels of Life: A User's Guide to the Chakra System. St. Paul, MN: Llewellyn Publications, 1987.

Myss, Caroline. Anatomy of the Spirit: The Seven Stages of Power and Healing. New York: Harmony Books, 1996.

Dale, Cyndi. The Subtle Body: An Encyclopedia of Your Energetic Anatomy. Boulder, CO: Sounds True, 2009.

Brennan, Barbara Ann. Hands of Light: A Guide to Healing Through the Human Energy Field. New York: Bantam Books, 1987.

Leadbeater, C.W. The Chakras. Wheaton, IL: Theosophical Publishing House, 1927.

Reiss, James. Chakra Balancing: A Practical Guide to Restoring Energy Flow. San Francisco: New Earth Publications, 2015.

Emotional and Spiritual Healing

Hay, Louise. You Can Heal Your Life. New York: Hay House, 1984.

Levine, Peter. Waking the Tiger: Healing Trauma. Berkeley, CA: North Atlantic Books, 1997.

Van der Kolk, Bessel. The Body Keeps the Score: Brain, Mind, and Body in the Healing of Trauma. New York: Viking, 2014.

Just for today, I will let go of worry and trust the flow of life.

Dispenza, Joe. Breaking the Habit of Being Yourself: How to Lose Your Mind and Create a New One. Carlsbad, CA: Hay House, 2012.

Zukav, Gary. The Seat of the Soul. New York: Simon & Schuster, 1989.

Naperstek, Belleruth. Invisible Heroes: Survivors of Trauma and How They Heal. New York: Bantam Books, 2004.

Hicks, Esther and Jerry. The Law of Attraction: The Basics of the Teachings of Abraham. Carlsbad, CA: Hay House, 2006.

Kubler-Ross, Elisabeth. On Death and Dying. New York: Macmillan, 1969.

Meridians and Traditional Chinese Medicine

Kaptchuk, Ted J. The Web That Has No Weaver: Understanding Chinese Medicine. New York: McGraw-Hill, 1983.

Beinfield, Harriet, and Korngold, Efrem. Between Heaven and Earth: A Guide to Chinese Medicine. New York: Ballantine Books, 1991.

Matsumoto, Kiiko. Clinical Strategies in Acupuncture. Berkeley, CA: Eastland Press, 1989.

Deadman, Peter. A Manual of Acupuncture. Hove, England: Journal of Chinese Medicine Publications, 1998.

Yuen, Jeffrey. The Philosophy of Chinese Medicine and the Meridians. New York: Yuen Publications, 2011.

Hammer, Leon. Dragon Rises, Red Bird Flies: Psychology and Chinese Medicine. Seattle, WA: Eastland Press, 1990.

Breathwork, Visualization, and Meditation

Nestor, James. Breath: The New Science of a Lost Art. New York: Riverhead Books, 2020.

Gawain, Shakti. Creative Visualization: Use the Power of Your Imagination to Create What You Want in Your Life. Novato, CA: New World Library, 1978.

Chopra, Deepak. The Seven Spiritual Laws of Success. San Rafael, CA: Amber-Allen Publishing, 1994.

Kabat-Zinn, Jon. Wherever You Go, There You Are: Mindfulness Meditation in Everyday Life. New York: Hyperion, 1994.

Tolle, Eckhart. The Power of Now: A Guide to Spiritual Enlightenment. Vancouver, Canada: Namaste Publishing, 1997.

Brown, Richard. The Healing Power of Breath: Simple Techniques to Reduce Stress and Anxiety. New York: Shambhala Publications, 2012.

Sound Healing and Vibrational Medicine

Goldman, Jonathan. Healing Sounds: The Power of Harmonics. Rochester, VT: Healing Arts Press, 2002.

Gerber, Richard. Vibrational Medicine: The #1 Handbook of Subtle-Energy Therapies. Rochester, VT: Bear & Company, 2001.

Just for today, I will let go of worry and trust the flow of life.

Halpern, Steven. Sound Health: The Music and Sound That Makes You Whole. San Francisco: HarperCollins, 1997.

Mitchell, Wayne Perry. The Secrets of Sound Therapy. Los Angeles: Sound Healing Press, 2004.

Alternative and Complementary Medicine

Weil, Andrew. Natural Health, Natural Medicine. Boston: Houghton Mifflin, 1990.

Pert, Candace. Molecules of Emotion: The Science Behind Mind-Body Medicine. New York: Simon & Schuster, 1997.

Northrup, Christiane. Women's Bodies, Women's Wisdom: Creating Physical and Emotional Health and Healing. New York: Bantam Books, 1994.

Dossey, Larry. Healing Words: The Power of Prayer and the Practice of Medicine. New York: HarperCollins, 1993.

Gerber, Richard. Vibrational Medicine: The #1 Handbook of Subtle-Energy Therapies. Rochester, VT: Bear & Company, 2001.

Suggested Internet Resources

These online resources provide valuable information on Reiki, energy healing, joint health, emotional release, and holistic well-being. They offer a mix of scientific insights, spiritual teachings, and practical techniques that align with the principles explored in *Reiki and the Power of the Joint Points*. Whether you're looking for research studies, guided meditations, or community support, these resources can deepen your understanding and strengthen your practice.

Reiki and Energy Healing

International Center for Reiki Training (www.reiki.org)

One of the most comprehensive resources for Reiki information, training programs, and research.

Offers articles, practitioner directories, and free resources for Reiki professionals.

Reiki Rays (www.reikirays.com)

A global online Reiki community offering articles, training, and insights from experienced Reiki Masters.

Includes detailed guidance on hand positions, techniques, and energetic balancing.

Reiki Healing Association
(www.reikihealingassociation.com)

Professional organization offering membership, training, and research on Reiki.

Just for today, I will let go of worry and trust the flow of life.

Includes downloadable resources and certification programs.

Shoden Reiki (www.shodenreiki.com)

Focused on the traditional Japanese origins of Reiki.

Offers articles and training materials on Reiki hand positions, symbols, and techniques.

The Reiki Alliance (www.reikialliance.com)

A worldwide association of Reiki Masters founded by students of Hawayo Takata.

Provides connection with other practitioners and information on Reiki lineage.

Joint Health and Emotional Healing

Arthritis Foundation (www.arthritis.org)

Offers research and articles on joint health and the connection between inflammation and emotional stress.

Provides guidance on exercises, diet, and alternative approaches to improving joint health.

American College of Rheumatology (www.rheumatology.org)

Scientific research and medical guidelines on joint health and autoimmune conditions affecting joints.

Includes research on inflammation, stress, and emotional health.

MindBodyGreen (www.mindbodygreen.com)

A holistic health platform that explores the emotional and spiritual aspects of physical health.

Features articles and videos on how emotional patterns impact physical health.

Psychology Today (www.psychologytoday.com)

Articles on the emotional connection to physical health and the impact of emotional patterns on body tension.

Includes research on stress, trauma, and emotional healing.

Chopra Center (www.chopra.com)

Founded by Deepak Chopra, offering articles, meditations, and research on mind-body connection.

Explores how emotional balance influences physical health and spiritual growth.

Chakras and Meridians

Anodea Judith's Sacred Centers (www.sacredcenters.com)

Anodea Judith is a leading authority on the chakra system.

Offers in-depth articles, books, and training on balancing the chakras.

The Shift Network (www.theshiftnetwork.com)

Online platform for spiritual growth and holistic healing.

Just for today, I will let go of worry and trust the flow of life.

Offers training on energy healing, chakra balancing, and emotional release.

Chi Nei Tsang Institute (www.chineitsang.com)

Resource on the meridian system and the role of chi in physical and emotional health.

Offers techniques on working with energy pathways and improving joint health through energy flow.

Emotional and Spiritual Healing

Emotional Freedom Technique (EFT) Resources (www.emofree.com)

Official site for Emotional Freedom Technique (EFT), which combines acupressure and emotional release.

Provides research, articles, and instructional videos on how emotional patterns are stored in the body.

HeartMath Institute (www.heartmath.org)

Research on heart-brain connection, emotional coherence, and energetic balance.

Provides training on emotional release through breathwork and heart-centered focus.

Dr. Joe Dispenza's Website (www.drjoedispenza.com)

Explores the power of the mind to heal the body through meditation and focused intention.

Offers research on brain-wave states, emotional release, and energetic balance.

Bessel van der Kolk – Trauma Research
(www.besselvanderkolk.com)

Leading authority on trauma and the body's memory of emotional experiences.

Provides insights into how trauma is stored in the body and how energy healing can release it.

Louise Hay's Website (www.louisehay.com)

Focuses on the mind-body connection and how emotional patterns influence physical health.

Offers affirmations and healing exercises to release emotional resistance.

Breathwork, Visualization, and Sound Healing

Breathwork Alliance (www.breathworkalliance.com)

Global network of breathwork practitioners and training programs.

Offers guidance on how to use breath to release emotional patterns and increase energy flow.

Insight Timer (www.insighttimer.com)

Free meditation and breathwork app with thousands of guided sessions.

Includes Reiki-specific meditations and energy-healing visualizations.

Just for today, I will let go of worry and trust the flow of life.

Sonic Bloom (www.sonicbloom.com)

Resource for sound healing and vibrational therapy.

Offers insight into the role of sound frequencies in energy balancing.

The Tuning Fork Store (www.tuningforkshop.com)

Source for professional-grade tuning forks for sound healing.

Provides training and resources on using sound to balance meridians and chakras.

Books and Educational Platforms

Goodreads (www.goodreads.com)

A large platform for book recommendations and reviews.

Search for books on Reiki, joint health, emotional healing, and energy work.

Gaia (www.gaia.com)

Online streaming platform for spiritual and metaphysical content.

Includes documentaries and courses on Reiki, energy work, and emotional healing.

Coursera (www.coursera.org)

Educational platform offering courses on holistic health, mindfulness, and spiritual healing.

Includes academic research on emotional health and energy work.

Open Path Healing Arts Collective (www.openpathcollective.org)

Low-cost membership platform offering holistic healing resources and practitioner directories.

Provides access to therapy, energy healing, and alternative health practices.

Professional Reiki and Holistic Health Networks

National Certification Board for Therapeutic Massage & Bodywork (NCBTMB) (www.ncbtmb.org)

Provides certification information for energy healers and bodyworkers.

Offers professional training and continuing education resources.

The Holistic Health Practitioner Network (www.holistichealthpractitioners.org)

Global network of holistic health professionals and training programs.

Includes resources on Reiki, bodywork, and energy balancing.

International Association of Reiki Professionals (IARP) (www.iarp.org)

Professional network for Reiki practitioners.

Just for today, I will let go of worry and trust the flow of life.

Provides training, certification, and resources for professional development.

Suggested Video Resources

Here are additional films that align with the themes of Reiki, energy flow, emotional healing, and spiritual awakening — without repeating the ones already listed.

These films explore mind-body connection, emotional patterns, spiritual insight, and metaphysical transformation, making them valuable for understanding the deeper aspects of joint-focused Reiki.

Year	Title	Director	Description
1984	The Karate Kid	John G. Avildsen	Explores the balance of mind, body, and spirit through martial arts and the energy of focused intention.
1989	Field of Dreams	Phil Alden Robinson	Explores trust in intuitive guidance and emotional healing through following inner wisdom.
1993	Fearless	Peter Weir	Explores emotional trauma, survival, and spiritual awakening after a near-death experience.

Just for today, I will let go of worry and trust the flow of life.

Year	Title	Director	Description
1993	Alive	Frank Marshall	Explores the connection between survival, emotional strength, and spiritual resilience after a plane crash.
1997	Contact	Robert Zemeckis	Explores spiritual connection, higher consciousness, and the search for deeper truth through interstellar communication.
2000	Chocolat	Lasse Hallström	Explores emotional transformation and the freeing of emotional resistance through connection and indulgence.
2001	A Beautiful Mind	Ron Howard	Explores the mind's power to heal and find balance through internal struggle.
2001	K-PAX	Iain Softley	Explores metaphysical awareness, higher states of consciousness, and emotional healing

Year	Title	Director	Description
			through an alien visitor's perspective.
2004	The Notebook	Nick Cassavetes	Explores the emotional and spiritual bonds of love and memory.
2005	Peaceful Warrior	Victor Salva	Based on Dan Millman's book, this film explores the mind-body connection, emotional balance, and spiritual awakening through athletic training.
2006	The Fountain	Darren Aronofsky	Explores life, death, and spiritual rebirth through the lens of metaphysical awareness and energetic balance.
2006	Déjà Vu	Tony Scott	Explores the concept of time, energy, and alternate realities — linked to spiritual perception.
2007	Into the Wild	Sean Penn	Explores emotional healing and self-discovery through

Year	Title	Director	Description
			reconnecting with nature and solitude.
2008	Seven Pounds	Gabriele Muccino	Explores emotional release, guilt, and redemption through acts of sacrifice and healing.
2010	Hereafter	Clint Eastwood	Explores life after death and the spiritual connection between the living and the dead.
2011	The Tree of Life	Terrence Malick	Explores the connection between human existence, higher consciousness, and emotional awakening.
2012	Cloud Atlas	Lana Wachowski, Tom Tykwer, Lilly Wachowski	Explores interconnected lives across time and how energy patterns repeat and evolve.
2012	The Perks of Being a Wallflower	Stephen Chbosky	Explores emotional trauma, healing, and the importance of emotional connection.

Year	Title	Director	Description
2014	Lucy	Luc Besson	Explores the untapped potential of the human brain and the metaphysical implications of consciousness expansion.
2014	Wild	Jean-Marc Vallée	Explores emotional healing and spiritual growth through a physical journey in nature.
2014	The Theory of Everything	James Marsh	Explores the intersection of physical limitations, emotional resilience, and spiritual connection.
2016	Arrival	Denis Villeneuve	Explores the connection between language, time, and consciousness from a metaphysical perspective.
2017	Lion	Garth Davis	Explores emotional healing, spiritual connection, and the

Just for today, I will let go of worry and trust the flow of life.

Year	Title	Director	Description
			search for identity and belonging.
2019	Soul *(Animated)*	Pete Docter	Explores the concept of the soul, purpose, and spiritual awakening.
2020	Sound of Metal	Darius Marder	Explores the emotional and spiritual process of adapting to physical limitations and finding inner peace.
2021	Nine Days	Edson Oda	Explores the spiritual process of choosing human existence and preparing for emotional life on Earth.
2022	Everything Everywhere All at Once	Daniel Kwan, Daniel Scheinert	Explores alternate realities, emotional healing, and spiritual awakening through shifting perceptions of time and reality.
2023	The Whale	Darren Aronofsky	Explores emotional pain, spiritual healing, and the process of

Year	Title	Director	Description
			forgiveness and acceptance.
2023	The Boy and the Heron *(Animated)*	Hayao Miyazaki	Explores emotional healing, grief, and spiritual growth through symbolic imagery and metaphysical themes.

Message From The Author

Joints are more than just physical connectors — they hold the emotional and spiritual weight of our lives. Every step we take, every burden we carry, and every hesitation we feel is reflected in the health and movement of our joints. What amazes me most about Reiki is its ability to reach beyond the physical — to touch the emotional and energetic imprints stored deep within the body's structure.

When I first began exploring joint healing through Reiki, I was struck by how quickly the body responds when energy flow is restored. Stiffness in the knees reflects uncertainty about moving forward in life; tight hips often hold emotional resistance or creative blocks; shoulder tension mirrors the weight of unspoken responsibility. Reiki works at a level beyond conscious awareness — dissolving these patterns and opening the body to new movement and emotional freedom.

Reiki has taught me that healing is not just about addressing pain — it's about restoring flow and balance at every level of our being. When energy becomes blocked in the joints, it disrupts not only physical movement but also emotional clarity and spiritual alignment. Reiki gently releases these blockages, allowing the body to return to its natural state of balance and ease.

This book explores the profound connection between Reiki and joint health — offering practical techniques and deeper insights into how emotional patterns manifest in the body. My hope is that it helps you see the body's messages more clearly and gives you the tools to work with them — not just to relieve discomfort, but to understand and heal the deeper emotional and spiritual lessons they hold.

True healing happens when we stop resisting and start allowing. When you trust the energy and let it flow, you'll find that both physical and emotional flexibility naturally return. Reiki shows us how to move through life — not with force or effort, but with ease, balance, and grace.

May you find freedom and flow in every step,
Dr. Constance Santego

Just for today, I will let go of worry and trust the flow of life.

About The Author

Dream BIGGER!

Dr. Constance Santego is a highly respected expert in the field of holistic health and spiritual healing, with a specialty in **Reiki energy work** and its profound connection to the body's energy system. As a **Grand Reiki Master** with over two decades of experience, Dr. Santego has taught thousands of students how to harness the healing power of Reiki to balance the mind, body, and spirit.

Holding a **Ph.D. and Doctorate in Natural Medicine**, Dr. Santego possesses a deep understanding of both the scientific and spiritual foundations of alternative healing modalities. Her work reflects a unique ability to blend modern research with ancient healing wisdom, creating a bridge between conventional and alternative medicine. This balanced approach allows her to address health concerns holistically — recognizing that physical health is deeply interconnected with emotional and spiritual well-being.

Throughout her career, Dr. Santego has been committed to empowering individuals to take control of their own healing journey. She teaches that true healing comes not only from physical treatment but also from emotional release, spiritual alignment, and energetic balance. Her approach to Reiki focuses on addressing the deeper emotional and spiritual patterns stored within the body — particularly in the joints — and guiding clients toward greater physical ease and emotional resilience.

In her **"Reiki Wisdom"** series, Dr. Santego draws upon her vast experience and expertise to captivate readers with profound insights into Reiki, energy medicine, and personal transformation. Through her writing, she offers practical tools and techniques for applying Reiki to all areas of life — including emotional healing, spiritual growth, and physical balance.

Her groundbreaking work in joint-focused Reiki explores the relationship between emotional patterns and physical health, revealing how stored emotional trauma and resistance can manifest as tension and discomfort in the body's energy system. Through her teachings, Dr. Santego empowers readers to reconnect with their body's innate wisdom, release long-held emotional patterns, and experience greater freedom and balance in all aspects of life.

Dr. Santego's teachings have touched the lives of countless individuals, guiding them toward deeper self-awareness, emotional healing, and spiritual growth. Her work is a beacon of wisdom and inspiration, encouraging readers to embrace their own healing potential and discover a path to greater harmony and well-being.

As a leader in the field of holistic health and spiritual healing, Dr. Santego continues to share her knowledge through teaching, writing, and personal practice. Her ability to blend spiritual insight with scientific understanding makes her a trusted authority and a guiding light for those seeking true transformation.

ALSO AVAILABLE

Play the game *Ikona* – Discover Your Inner Genie

For additional information on

Constance Santego's

wide range of Motivational Products, Coaching Sessions,
Spiritual Retreats,
Live Events and Educational Programs

Go to

www.ConstanceSantego.ca

Follow on Instagram – Constance_Santego and
Facebook – constancesantegoo

Subscribe and receive Free Information and Meditations on
my
YouTube Channel – Constance Santego

Just for today, I will let go of worry and trust the flow of life.

Just for today, I will let go of worry and trust the flow of life.

Just for today, I will let go of worry and trust the flow of life.

www.ingramcontent.com/pod-product-compliance
Lightning Source LLC
Chambersburg PA
CBHW051128120626
46547CB00012B/721